"The testimonies of these women are [...] especially because of their heart for r[...] ship and love for one another. People [...] [...] [...] [...] these stories—as we have been separated by race and by gender—so that we can be inspired to overcome our own prejudices."

Dr. John Perkins, Chairman of the Board
Christian Community Development Association and
President of John Perkins Foundation for Reconciliation

"Rare and wonderful. An extraordinary book by young Christian women telling the whole truth about race, their faith, and themselves. A true cross-cultural achievement. So honest, modern, and real. Both brave and hopeful. I loved it. I highly recommend this book."

Patricia Raybon, Author, *My First White Friend*

"No fake or feel-good Christianity here: These women give us the raw truth on finding themselves, God, and one another in a country with a race hangover. If a great book is one that exposes us to ourselves, this book succeeds—I see my reflection in both the black girl who discovers that America despises her and in the white girl whose privilege makes her feel guilty. Yet this story's real gem lies not in what pain it helps us to unearth, but in the message it leaves us with—that color aside, we're all in bad, bad shape without God."

Michelle Burford, Associate Editor, *Essence*

"By sharing their stories, these four women have offered us a powerful glimpse into just how difficult—and worthwhile—it can be to pursue committed relationships across racial lines. Ultimately, their journeys show us that the solution to our nation's race problem lies not in legislation or evangelical lip service, but in the gritty business of relationship and loving our neighbor with a Christ-inspired love. Listen closely, brothers: this book is for you too."

Edward Gilbreath, Associate Editor, *New Man*

"Four unique women from four very different worlds invite us into the private places of their lives and expose to us the hidden struggle of coming of age in a racist society. With sensitivity and candor, they draw us in close enough to feel the confusion and hurt, the surprises and delights of finding their way through hostile territory into racially reconciled relationships. *I Call You Friend* shatters stereotypes and opens the way to deeper understanding and appreciation among God's diverse family."

Robert Lupton, FCS Urban Ministries

"Jo, Pam, Andrea, and Elvon are friends by divine intention. From four different backgrounds—two white, two black—their individual journeys of spiritual definition take them through good times and bad. But in the end, spurred by God-directed confidence, these women effectively and personally demonstrate racial reconciliation. They truly are doers of the Word, and not hearers only."

Bonne Steffen, Editor, *Christian Reader*

"Few works weave the human factor into such a tapestry of honesty, hope, and harmony in dealing with the tangled threads of racism in our country. The stories of these four women—two black, two white—compose a fugue of friendship that is beautiful and compelling. The hope for the church in transcending our prejudices is to be found in the interwoven narrative of these wildly and blessedly colorful Christian women. The best civil rights program is the forging of friendship, of letting God's Spirit gather us from every nation, tribe, people, and language. *I Call You Friend* is a stunning gallery of four diverse portraits that revive our awe for God's glory. This is a book which one is honored to call friend."

Terrence R. Lindvall, Ph.D., Distinguished Chair
of Visual Communication, Regent University

"An entertaining as well as illuminating book. These from-the-heart stories give us important insights into cross-cultural relationships from which Christians desiring racial reconciliation can learn."

Dr. Amy L. Sherman, Director, Urban Ministries,
Trinity Presbyterian Church, Charlottesville, Va.
Author, *Restorers of Hope: Reaching the Poor in Your
Community with Church-based Ministries That Work*

I call you Friend

four women's

stories of race, faith,

and friendship

pamela A. toussaint
and jo kadlecek

BROADMAN
&HOLMAN
PUBLISHERS

Nashville, Tennessee

0-8054-1762-1

Published by Broadman & Holman Publishers Nashville, Tennessee
Page Design: Anderson Thomas Design
Typesetting: SL Editorial Services, Brentwood, Tennessee

Dewey Decimal Classification: 302
Subject Heading: CROSSRACIAL FRIENDSHIPS
Library of Congress Card Catalog Number: 98-48099

Unless otherwise stated, all Scripture citation is from the Holy Bible, New International Version, © 1973, 1978, 1984 by International Bible Society.

The names of some of the people in these stories have been changed to protect their identities.

The photos in the epilogue and on the back cover are by Christopher Gilbert.

Library of Congress Cataloging-in-Publication Data
Toussaint, Pamela A.
     I call you friend : four women's stories of race, faith, and friendship / by Pamela A. Toussaint and Jo Kadlecek.
        p. cm.
    Includes bibliographical references.
    ISBN 0-8054-1762-1 (trade paper)
     1. Female friendship—United States—Case studies. 2. Afro-American women—United States—Case studies. 3. White women—United States—Case studies. 4. Racism—United States—Case studies. 5. Self-perception in women—United States—Case Studies. 6. Women's rights—United States—Case studies. I. Kadlecek, Jo. II. Title.
HQ1206.T68   1999
3302.3'4'082—dc21   98–48099
                                          CIP

1 2 3 4 5 03 02 01 00 99

To the black and white women and men throughout our country's history whose shed blood, God-inspired words, and united vision for racial justice made it possible for us to come together as friends to write this book.

Thank you.

I have called you friends, for everything that I learned from my Father I have made known to you.
—Jesus, John 15:15

Contents

Foreword
ix

Introduction
1

Section One: Coming Up . . .

CHAPTER ONE: . . . IN THE CITY
PAMELA A. TOUSSAINT, 7

CHAPTER TWO: . . . IN THE SUBURBS
JO KADLECEK, 26

CHAPTER THREE: . . . IN THE SOUTH
ELVON REED BORST, 38

CHAPTER FOUR: . . . IN THE NORTH
ANDREA CLARK, 52

Section Two: Coming of Age

CHAPTER FIVE: THE BEST OF TIMES
PAMELA, 67

CHAPTER SIX: BEYOND THE 'BURBS
JO, 84

CHAPTER SEVEN: SOUTHERN ROADS
ELVON, 101

CHAPTER EIGHT: COASTAL CARES
ANDREA, 115

Section Three: Coming Together

CHAPTER NINE: A BITTERSWEET EMBRACE
PAMELA, 135

CHAPTER TEN: HABITS OF COMPANIONSHIP
JO, 155

CHAPTER ELEVEN: CHANCES ARE
ELVON, 183

CHAPTER TWELVE: MIRROR, MIRROR
ANDREA, 205

Epilogue
A DIALOGUE FOR THE FUTURE
227

Suggested Reading
244

Foreword

My days are controlled by carpool schedules, assignments, board meetings, and writing deadlines. In the midst of these responsibilities, and often in spite of them, I long for a still point, an oasis where I can stop the whir—step outside of the obligations that hem my days—and be known by another friendship.

In many moments, my husband meets this need. But I find myself hungry for more: for friendship with others, mothers, women, sisters. I want relationships both with those who mirror me in likeness and those who reflect the diversity of God's human creation and challenge me to see and think and feel all of who he made me to be.

I wasn't always at this point in my appreciation of the deep texture of friendship. My junior high days demanded clonelike commitment. A friend was someone who thought and felt and most importantly *looked* like me. This friendship formula carried me on through high school and most of college.

Until I met Argelia. We worked together one summer filing thick manila medical charts in a doctor's office. Argelia was not my clone. She was more my complement. I spoke English; she spoke Spanish. We lived on opposite sides of Houston, Texas. My twenty-something hair hung limp and brown. Hers was coarse with body and streaked with gray. I had yet to taste deeply committed love. She was a grandmother. On the surface, it seemed we had little in common.

That summer, sitting at the office picnic table over our brown bag lunches (mine tuna fish, hers tortillas), we discovered a mutual love for the one true God. Suddenly our very different worlds were connected by a united hope. Daily, we crossed the bridge of our newly formed friendship, discovering the richness of unexplored life.

It's been over twenty years now since my summer lunches with Argelia. The lessons learned at that picnic table have stuck in my spirit. Obviously, there is more than the at-our-elbow friendships of our everydays. There are cross-generational connections between those who've "been there, done that" and those who haven't. There are enriching relationships with those who hold to another faith or none at all. And there are sisterhoods to explore with those whose skin color, eye shape, and hair texture differ from ours because they hail from another race.

In the pages of this book, Jo, Pam, Elvon, and Andrea stir us to realize that what God has for us in friendship is more than we typically allow him to deliver. The weavings of the lives of these four women are complex. Only a sovereign God could accomplish their connections.

So I journey with these four women and find I'm turning yet another bend in my own friendship journey. Here are guides and travel companions for the days ahead. In the archiving of their struggles and victories, I gain direction for my own crossroads ahead. And you will too

Come along, friend. There is more available for you in friendship than you've yet dreamed. Find an Argelia. Sit down at the picnic table. Open your brown bags and your hearts and begin the bridge-building journey from your world to hers that is friendship.

—Elisa Morgan
Author and President of MOPS
(Mothers of Pre-Schoolers, International)

Introduction

God is good.

There is a race problem in our country.

And we have experienced both.

But ours is not the story you might read in the newspapers or hear on a television talk show. Yes, two of us—Pamela and Elvon—are black women, while the other two—Jo and Andrea— are white women, but that's where the labels end.

You might assume that Elvon grew up in the ghetto and walked twenty miles with no shoes to get to a second-class school each morning because she didn't have enough money for the bus. You might think Pamela was raised on collard greens and chitlins for breakfast, that she grew up on welfare in the projects with her mother, and that she struggled to make it through the sixth grade, let alone thought of achieving anything when she grew up.

You might think that Jo grew up playing with Barbie dolls, that she was a model student (especially in home economics and typing), and that Donny Osmond was her hero. And you might assume that Andrea had a perfect suburban existence where she was given everything she ever hoped for, that she couldn't imagine becoming anything but a bouffant-wearing wife and mother with 2.5 children and a white picket fence.

We are not these stereotypes. No one is. Sure, we are products of our backgrounds—two black, two white. But we have unique cultural perspectives and tastes, personal quirks and idiosyncrasies, and individual gifts and talents. We have been shaped by our upbringings and affected by our society. And given the current climate of racial tensions in our country, you might think we could never be friends . . . .

Real friends. More than colleagues who nod to one another each morning behind their coffee cups. More than acquaintances who say hi and bye to each other as they bump shopping carts at the supermarket. More than members of the same health club who smile at each other across the Thigh Masters . . . .

Real friends. Imperfect. In process. Growing.

Two black, two white.

God is good.

He has shown us we have more in common than we think. We all hate chitlins, love tennis, hate injustice, and love the written word. We all think Denzel Washington is *f-i-i-i-ne,* that gangsta rap is obnoxious, and that Flannery O'Connor was one of America's most gifted writers. It is easy for us to talk about the latest hit movie, the men in our lives, the last good sermon we heard, or our most recent family squabble. We have each felt the sting of being different, stared at, patronized, and singled out because of our skin color. And we have celebrated the rich cultural heritages of people different from ourselves.

It is our commonalties that make us friends, but it is our faith and convictions that make us persevere. What else but a supernatural something-or-other could explain why two white women and two black women would hang out together for hours over coffee or pizza talking about Maya Angelou or Annie Dillard, welfare reform, or the kids in our neighborhoods? What other possible reason could there be for four women from very different backgrounds, with very different life experiences, to form a friendship? And to talk about it on paper?

History did not bring us together.

Legislation did not bring us together.

Political rhetoric did not bring us together.

The church, sadly, did not bring us together.

Though, certainly, each made the road a little smoother, only a good God could bring us together. And did.

And so he has given us the stories that we share with you here. Stories that reflect on actual encounters, that ask hard questions, that describe our experiences—good and bad—in America. Stories that are simply part of our journeys, a process toward understanding and healing and unity.

We share them because we hope in some way they will move you beyond the cultural politeness of, "Hi. How are you?" to the meaningful dialogue of, "Hi. *Who* are you?"

We offer them *not* because we think we have the last word on race relations, but because we have come to realize we are incomplete without one another. Period. If we hibernate in our little corners of the world, never allowing significant interaction to take us across cultures, then we are not fully who we were intended to be.

We give these stories hoping that maybe they will keep children from growing up believing all black people live in the ghetto and all white people live on Easy Street. Maybe the story of our friendships can help them (and their mamas and daddies) be friends. Real friends . . . .

That is our prayer.

We hope people of all colors will be inspired to become friends in spite of and *because* of their cultural differences. Yet, because of our particular experiences, we want this book to challenge white suburban women to face any fears they may have about the black community, moving them beyond what is often a world of comfortability and privilege to experience some of what it's like to be black in America. A story like ours could also show women of color that not all white women are clueless about racial issues, and that just because a black woman calls a white woman friend does not mean she's a sellout.

It is not a simple matter—this race thing—one nicely packaged with easy-to-follow directions on the back of the box. Relationships are hard enough. We understand that the extra ingredient of race mixed into a batch of friendship can sometimes be hard on the palate, especially if you pour in too much of it at a time, forgetting to stir, sift, and let cool before eating. Race overdose, we call it.

Sometimes when it hits us—that is, when the constant stress of race becomes too much—we retreat to our separate corners to refuel. Mostly, though, our friendships find us lunging, sliding, and (sometimes) hobbling on local tennis courts or walking through parks. Or we take in a movie or a play together and talk about it afterward over Indian food. Or we plan imaginary trips to lush Caribbean islands where we live the "writer's life." In a word, our friendships are ordinary. Yet, in our ridiculous world, people tell us they are *extra*ordinary.

That is the balance we want to show here. Friendships where the issues aren't always black and white, the lines aren't always neatly kept, and the answers are found in a lot of questions—but where the reward, regardless of the struggle, is great and refreshing and fun. In the process, the steps each of us take toward one another become a little easier.

Yes, God is good.
There is a race problem in our country.
And we have experienced both.

—*Elvon Reed Borst*
Andrea Clark
Jo Kadlecek
Pamela A. Toussaint

Section One:
Coming Up . . .

Chapter One
. . . In the City

On most days I am a card-carrying, New York City-raised, African-American woman. I attend a church where we shout and raise our hands in praise (major prerequisite). I love

Pamela

banana pudding with Nilla wafers (a southern throw-back even though I'm not southern). I read *Essence, Emerge, Black Enterprise,* Cornel West, bell hooks, T. D. Jakes, Bebe Moore Campbell, and Maya Angelou. And I listen to jazz, funk, and even a little rap on occasion. I am not a Republican.

Some days I'll spend afternoons whacking little green balls at a gleaming, chrome tennis club. Or, I'll turn on a classical music station in my car and conduct passionately right along with Tschaikowsky while I'm at stop lights. On those days, I might prefer a cup of iced Twinings, some tiramisu, and the *Wall Street Journal* stock pages over Nilla pudding and Maya. And still at other times, I am a cool-twanging West Indian-American chile who can eat fried plantain and codfish cakes, drink sorrel, and dance calypso as well as the next "mon."

In each of these modes I am still black.

My mother and father stepped onto America from the West Indies in the late 1950s, visas and borrowed coats in hand, in hope of making a "betta" life. Like thousands of others, they heard about an America where opportunities abounded for blacks, where it was rumored that quarters lay on the sidewalks waiting to be picked up, and where an American ten-dollar bill sent home bought two pairs of good Sunday shoes.

America the "beyu-tee-ful."

I consider myself a fortunate brown girl in America because of them. My parents were raised on an enchanted, unspoiled Caribbean island called Grenada. West Indians seem to remember little of the history of the nasty English slave trade that occurred there in the eighteenth century. In fact, many islanders revere the British in a way that's incomprehensible to my black American friends who know the deal about our history.

When they got married, my parents chose a spacious, three-bedroom, co-op apartment in a Jewish-Irish neighborhood in Queens. Never mind that they were one of the only black couples in the entire seven-building complex, which included thousands of apartments. No problem. You see, my parents had no hate to pass down. They mingled appropriately with white folk and tried not to buy into the American "race problem." Growing up and becoming young adults in Grenada, they didn't have to wrestle with their self-identities the way we do here. In their home country, if opportunities for advancement were denied, it was because of a poor economy, inadequate preparation, or, at worst, classism. But rarely was it racism. So in our house, no cautionary speeches were given on "how to handle oneself with whites." We were just as good and just as able.

That doesn't mean things didn't happen in our little world, both subtle and blatant, that made you want to holler.

"I heard a *white* woman takes care of their baby," a short white man said in a hushed, conspiratorial tone to a blond woman with a beehive in the laundry room of our apartment building, just as my mother entered. "And what of it?" Mother replied, giving them "a look" and going right on with her laundry, leaving them in stunned silence at having been caught. A moment later they nervously tried to make small talk with her. Mother continued to attend her laundry.

On another wash day, a lady gruffly asked her—or told her—"Why don't you go wash in the laundromat across the boulevard?" My tired mother stopped and replied, "And why should I?" The lady gave no reply. I guess she thought my mother was a washerwoman. Another time Mom came through the lobby door with a white woman. The woman looked at her, clutched her bag, and said loudly to her companion ahead, "Gee, I'd really better watch my purse." These little encounters can wear down even the best of people after awhile.

The "white woman" the laundry room gossips were referring to was my nanny for the first year of my life. DeeDee, which was her nickname, took excellent care of me (or so my mother finally decided after weeks of calling home every few hours to make sure I was OK.) She bathed me, creamed me, dressed me, fed me, played with me, and was very protective of her little brown-skinned charge. (She wouldn't let my father near me unless he put out his cigarette *and* washed his hands.)

You can only imagine what a spectacle it was that the only black family in a complex of thousands had their baby wheeled around the playground by a white nanny. In the '60s? Girrrrl! "The eyes" were out and about, taking it all in to relate to their friends and spouses that night at the dinner table or during the next laundry room "Chatfest." (Thinking back, I would give anything to have been old enough to look down at myself being wheeled around in my smart, navy blue carriage and gloat a little.)

DeeDee was very content in her work. To her credit, she didn't seem at all bothered to be a white woman drawing her paycheck from a black family in 1965. Then "the eyes" began to question her when she took me out for strolls around the complex. "Why are you taking care of this little *black* child? (At least *black* was the word DeeDee used when she told my mother the stories.) "How much are they paying you?" the inquisitors asked another day. "Is this the *only* job you could find?" And so on. Seemingly unperturbed, DeeDee would relate these inquisitions to my mother, who would say that they were just ignorant and that she shouldn't worry about them.

But these encounters began to wear DeeDee down, and she wasn't even the real object of their distaste. She was guilty by association with a black family. Not long after, DeeDee announced that she would need much more money than we were paying her if she was to continue. It wasn't negotiable. She resigned, with notice. After just one year of experiencing the questions, suspicious looks, and small indignities that many African Americans experience as a matter of course, DeeDee was worn out.

Not surprisingly, other white sitters who came after DeeDee's unfortunate departure had similar encounters. When one sitter took me on the subway, she was asked by a stranger, "Why are you taking care of this nigger?" If only that person had known that this woman, also a co-op resident and mother, had come right up to our front door, rang our bell, and *offered* my parents her baby-sitting services.

We developed a useful survival tool to deal with these "incidents": it's called selective hearing loss. Racist comments could be made to go away at will, as if they didn't occur. If you play nice, look nice, and sound nice, everything will be nice. Everything *is* nice, isn't it? "Oh, you *live* here? *Really?*" the bee-hives asked. "Oh, you have a *nanny?*" Locked behind the lime-green, steel door of our apartment, we escaped the peering eyes, the sneering eyes, and the curious eyes—and just the eyes.

Then it was time for school. I entered the graveled playground filled with running, jumping white children in blue and gray plaid uniforms. It was Catholic school. Suddenly the bell rang. Hundreds of little, cream-colored Irish children paired up in twos and lined up against the brick wall to go into the building. My brown eyes darted back and forth across the long row of freckled-faced pairs. Panic washed over me as I realized I was partnerless. Only a few minutes ago, Daddy was saying, "OK, study your head" (which is West Indian for, "Be good and learn something") and trying to let go of my hand so he could go to work. I resisted. What exactly will I be "let go" into?

Then, standing alone on the gravel and facing the rows of pairs, I saw why I was afraid to let go. I looked toward the nuns monitoring the line for a helpful hint or smile. I found none. In the same moment, I saw my daddy with his leather briefcase and folded *New York Times* under his arm disappear behind the school fence into the faraway world of adult matters.

In that frightful instant, up walked little Maryellen O'Connor, the bangs of her blond pageboy falling in a neat row just above her eyes. She extended her upturned hand to me (this was the universal symbol at St. Sebastian's Elementary for, "Will you be my partner?" but who knew *that?*). I responded by doing the only thing I could think to do. I slapped her five. She stared at me in a funny way. I didn't move. Uh oh, I had done the wrong thing. Hours passed (seemingly) before she smiled nervously and beckoned me to join her on the line of pairs. I followed and fell in line. I had a partner! I was still nervous but hopeful. Maybe, just maybe, this Catholic school thing was gonna be OK.

Actually, it had better be OK. I didn't know it, but my mother had been politely visiting the principal at that school for years, asking for her daughter to be admitted. "No room." "Too late." "Maybe next year." "Didn't fill in the form correctly." "Ehhh, we'll call you." . . . Not to be denied, Mom persisted in the incredulously decorous manner I believe only a West Indian mother could pull off in such a situation.

Years of lame excuses that masked, "Don't you see we don't want you here?" went by. For those years I went to the public school nearby. PS 229 (that's "P" for public and "S" for school in New York) was full of children of all colors who weren't constrained by uniform jumpers and buttoned-up blouses with Peter

Pan collars. Life was good there. Life was free there. I didn't want to go to the disciplined, uniformed halls of the parish school where everyone seemed to be named either Shevaun or Brendan and everyone's mother spoke with an Irish brogue. I cried floods of tears when the decision was made: she will go to the Catholic school.

This wasn't any Dr.-Spock-sit-your-child-down and discuss with her rationally, like, what her feelings are, like, about, emotionally detaching from, like, one environment into another. Instead, I was asked, "What's all this silly crying about?" I was going to a *better* school. The battle had been fought and won for me by scores of black people before Mr. and Mrs. Toussaint ever existed. These people gave their *lives* so I could set foot in a "white" school. It was not my place to whine or argue. Mother and Father knew best. I went.

I grew up privileged. Only child. Wearing Bloomingdale's dresses to church every Sunday with matching velvet ribbons and patent leather shoes from Stride-Rite. I felt pretty secure—as secure as a black child could be in an all-white setting. But something wasn't right. As a child I couldn't pinpoint what it was— like a constant itch that you scratch daily but never ask the doctor about.

Fortunately, my mother understood the itch. She began to import black friends for me from wherever they could be found—usually from a strange, exotic land called Brooklyn (actually a fifteen-minute drive away). All other blacks supposedly lived there, except us. They put in their time, those little brown girls, and then went back home, not to be seen again until the next time their parents could trot them way "*out here.*" It was all quite pleasant, this smattering of Caribbean and American black friend-visitors, amid the omnipresent MarygraceColleens. But the MCs stayed, while the brown girls always went home.

These two groups of friends rarely mixed. I played with the brown girls in our apartment and played outside with the MarygraceColleens. It just worked out that way. Somehow, I didn't think my brown friends would be accepted anyway. I feared they would be looked at funny. And if one of the MCs made a dumb comment, I was more afraid that these girls, who seemed to know their black identity much more than I, would say or do something to disturb the tacit peace I had with the MCs. I couldn't allow that, nor did I have confidence in my ability to facilitate such a clash. The MCs could tolerate me, but I didn't want to find out if they could deal with my black friends from Brooklyn.

Small doses of blackness. That's what those visiting brown girls gave me. A piece of rhythm here, a flash of familiarity there. A look and a touch of another girl who had hair like mine. Had a body shaped like mine. A taste of soul. They held up a mirror for me, those girls. And it was a good and strangely familiar and exciting reflection, but it wasn't enough. Only I didn't realize that for a long time.

When puberty arrived, I realized I was fat. I wasn't really; I was just shaped like the Caribbean-American girl that God made me. Only I didn't realize that for a long time either. I had thick thighs and a round rear they might call "ample" these days. But my ampleness was unable, despite the utmost of shoving, to fit into the size 26 Levi jeans that all the MarygraceColleens were sporting. You know, the ones where the size is on the tag that shows on the outside for all to see. No way, no how was I getting into those. The intrinsic design of the pants mocked me— cut wide in the waist and hip area and skimpy in the butt and thighs. I needed to diet immediately. Ample butt and thighs must be eliminated, assimilated, extinguished.

The new, multiaisled drug store in town introduced me to Dexatrim at age twelve. I popped those diet pills faithfully, unbeknownst to my parents, and lost fifteen pounds in a jiffy. A few weeks of headaches and funny feelings in my stomach was a small price to pay to fit into a size 28 Levi jean and be accepted. I was acceptable, if not quite perfect, as my friend Laura reminded me when she remarked negatively at the size I had starved to fit into. My slimmed-down black body was acceptable. If not quite perfect.

And what was I going to do with my *hair?* It was not drying into a nice, smooth ponytail like the MarygraceColleens' did after swim practice and a quick rinse 'n shake. Blow-dryers were death to my Motherland locks. In fact, my own mother loathed swimming team practice. It was she who sat up until all hours of the night, fighting like a she-warrior with my coiled, African hair gone stiff with baked-in chlorine. What exactly *is* wrong with my hair? I wondered. My tenure on the swim team lasted exactly one season. Finally, an Ultra Sheen Hair Relaxer Kit with the smiling brown-skinned woman on the box rescued my self-image. My hair and I both became more relaxed, for awhile.

At the same time I was having my hair/body angst, the MarygraceColleens were discovering our differences too. "How come your lip's poked out like *this?*" they asked, teasing, pulling their thin bottom lips out with their fingers. "It is *not!*" I responded most assuredly, but not quite sure. "And you walk with your bee-hind stuck out like *this,*" chimed in another one rudely as she attempted to poke out her flat rear. "Do *not!*" I answered again, much less assuredly now, looking away as if uninterested, ready to move on to the next thing. Block it out of your ears. Then it doesn't exist.

There was something very frightening about the MCs. They were my so-called friends. They laughed with me, walked home with me, played with my Barbies, came to my birthday parties, and invited me to theirs (well, some of them). But at any given moment, some difference would make itself known to them. The more differences I tried to fix, the more they seemed to find. I couldn't keep up. They could turn on me in a flash—whip my self-image, my very self, with their tongues and eyes and antics. Whatever the object of the difference, it was *my* problem, *my* fault. Then in a moment, they would turn back into so-called friends again and act as if it never happened.

"Well, white people are just better than black people any-way," insisted one particularly annoying freckled-faced girl.

"They are not," I insisted, waiting, worried. After a round of "Are so's!" and "Are not's!" my little tauntress said, "So, name some black movie stars. Betcha can't." A quiet panic came over me. The weight of the entire race was resting on my seventh-grade shoulders.

It was the final round of Jeopardy, and the category was Black Stars for $5,000, please. Winner take all. I searched the Rolodex of my preteen mind to come up with a name. Would it be good enough to save the race from eternal embarrassment? The clock ticked. The Jeopardy music played. I pushed my buzzer. Alex Trebec looked up from his cue cards at me. "Pamela?" he said, in that Alex Trebec voice, as the black and white worlds watched, waiting for my answer. "Michael Jackson!" I said in an overconfident-of-course-everyone-loves-him tone. (I loved Michael and planned to marry him and have a long, happy relationship as part of the singing Jackson family.) I threw in Diana Ross for good measure.

A hush fell across the studio audience. Trebec looked doubtful but finally said, "Yes, we'll accept that." The black community breathed a collective sigh of relief in living rooms all across America. The MarygraceColleens were temporarily appeased.

Toni Morrison noted in her first novel, *The Bluest Eye,* that some people "don't have home towns, just places where they were born." She was talking about me. There was nothing "my" about my neighborhood. It was "theirs." We were unsuspecting interlopers. My parents, though middle-class, polite, intelligent, and well spoken, were still not in the know, the way parents need to be to keep up with important things: neighborhood opportunities for their children, information about property values, the inside scoop on local politics, warnings about "bad" kids, and the like. They were out of the loop, as it were, both because they were ostracized from it and because they ostracized themselves, I suspect, out of sheer tiredness.

White mothers did not stand around with my brown-skinned mom after swim meets and chat about the team's chances, various girls' athletic abilities or lack thereof, rising tuition costs, and upcoming birthday parties. She did not go to Friday night bingo or sit with her husband in the local Irish restaurant on the weekend, munching peanuts and chatting with the bartender. And they certainly would have been a spectacle at B'Nai Brith meetings, the local and quite active Jewish social group. My father did not stand in front of the building on evenings to smoke a cigarette with the bald-headed white men that gathered there to escape their wives and exchange gossip and complaints. We did not know things like the mailman was about to have triplets or a neighbor's young daughter was dying of leukemia two floors above us. We were out of the loop. What else could you be when the majority of your exchanges with people consisted of, "Hi. How are ya?" and "Good night" as you got off the elevator?

Where could a brown couple go for real, come-over-for-dinner camaraderie in this neighborhood? My parents found comfort, real talk, and a few good laughs among their West Indian friends when they visited, but those opportunities were few and far between. Meaningful relationships with the people were sacrificed on the altar called "A Better Life."

Every other summer or so, my parents took me to visit the beautiful, tiny Caribbean island where they were born and raised. I had never seen a place like Grenada before. There were black people of all colors, some with strange and mystical hair/eye combinations, like red coiled hair, blue eyes, and freckles. Or dark hair, light-brown skin and transparent green eyes. They had cool accents that I commenced to imitate immediately. In fact, I got so good that new people I met there would say, "You doon sung like no American *ataaall.*" Good. Because now I wanted to try on this place, as one would a dress in a store, and see if it fit. Then I could take it home as my own. *Maybe this is where I'll be from,* I thought.

One striking thing about these West Indian folks; they had fierce ambition and no lack of confidence. They had no qualms about what they could be or do. It was much later that I realized that they had on this little island what I couldn't find in my big, privileged metropolis—an identity. As children they would go to a store and purchase items from a black store owner; opened their first bank accounts with a black branch manager; opened their mouths and said "ahhh" and a black doctor peered down their throats. Even the president of their country was black. It was much later when I realized that it was the grounding my parents received there that was passed on to me, maybe unwittingly. But here in America, that confidence was constantly being put to the test. Just living began to feel like one long exam.

The adoption of Grenada as my new home was not to be. Try as I did, I never became one of the crowd down there—still haven't, though I love my visits. I always managed to do or say something that showed I was from "the States." Like insisting on cold, homogenized milk for my breakfast cereal (instead of hot and evaporated) and not knowing that you say good night when you *enter* someone's house for dinner, not when you leave.

But being from America had its advantages and held my West Indian friends sufficiently enthralled. Interestingly, many were hoping to migrate *here* to find their way, and I, the privileged American, was longing for belonging on an island one could drive completely around in an afternoon.

It was almost Christmas break during junior high, and a Kris Kringle was being held in my homeroom. For those who don't know, Kris Kringle is the cost-saving holiday ritual where everyone draws one person's name from a hat and buys a gift for that person. Usually a limit is placed on how much can be spent on the gift so that everyone gets an equally nice present. My conscientious mother obliged and purchased an appropriate, thoughtful item for me to wrap and offer as my gift. We may have gone slightly above the limit just so I could make a nice showing (being the only black child in the school and all).

I remember my mother teaching me how to wrap a box, ever-so-perfectly: Turn the box upside down on the paper so the smooth side would show on top; fold the edge of the paper over to hide any jagged edges where your scissors may have gone awry; crease and fold the corners so they line up in a perfect upside-down vee. My box looked as nice and crisp as the empty ones that sat under those fake Christmas trees in department store windows downtown.

On the day of the gift exchange everyone in class was restless with anticipation. The cloakroom was abuzz. This room for cloaks amounted to a long, walk-in closet where we were supposed to just hang up our coats and boots and walk through, but where we actually played games of pinch-me-and-run, snapped newly acquired bra straps, passed notes, shared secrets, giggled, pulled hair, put on bubble-gum-flavored lip gloss, and rolled the tops of our uniform skirts so we could show more leg (since I didn't like my thick legs, I only dabbled in this ritual).

"I know who you've got!" said one boyish-looking blond girl to a boy who looked like he couldn't care less. "Ooooh, you forgot yours!" one girl said, her face a mass of tiny brown spots with ivory underneath, pointing to a bewildered girl as she searched through her bookbag looking for what wasn't there. We had our fun in the closet and then exited with a fake-serious, I-just-wish-we-could-get-on-with-the-business-of-learning look on our faces, as our teacher watched tiredly from her desk.

Everyone was instructed to walk over to his or her person, say "Merry Christmas" (this was Catholic School in the '70s, so there was no need for political correctness), and hand the person the gift. I walked over to the girl whose name I had drawn and gave her the gift, for which I received an awkward but sincere smile and a, "Wow. Thank you." I know she couldn't help but be totally impressed with the wrap job, if not with me. I went back to my desk smiling.

I spied a sheepish-looking, unsmiling girl inching toward my desk with a box in her hand—an unwrapped box. I noticed that its thin, cardboard sides ached and that it had a rubber band around it, masquerading as a bow. She handed it to me. "Merry Christmas," she said flatly. "Thank you," I remember saying, skeptical but hopeful.

I opened the box to find it half-filled with paper. Not sta-
tionary or a drawing pad. Loose-leaf paper. *Old* sheets of loose
leaves. Some sheets had curled edges, and some were tinted yellow on the sides, as if aged. This girl gave me *paper* for
Christmas. And there were some pencils, a few with run-down
points and half-used erasers. I was shocked and embarrassed.
(*Oh my God, who from the cool group is watching this?* I thought.
Is this a joke?) I politely searched through the paper to see if any
hidden treasure was to be found between the pages. Fat chance.
She offered neither explanation nor apology. She just stood
there.

My home training taught me to smile and say, "Thank you,"
so I did. She, who never cracked a smile throughout the entire
process, flung her long, thin brown hair, whipped around, and
went back to her seat.

Later on, when all my friends were showing off their gifts, I
was hiding mine. Would I get sympathy or snickers? I wasn't sure.
Even the friends who got inappropriate gifts, like bunny slippers
or something much too juvenile for our sophisticated eleven-
year-old tastes, could get everyone to laugh at the dumbness of
the giver's choice. No one else got a half-used gift but me.

Walking home, I wondered what message was really hidden
in the cardboard crevices of that girl's mangy box. Hatred?
Disgust? Disregard? Forgetfulness? Poverty? Did she go home
from school and tell her parents she drew the name of the only
nigger as her Kris Kringle? As always, who knew? Block it out of
your ears and move on.

Though some strange incidents were open to "interpreta-
tion," there was no mistaking the motives of a boy named
Eugene Jackson, who chose me as a target for his twelve-year-
old racial anger. He patiently and purposefully waited in the
bushes for me on several occasions, aware of the route I took
home. He seemed to know just the point at which the last boy
who walked home with our group turned into his corner
house, leaving only girls—and sometimes only *me*—to walk
the rest of the way. At that point, he would jump out of the

shrubs suddenly, like an eerie horror-movie character, then block my way as I tried to continue walking.

"Yeah, nigger, think ya goin' home, nigger?" he'd say, jerking my arm. Taunting turned to shoving and then kicking. He tripped me, and I fell on the concrete. "Awww, is that hurting you, nigger?" he'd ask as he yanked the braids my mother had fixed so carefully that morning.

I fought back as well as I could, but I was overpowered by his boy-strength and his anger. With his face all screwed up, so close to mine as he snarled, and his grip on me so firm, he appeared incredibly superior. In a macabre way, it somehow seemed like he had a right to have "little outbursts" like these.

He knew he'd be protected from intervention if someone saw him. Adults walked by and watched this boy hurting me, but no one offered help. I was defenseless and alone.

After these beatings (they happened several times), I'd get up, brush off my school uniform, pick up my belongings, which had gotten strewn about the sidewalk, and cry a little. These "little outbursts" were to be endured and gotten over with. I took great pains for a few days after these attacks to walk far out of the way to avoid Eugene, even leaving home early to do so. But eventually I slipped back into my normal routine. I still had angst in my heart, even as I resumed walking home with the MarygraceColleens, knowing fearless Eugene could be lurking in the bushes . . . waiting to pounce.

Who could I share this trauma with? If I thought the MarygraceColleens would have defended me, I might have told them. But I wasn't so sure. This kind of thing never happened to them, so how could they help me? Once my good friend Kathy saw him bothering me and told him he'd better leave me alone. But this only seemed to fuel Eugene, making him craftier in his pursuit. Nonetheless, I appreciated Kathy for doing that. I never told any adults about the incidents. I brushed them off like I did my dusty school uniform, and went on.

Meanwhile, I had the nerve to be totally in love with blond-haired, brown-eyed Patrick McLaughlin, who lived across the street. Oh, how worthwhile it was to linger around after school in hopes of falling into his walk-home group. I was very good at this and am still grateful for the assistance of my then-best friend Evelyn Gonzalez, who went to pains to assist me. (Though, being the frank girl she was, she probably wanted to say, "Pam, this guy is never going to like you." Maybe she did say it, but I wasn't listening.) I had the confidence of my convictions. I would win him over.

To attract Patrick's attention and build a friendship, I was always looking for the opportunity to exchange a joke, ask an unnecessary but serious-sounding question, initiate a story, or poke a little friendly fun at him. Just to be around him made me happy. He was so cool, yet quiet and unassuming. He wore a chain of what we called pooka shells around his neck. Patrick loved the ocean more than anything. He surfed all summer long at his family's beach house and came back tanned, peeling, and beautiful in the fall. I spent hours devising ways to get myself out to the beach (about a three-hour drive away), so I could accidentally bump into him during the summers.

Patrick tolerated me and may even have thought I was OK. We stood outside of his house many afternoons, chatting about nothing in particular. Him inching his way back toward his driveway, me inching my way forward, hoping to be invited in.

Finally, I got my wish.

One afternoon, when his father found us studying for a math test in their basement, something I had cajoled Patrick into doing, panic struck his reddening, freckled face. He rushed over to where his father stood at the foot of the stairs, sort of blocking him from coming any farther. "Oh, this . . . uh . . .girl, she's in my . . um . . . class and we're just . . . um . . . studying for this test . . . uh . . . ."

This girl. Somehow, even my Dexatrimmed, straight-haired, Levi's-wearing, sweet-smiling self was *still* some kind of embarrassment. I was *this girl*. I felt so thrilled and privileged to be sitting in that house too. I thought I was getting somewhere. We were more than walk-home friends. We were study friends. Maybe that would bloom into hang-out buddies and then maybe . . . .

Maybe I had misunderstood, maybe Patrick was telling his dad, "This is my friend Pam, Dad. We're studying for this test tomorrow, OK? Can she stay for dinner?" To which his dad would reply, "Oh, nice to meet you Pam, dear" and extend his hand. "Please, stay and eat with us," he'd say. Later that evening, Mrs. Cleaver would yell down, "Kids, I've got cookies and milk on the table. Why don't you take a break?"

Isn't that how it goes?

That dream self-destructed as Patrick thrust my books and belongings at me and hurried me out the back door. His dad had taken him into the corner and told him, through clenched teeth and held-in fury, to show me out. I still remember his dad's very red face and angry eyes. I smiled nervously back at him, wondering if I should stay or run or try and sink into the carpet. Adults weren't supposed to look at little kids in the angry way Mr. McLaughlin was looking at me. What had I done?

Mrs. Cleaver never showed up for her part. And I never saw the inside of that house again. A snobby girl with long, silky red hair ended up being the real object of Patrick's affections. I never had a chance. Only I didn't realize that then (which was probably a good thing).

My crush was sufficiently crushed.

As a family we attended church every Sunday and had a big breakfast at the local greasy diner afterward. As I got older, my mother and I had terrible fights about dresses with puffed sleeves, patent-leather MaryJanes, and floppy hats. She was in favor of them; I was nauseated by them. The MarygraceColleens usually wore pants or even jeans to church, I argued. *I* was not *them,* I was told flatly. The battle raged.

St. Sebastian's was the large parish church that spawned the school I went to. It had three large sections of dark wooden pews that led up to an ornate altar with a crucified Jesus in the middle, a statue of Mary on one side of him, and a statue of Joseph on the other. Jesus looked skinny, hurt, and sad up there, with blood streaming down his brow.

Church was not fun when you had to attend with your parents. Forever restless, I always found something more interesting to do than listen to the drone of the sermon. Sometimes I would see school friends and smile or try to exchange conversation with whispers and sign language. I always got my mother or father's evil eye for those kind of antics. My favorite part was reciting the long, involved prayers and responses that I had memorized after years of constant repetition. Now it was a contest to see if I could say it faster than it was supposed to be read. Where there were pauses, you would hear Pamela's voice, hurrying on to the next verse. Thankfully, the service was just under an hour long, and I could escape to the smell of bacon, scrambled eggs, buttery toast, and hash browns.

By junior high, church actually began to affect me. I had just made my Confirmation (where you officially declare your allegiance to the faith) and had gotten a new middle name along with it (Elizabeth). Now that I was "confirmed," I was allowed to go to the Saturday night service with my friends, which allowed me to stand in the back and fool around the entire time if I wanted to. Instead, I wanted to listen. I looked at the Stations of the Cross, which were wall statues all around the church that depicted each stage of Jesus' journey to Golgotha. Those statues now made me teary. Why did poor Jesus have to go through all of that? Somehow, I knew I had something to do with why He was up there looking so poorly. And I wanted to fix it.

When the offering came around, my friends dropped their obligatory quarter into the velvet-lined basket and looked at me surprised when I put in a dollar. Really, I wanted to empty my pockets. I wanted to shed those welling-up tears. I wanted to stay afterward and say something—who knows what—to Jesus. But my stand-in-the-back peers were beckoning me.

It was time to move on.

Taking the high school co-op exams was the first time I ever remember praying for real. I wanted to get into Saint Francis Prep School (Prep, for short) so bad I could scream. Open house night was a dream come true. My mother and I toured the shiny halls and wondrous rooms with science equipment, electric typewriters, brand new desks, and lockers for every student. I was amazed as I watched the smiling Franciscan brothers, the order that ran the school, wearing their long, hooded black robes with loose white ropes as belts. Prep was tops in academics and in sports, too, which made it all the more exciting, as I was a budding athlete. A number of other brown-skinned parents and students were touring also. We exchanged the UBN (Universal Black Nod) that means glad-to-see-*you*-here.

All I knew was that I *had* to get into that school.

It was the number one choice of the brightest kids in my elementary school. I was one of them. When the envelope finally came, I opened it with trembling hands. It was a yes! I was going to be a Prepster! I remember thanking God for the first time, too, for that (from the heart, not in a rote prayer like at church). My mother said a chorus of "Thank you, Jesuses." My father must have murmured something affirmative from his parked position on the living room recliner.

The next day at school, I could hardly wait to tell my eighth-grade teacher, Miss Wincett. She was the first person I knew who had an adopted daughter and no husband. Everyone, including me, thought she was kind of funky and cool. She secured my good graces by excusing me from eating the greasy fried school lunches that sent me to the bathroom. She wore weird hats and always said, "Calm down, pee-pull!" when we got too rowdy.

Miss Wincett had to sign each acceptance card for whichever high school the student decided to attend. I approached her desk when my name was called, and I was so proud I'm sure I had my chest poked out. As she held her hand out for the card, she asked, "St. Agnes?" automatically assuming I had to take my second-choice school. When I replied confidently and with the sweet air of one-upmanship, "No, St. Francis Prep," you could have knocked her down with a mimeograph sheet. My own teacher never thought I could make it in. I was a B+ student. Miss Wincett, her lips forming a thin line, managed to mutter a fake-sounding, "Oh, congratulations," speaking more to the top of her desk than into my face. She scribbled her signature and thrust the card back at me. "Next!"

Despite *her* disappointment, *I* couldn't have been more thrilled. I saw the multihued faces during the open house and was giddy with excitement. I couldn't wait to see those faces again. I didn't know a single one of those black students, but I loved them all at first sight. I wanted to run up to each one, throw my arms around them, and say, "Thank you so much for being here," pumping their hands enthusiastically like a political hopeful, "Thankya, thankya ver much."

I had found Utopia—right there in Queens. Black friends, white friends, all together under one roof. All smart, talented, and high-achieving, on a level playing field, going places, doing things. Future movers and shakers. Imagining it—and the fact that *I* was a part of it—felt like having a tall, cool drink after a lifetime of living in the desert, when you didn't even know your throat was parched.

I just wanted to go there and drink it up.

Chapter Two
. . . In the Suburbs

I am a white American woman with suburban, eastern European roots and a life steeped in privilege.

Many times during my forty years, though, I have not been

Jo

aware of just *who* I am. When I do stop and think, when I stare at my baby pictures and my college graduation photographs, when I glance from the mirror to the world, I confess: I don't quite know what to do. Especially when it comes to race.

So I pray. I know deep in my white soul that only God can help me make sense of what I see and what I've experienced and what I will encounter. And where I came from.

I grew up on a block where all the houses were built exactly the same: brick boxes with small lawns and two-car garages with short driveways. All of the families who lived in the brick boxes looked like mine: a father who worked long hours, a mother who stayed at home and cooked, and children who ran and played and laughed and teased. We were blond and tan in the summers, bundled and pale in the winters. Lilacs bloomed every spring, and dry, colorless autumns ushered golden-haired, blue-eyed children into each new school year.

Every street in my suburban neighborhood was lined with wide sidewalks and bushes, every driveway had a station wagon, and every front yard had a child's bicycle and a short tree or two. Maple Grove Elementary School was right next door to the junior high, and both were just around the corner from the Safeway grocery store and a couple of churches. If ever there was a picture of uniformity—that is, of white, middle-class America—it was Applewood, Colorado, a twenty-minute drive to downtown Denver.

My parents, Jack and Jan, worked hard to give my older brothers, Jim and John, and me what they never had as children: comfortable stability. That's what suburban parents did in the 1950s and '60s. Even our initials were all the same.

But I was a restless child.

Don't get me wrong: I am grateful for the tennis lessons my parents paid for every spring at the private club down the street. I am thankful they signed me up for a ski club in the Rockies five winters in a row so I could learn what it meant to risk, fall, and survive the cold for the joy of skiing. I enjoyed playing softball every summer from the time I was eight years old until I graduated from high school (so I could learn the value of teamwork). And I appreciate the piano lessons (even if I can only play "Swans on a Lake"), the ballet classes I bungled in second grade, the Girl Scout troops that endured me in sixth grade, and the YMCA camp outings in the mountains.

In fact, it is difficult for me to imagine what life would have been like *without* riding my turquoise Stingray bicycle in endless figure eights on the backyard basketball court. Or hosting slumber parties with my softball friends in our basement. Or sledding down wintry hills at Maple Grove. Our life in Applewood was full of hamburgers on the grill, vacations in the car, and hide and seek in the yard.

And it was full of awkward distance.

But the opportunities were gifts, I see now. Gifts of privilege and access and choices, symbols of a lifestyle that America forged in the afterglow of a world war victory along with the Cleavers, Ed Sullivan, and Dick Van Dyke. Gifts available for *all* the people in the United States . . . who looked like I did.

Didn't all little girls grow up riding Stingray bicycles and taking ski trips? Did other little girls want time and talks even more than tennis lessons? Did they sometimes feel like they were on the outside looking in, like they weren't quite good enough, no matter how hard they tried and no matter how many times they were told they were?

Golden hair, blue eyes, suburban, athletic, western: I was the "all-American" kid.

I was eight years old when I first learned there might be people different from me. My parents took us to Honolulu to visit my mom's brother and his family. One night we went to a hula show put on by Hawaiian natives, and I looked up at these dark-haired, dark-skinned women with awe and respect. Red, pink, and white flower necklaces covered their chests and adorned their coal-black hair, which moved gently from side to side like a breeze. But it wasn't the dance that caught my attention; it was their . . . difference. Their very presence was as surprising and delightful as the first time I swam in the ocean. I could not look away from their brown flesh. All I had ever seen before were families who looked like mine. This difference was intriguing and somehow comforting to me as a child.

Still, the vacations and bicycles and lessons weren't enough for me. I had the strange luxury of feeling alienated *and* provided for, misunderstood *and* sheltered, like an underdog or a misfit in a typically dysfunctional (white) middle class family, amongst a bunch of other typically dysfunctional families in my white suburban neighborhood.

So I lived for the fun of activities, the pleasure of a busy schedule. Never mind if it left me empty, a hollow drum that played whatever rhythm was in the moment. Funny, though, how instead of filling me up, it only fueled my craving for more, directing me into more and more arenas where there were people, potential friends . . . relationships. I joined teams or clubs or cliques, hoping for some point of connection, for some significant interaction that would make me feel like I belonged.

Most suburban kids want to belong.

Maybe that's why I dreaded family reunions—gatherings of people I hardly knew but somehow was "related" to. Every other summer or so, my father would take us to a small rural town in eastern Colorado where my relatives lived. He had grown up on a farm during the Great Depression with six brothers and sisters who worked the land and milked the cows. My grandparents, Joseph and Vilma, met on a Czech settlement in a Nebraska farming town, first-generation children of immigrants who had left oppressive regimes to forge a new life on America's frontier. They were nice people, my aunts and uncles and cousins; they ate and laughed a lot and pinched my cheeks and told me how much I had grown since the last reunion. We would play softball in the fields, eat corn on the cob, hamburgers, and kolatches, and drink Pepsi-Cola out of bottles.

And it was confusing for me. Though I liked my relatives, I felt self-conscious around them, as if the only thing we had in common was our last name. Grandma never taught us much about Czech culture; we were Americans now, that's what mattered. Here we could have any job we wanted, eat as much as we could, drive any car we chose, and watch Tinkerbell on the big color television as she flew across "The Wonderful World of Disney." These were family reunions, places where I would fight and play with my brothers and cousins, stand up for the younger ones, and try to be nice to all the strangers I had never seen before. I knew I was supposed to feel connected. We were family, after all. And I tried to belong. For my dad's sake.

It wasn't easy. I felt too . . . odd.

School wasn't much better. In second grade, when I asked Miss Gibson to call me Jo instead of Joanne (as a tomboy who lived in a neighborhood of mostly boys, "Jo" just worked better), she laughed at the request. "What a crazy idea. Why would you want to do that, Joanne?" she said. In front of the class.

In third grade, I played Goldielocks in our class play. In front of the class, my teacher, Mrs. Lovely (yes, her real name), said I had the blondest hair. That made me "better" than the other kids.

In fifth grade, when the rest of the country was listening to Dr. Martin Luther King Jr. and Malcolm X and the Black Panthers talk about this "new" idea called civil rights, I couldn't believe my little white ears one day. Mr. Archebeque was teaching us about slavery. He was my favorite teacher so far; he was kind to me. His bald head, long sideburns, and bell-bottom plaid trousers communicated to me a confidence I knew I could trust. That's why I knew he wouldn't lie to me about something like *this*.

I shot up my hand and blurted out, "You mean, white people *owned* black people? Why would they do that, why would they do that?" The horror slapped me like the Colorado cold in January. My Hispanic mentor was patient but firm: "Yes, Jo, that's right. Slavery is a part of the history of our country."

I hadn't cared much about school before—except gym class and reading—so I have no idea why this history lesson bothered me so; I didn't even know a black person and had barely seen one in my ten-year-old life. In fact, the only black people I knew of were the Jackson Five and Sammy Davis Jr. All of a sudden, though, I was wide-eyed and open-eared as I listened to Mr. Archebeque recount how many white families in several southern states had bought and paid a lot of money for black men, women, and children to work their land.

As if they were buying groceries or pets.

He told *me*—I was completely unaware of the other children in the class by now—how thousands of black families had been sold from one another, many were beaten and tortured, most were denied opportunities to own land or businesses, and it was illegal for them to learn how to read, write, and gather together. He said the government passed laws to make it so.

Mr. Archebeque had always told me the truth before, but this seemed impossible to believe. How could the government have done such bad things? My elementary mind just could not fathom why people could be so mean to other people just because of what they looked like, or didn't look like.

I had to think about this some more.

And my fifth grade teacher *let* me think about this strange evil called slavery. Rather than glossing over its place in our country's formation, he allowed me to feel it, as much as a ten-year-old suburban blond could. He handed me a fifth-grade-level biography of a former slave who became what was called an "ab-o-li-tion-ist." His name was Frederick Douglass, and in that book I met my first black hero. I wrote a short paper on him, drew his wild thick hair with black and white crayons, and handed my report to Mr. Archebeque with great pride. He smiled, and somehow, deep within my little belly, I was really, really glad. I had found a new friend, and I had pleased my favorite teacher.

But what of the little slave girls and boys? I was still confused.

Did Mr. Archebeque know what he had done? Did Mrs. Lovely know what she had done?

Funny, all my other teachers—the ones who looked like I did—never talked about slavery. Or Frederick.

The year of my first "black" revelation was also the year that George Wallace was running for president. My parents were active Republicans—we had red, white, and blue Barry Goldwater buttons all over our house—so I was exposed early on to the political process. Some big white kid from the junior high told me that Mr. Wallace wanted to separate the country: put all the black people in one place and the whites in another. Make it legal and neat and orderly. That way everyone would know his place, he said.

"Segregation now . . . Segregation tomorrow . . . Segregation forever." These were the exact words of his inaugural speech when he became governor of Alabama, the same campaign cry we heard that election year. Again, a burning confusion swept through my being. I fired back to the boy, "Nu-uh. No one would *ever* do that!"

"Sure they would, dumbo. Niggers got to know what's good for them."

The big white kid might as well have slugged me in the stomach.

I caught my breath and quickly staggered away from the demonic-looking white youth. The cool spring afternoon suddenly seemed to change to one hundred degrees plus humidity. I walked alone, slow, heavy step after slow, heavy step, toward our brick box house, eyes searching the black pavement on the side of the road as station wagons swirled past me. My fifth grade mind was busy, and I began to compose in my head a speech that was sure to put Mr. Wallace in his place. I tightened my fists. He'd hear from me why that racial segrega-thing was such a bad idea. Who did he think he was anyway? Oh, I'd let him have it if I ever met the man.

I shivered as I thought of him becoming president, this boy I had just met at the junior high, and the slaveholders Mr. Archebeque had told me about. What would Frederick think of all this? What did *I* think of all this? I looked around at all the driveways and yards and windows.

And I felt lonely.

I didn't like it. So I walked through the door of our brick house and did what most suburban children did to escape the pain that comes when reality invades your artificial, comfortable world: I turned on the television. The "Dick Van Dyke Show," to be exact. Soon afterward, my mom called me for dinner. My brothers played basketball in the backyard. And that night my dad went to a Kiwanis Club meeting.

School ended that year much as it began for me every school year: with little-girl excitement for something different. Softball tournaments and swim club crammed my summer, and I all but forgot about the strange brush with racial injustice I encountered in fifth grade. Once in a while I remembered Frederick, but now I was exploring Laura Ingalls Wilder's *Little House on the Prairie* and Nancy Drew mysteries. By the next school year, I began to notice other strange things: boys.

My friends and I loved to tease Timmy and Brad and Danny and all the other boys in our class. We would meet them secretly for routine rounds of spin the bottle, hide and seek, and truth or dare. We laughed and reveled in discovering this new world of "he likes you—she likes you" and note passing and long telephone conversations. We'd meet at Lakeside Amusement Park (being careful to steer clear of the tough Hispanic girls I had heard liked to beat up blonds) and stroll through haunted houses with the boyfriend of the week.

Social life was settling in like a habit.

So my parents did what any logical parents would do to protect their only daughter from a premature and wayward life: they sent her to camp. Camp Chief Ouray in Colorado's tiny mountain town of Granby would distract and toughen her up a bit, they thought. So I sold cookies to rich white people in neighborhoods a few miles away to help pay for my two-week trip. This would make me more responsible, my parents reasoned. Soon I had earned my way to Camp Chief Ouray and was on the train riding through the majesty of the Colorado mountains, ready to learn how to ride horses, hike trails, and carve wood plaques.

What my parents must have forgotten, though, was that Camp Chief Ouray had a unique policy (that many YMCA camps did not have at that time): it was coed. Plenty of boys my age had come for two weeks of mountainous adventures; the idea of BB-guns, canoeing, and girls had tantalized them as well. Maybe my mom and dad thought I'd be so busy learning crafts and archery that I wouldn't have time for crushes.

They were wrong.

Within a few days, I had a new cute boyfriend named Randy. Most of the girls thought he was the cutest boy at camp, with his rich brown eyes and sweet smile. He wasn't much taller than I was, but I was impressed at how well he could play softball and basketball. He was a good athlete, a funny guy, cute, and . . . black. In fact, Randy was one of only a few black kids who had come to camp. So now a white blond seventh-grade girl was holding hands with a young black boy. I never even thought about his skin color; I just thought he was cute and nice.

Two weeks of junior-high romance is hardly the stuff of great love stories. Randy and I talked on the telephone a few times after camp—he lived in a nearby town, but it was too far to continue boyfriend/girlfriend status. Still, the summer of my first (and only) black boyfriend speaks clearly to me now: I had no barriers that would have kept me even from having a crush on Randy. There was no reason *not* to like him. Besides, my parents were "open" enough not to worry too much when they saw his picture on my wall. I heard no lecture about race matters, no discussion about boyfriends in general. Just a periodic holler to "get off the phone, Joanne!"

But did junior-high girls in the southern states Mr. Archebeque told me about do the same? Would they hold hands with a black boy or think he was cute? Or would they have expected Randy to "know his place"?

No matter. I lost interest in Randy when I became popular in eighth grade. I was the class president. I was somebody. For a whole year.

The next year I was odd again. Rebellion's roots ran deep, and authority figures were impossible to deal with. In science, math, and even physical education, my teachers would not tolerate my temper or my tantrums and often demanded that I leave. Fine with me—I wanted to do what I wanted to do, and no amount of rules was going to change that. I made many visits to the principal's office.

But my English teacher, Mrs. Manning, was different. Every day her neat brown hair flipped up at the ends. Her flat shoes always matched her skirts. In fact, every day Mrs. Manning looked as if she were dressed for the most important job in the world. She never raised her voice, never changed her tone. Her classroom was organized, her rules were clear, and her words were always kind.

I respected her.

Mrs. Manning must have heard in the teachers' lounge that I was not the most attentive or cooperative child and that I had a reputation for mouthing off at teachers. If she did hear this, she never said anything to me. Instead, she assigned me "special tasks." Besides diagramming sentences on the chalkboard, she trusted me enough to send me to the library and check out books about Dr. Martin Luther King, poetry by Langston Hughes, and short stories by a variety of black authors. I wondered why I was the chosen one, but I paid attention; this was much more interesting than detention hall or the principal's office.

As I began to read, something in the works of these writers got lodged in my soul. Somehow I connected with their stories, with the struggles they felt, with the fights they endured against authorities, with the justice and understanding and acceptance they sought. The poems, the characters, the trials all spoke of an unusual determination and vision. I guess their words showed me a depth of life I had never come close to but always imagined. While I was getting kicked out of my other classes, black literature and Mrs. Manning kept me in English. In junior high altogether.

For the first time, belonging was not so confusing. If only in books.

The more I read, though, the more the wrongdoings nagged me like an elbow pressed against my ribs. I could not indulge too often in this thought of injustice—it was too depressing and, I see now, I was too insecure. I obeyed Mrs. Manning but put away the books. My quest for relationships and acceptance always overshadowed any emerging social conscience. The next year I joined every club and team our high school had. I would try to tolerate authority figures. And above all, I would make friends.

I would make the kind of friends I had seen that summer in my favorite movie, *To Sir with Love*. Sidney Poitier, a fine black actor, played a teacher who was determined to help a bunch of white, misfit teenagers in London. Other teachers had all but given up on them. Lulu and the others stuck together, even when their deviance and rebellion got the best of them. Eventually they began to change their ways, especially when they realized this black Sir, this different teacher, believed in them.

I sang along with Lulu, all the more determined to belong. Never mind that I came in third or fourth in all the sports or speech tournaments or student government campaigns. (Mediocre. Looking on. *Potential*.) A few times I let myself notice the others who were "different," the handful of "minorities" in our high school of two thousand, a school whose mascot was still "Farmer," though there wasn't a cornfield for miles in this newly developed suburban sprawl.

Our mostly white high school was full of Beavers and Wallys in 1974, full of other "all-American" kids. We had a state championship football team and a pep club—the "Farmer's Daughters," who wore denim overalls with yellow-checkered blouses under them. At home, in the car, or at parties, we listened to Simon and Garfunkel, James Taylor, and Carole King. During the weekdays, we smoked cigarettes and drank coffee at the Village Inn coffee shop while we ditched biology or geometry class. And on the weekends, after football games, we crooned and drank beer at "kegger parties," though I hated the taste of Coors (brewed three miles from my house). I went to the parties to be with friends. Socializing was consuming.

And the hollow, restless drum still echoed in me.

Did all high school sophomores ache for acceptance, for some sort of meaning? Did Randy?

After football season and just before basketball, a friend told me of another social event. Was it a party? I asked. No, it was something called a "youth group," a weekly meeting where most of the popular kids went to someone's house, playing crazy games, singing strange songs, talking about life. The cutest guys were often there. So were many of the jocks and the cheer-leaders. Even my oldest brother.

But I was completely confused. Why would these cool, upper-middle-class teenagers go to a party where there was no beer? No cigarettes? No slow-dancing? Just a gathering with a "religious" emphasis, they told me.

Weird.

My family had gone to Shepherd of the Hills Presbyterian Church most Christmases and Easters, but I didn't know much about God. Besides, what possible use did all-American kids have for religion? Who needed something else to believe in besides yourself? After all, if you wore stylish clothes, drove a Mustang, and played on the football team or dated an athlete, you were in. Popular. Accepted. You had arrived.

Why would anyone want anything else? Why did I? So desperately.

I was about to find out.

Chapter Three
. . . In the South

When you're the newest baby born into a farming family that already has fourteen children—all by the same mother and father—your parents tend to run out of names. That might be how I got mine. They already had a Johnnie Mae, Forrestine, Hazell, Dorothy Jean, Pearlie Sylvester, Tommie Dale, Eddie, Faye, Janice, Beatrice, Elroy, Mary, Cliffie, and Gennora.

When you're the youngest of fifteen children, baby photos are a luxury!

Elvon

Then me. When I was born in 1967, it's as if my folks looked at me, glowing in all my newborn colors, then at each other, and said, "Number 15. Hmmm. Let's call her El . . . von. Yeah . . . that's it."

I'm told Elvon means "colorful" in Arabic. My brothers and sisters have always called me Penny because my sister Bea thought my little-girl skin was the color of a penny and that I "wasn't no bigger'n one." I've been Penny to them ever since.

Seems appropriate, too, since mine has been a life shaded by a region of our country where dark and light really do sit next to each other, like the train tracks that still segregate many southern towns. I've experienced blatant racism at churches and businesses—the kind that stings and makes you cry. Yet I've also received gracious acceptance from neighbors and peers—the kind that soothes and offers a tissue.

I am a southern, African-American, Christian wife, mother, and teacher who knows, really knows, that black pride and white friends are not diametrically opposed. I am as familiar with collard greens as I am with Caesar salad, with Pentecostal worship services as I am with reformed Presbyterianism, with small town Arkansas as I am with New York City.

I have to be. I live on the corner where black and white intersect. Every day. And I don't mind.

Not now anyway.

Growing up black in the rural South means you automatically learn that there are two Americas. For instance, the place I was born, Forrest City, Arkansas, was named after a former Confederate general, Nathan B. Forrest, who founded the Ku Klux Klan. It was the nearest town with a hospital, about eighty miles west of Memphis, Tennessee, and about fifteen from our forty-acre farm in Hughes. Medical care wasn't readily available, so my mother hadn't even seen a doctor (when you're having your fifteenth, you kind of know how this thing works) until she got to the Forrest City Memorial Hospital and had me prematurely. Smallest, youngest, and the color of a penny, in a town named after the KKK's original grand wizard.

Welcome to the world.

Our mailing address—where my parents still live—reads Rt. 1 Box 61, Heth, Arkansas." But Heth, which consists of a post office and a truck stop, is really about eight miles from our nine-room red brick house. We had a huge yard where pecan and Cypress trees surrounded our house like a shield, where we children would hide behind tree trunks and thrown-down picnic benches and bombard each other with Cypress balls. If you stood on our back porch, you could see the cotton fields I picked until I was in seventh grade, the patches of okra, peanuts, butter beans, cucumbers, tomatoes, and peas we grew and sold every summer at the farmers market in Memphis.

Those summers in northeast Arkansas were as hot and as humid as they say—great for growing rice and mosquitoes, not so good for working. But we did. Hotter than Hades, too, as each May we'd watch the thermometer hit eighty degrees, preparing us for a dripping one hundred by July and hanging around until September. Summer for us was not a vacation, unlike what it must have been for suburban or city kids. We were up at sunrise and in the sweltering fields before we knew it, picking the crops and preparing them for Memphis.

Evenings were just as hot and muggy. We were fortunate enough to have an air conditioner that we'd sit under while we ate fresh cantaloupe or watermelon. And we were always ready to go back to school to end the work, to enter the fall months where life would actually cool off—back into the eighties and nineties, that is—so that by November we'd even have chilly evenings. Winter only visited in January or February, ushering in green, colorful springs by Easter. Different colors—greens, pinks, yellow, whites—blossomed everywhere.

Our nearest neighbors were a white family named the Wests. They only lived a quarter of a mile away, separated only by our fields, but I don't recall ever seeing them. I know they lived there—their crops proved someone was working the fields—but the Wests were as invisible to me as ghosts. Maybe it's because the father and sons were members of the local KKK. In fact, I didn't even know they had two boys—or such Arian leanings— until I came home from my freshman year of college and my father told me. He had waited until then. Didn't want to scare me, I guess.

I can't remember when I first heard about the KKK—or slavery—or lynchings. They've just always been there, settled into my head like dust on a country road.

Our neighbors in the other direction were another large black family whose boys and girls often came over to play Cypress war with us or to play basketball with Elroy on the homemade court my father had made out of a log and two-by-fours. Not many black people in Arkansas owned their land then, much less a house worth something. But we were *the Reeds*—my daddy made that clear to us with a belt or a look—an upstanding family in the community whose children all made good grades in school and were expected to graduate from college (and did). Reeds did not go out on Saturday nights to the juke houses, and didn't drink or smoke or hang out with those who did. Though neither of my parents ever made it past the eighth grade, they understood the meaning of hard work and sacrifice and expected the same from us. They had, after all, built our home with the money they received from my oldest brother's military pension from the war. Junior had died in Vietnam in 1968. I never met him.

So our family was considered well-off by blacks who knew us and somewhat respected by whites we'd encounter in town.

Never quite equal though. That was clear.

"Hey, *Floyd,* how's the crops?" the local white farmers would ask my father as he pulled into town. "Hey, *Floyd,* something you need today?" the store-owners would say to him. Then they'd stare at him, white eyes on black skin and a centuries' old glare, waiting for the polite reply of this "Negro" who was probably older than most of them, "Yes, sir, *Mr.* Banks," or "Fine, *Mr.* Smith," or "How 'bout you, *Mr.* Jones?"

What they didn't hear was his, "I see what you're doing. Who do you think you are, anyway?" that he'd scowl under his breath when they turned their backs. My dark father, who spent most of his days working hard on the land he owned to support the children he loved, would stare back at these younger white men, flash "the grin" that all southern black people learned to give white people, and go on about his business. And my mom's tiny five-foot-four-inch "high yella" frame (that's what we'd call it in the South because she's light skinned) would stand proud and still next to my father. She would smile sincerely at the white faces, especially if she felt sorry for them. It's a smile I still see today in her seventy-seven years, one that reveals a pretty row of pearly white teeth—all her own, too, which is no small thing considering she was forty years old the first time she went to a dentist.

I think she's beautiful. Smiling when she had to and when she wanted to.

I think my father was wise. He had to be. He still is.

My parents grew up in Arkansas, though my mama's folks came from the Mississippi Delta. Her grandmother was full Cherokee Indian, and her papa was a teacher in the Negro school. My father, on the other hand, built his muscles and his pride from harvesting the land—he came from a long, proud line of southern farmers. At least until many of his aunts and uncles heard there was work up north and moved into the cities. Some even made it as far as Chicago.

I'd only see them and my cousins at family reunions every other August or so when they'd gather in, of all places, Forrest City, for barbecue and hamhocks and corn and catching up, all in one-hundred-degree heat. Then they'd come out to Route 1 and visit us on our farm. My father didn't like us going to Forrest City, so he avoided the reunions, telling his relatives that if they wanted to see the Reeds they'd have to come to the red brick house. He never quite understood why they left country life to begin with. What was so great about the city anyway?

New adventures and letting go of grudges were not high on my father's list of priorities.

Discipline in our house was. For my older brothers and sisters, that meant a switch from the tall persimmon tree out back. Get out of line or fight with a sibling, and my father's stern look (translation: "You're gonna get a whoopin'!") would push us back on the right track. A belt, a switch, or a hand across our backside was his method of keeping his children in line, all fifteen. But since I was the youngest and the smallest, I rarely experienced my father's correction. I could hide behind the others or watch from a distance or learn from my elder siblings' errors. I knew enough to stay clear of my father.

Always the smart kid. Had to be.

But the couple of times I did stray from the path of obedience and into the painful chastisement of my father are still clear in my mind.

One spring afternoon I decided to stay after school to hang out with my friends. High school games and gossip had become more exciting than staying home. My older brothers and sisters had all left home by then, and the last thing I wanted to do was sit around the house or pick vegetables with controlling adults who also happened to be my parents. Never mind my father's deep voice, still echoing in my adolescent head: "Better get home directly after school or *else!*"

I stayed at school anyway. Testing the waters.

Direct disobedience. That's what he called it.

I think it was his right farming hand—the one that dropped seeds into the ground or pulled up weeds—that slapped my tender, penny-colored cheek and made it redder. Of course, he waited until we left the halls of the school, away from eye view and earshot of friends and potential boyfriends, away from any possible embarrassment that a disobedient child might cause a proud, controlling father. The only way to teach me to obey him, he said, was to feel his hard, blistered, farming hand on my cheek.

I learned.

Don't get out of line.

You can imagine what happened when one of my older sisters came home at sixteen years old, acting aloof and moody. She looked different to my then six-year-old eyes, though I wasn't sure why. Something was funny. Then she started throwing up some mornings. Finally, another sister caught on and without thinking one day loudly inquired, "Are you pregnant?" The guilty one looked out the window as she whispered that, yes, she was "going to have a baby." At sixteen. Without getting married. I understood enough to recognize that our daddy was not happy.

Rage is a better word. Rip-through-the-house-and-throw-things-off-the-shelf-rage. The Reeds did not get pregnant at sixteen, unmarried, without finishing high school. Didn't she know any better?

At the age of six, I became an auntie to our family's first "illegitimate girl," Baby Audrey. And our daddy became a proud, stern, disciplining grandpa.

He loved Audrey like he did all of us.

Raising fifteen children and watching them go through a million changes, and then become parents themselves, was no easy matter. Thankfully, my mama had known enough to ask for divine help through all those years. It was she who first thought that praying before dinner would be a good idea. And she was the one who insisted that church was something we all needed.

So, when I was barely old enough to know any better, we were faithful Sunday morning members of St. Paul's A.M.E. (African Methodist Episcopal) Church in a place called Wavery, not too far from Heth. Before that we went to St. John's A.M.E. in Hughes for years and years. We stopped going to St. John's because my father had had a falling out with the minister—something he said, I guess—and grudges had a way of hanging around my father like summer humidity.

My asthma was acting up one Sunday morning when we went to St. Paul's. We sat on wooden pews, looking out the four-pane windows. Flies buzzed around church hats and baby strollers and choir members. It was hot, and I was especially hot because I had been wheezing and coughing. Everyone else had on cool summer outfits, but I wore a thick black coat; my parents thought I might get chilled from the asthma, though I had no idea how that was possible in ninety-degree heat. The congregation fanned themselves with the fans supplied by Watts Funeral Home—standard "air conditioning" for small southern black churches. This Sunday I was sweating, dripping really, feeling light-headed even, but I didn't want to tell my mom. I just couldn't interrupt church.

If the pastor was talking about God that morning, I didn't hear him. I was just trying to stay alive. In fact, I'm not sure I heard him the other mornings either. I don't remember the sermons or Bible stories or church prayers of those early years. I just was always hot and wheezing. And miserable, sitting for two or three hours solid on hard wood benches, fighting flies and stuffy air and boredom.

But I did get distracted during the money part of each service. The offering was counted faithfully after Sunday School classes by one of the teenage girls who would then report to the congregation how much had been given, how many people were in attendance, and what announcements we needed to be aware of. Then the singing would start, the pastor would preach, and I would wheeze and sweat.

That was church life for me until I was eight. I didn't go again until I was in college. Unless, of course, there was a funeral or a wedding. Or unless I was visiting my sister and her husband in Memphis. For some reason, a few of my siblings never stopped going to church. Mama's influence was stronger than the flies, I guess.

Now that I think about it, growing up for most of my brothers and sisters was different from what I experienced as the youngest. Some of them literally grew up at St. Paul's A.M.E. Church, whereas I only attended every now and then as a young girl. Most attended all black schools and colleges, whereas I, the post-civil rights baby in the South, was enrolled in integrated schools all of my life.

I went to school in Hughes eight miles from our house in the other direction from Heth. Most of my siblings went to the "colored" school, Mildred Jackson High School, just outside of Hughes—Stump City, they called it, which was close to Greasy Corner. (I promise, I'm not making this up.) My brother Eddie was in the first class at Hughes High that graduated as an integrated class. That was in 1972. His picture is still hanging in the halls there because he was Hughes High School's first black valedictorian.

That makes my father smile.

Still, no amount of home discipline could have made school life any easier for us. Like most southern black children after the 1960s and '70s, all of us confronted a host of challenges and obstacles that gave learning a skin color. My first grade teacher,

Mrs. Cross—a large black woman—thought I was stupid and immature. Because I was little, I had been sick a lot, which meant that everyone babied me. Mrs. Cross, however, thought that should change. She was sure I was taking longer to read than the other kids (white kids), and every day her face told me she thought I somehow had the misfortune of inheriting dumb genes. I guess Mrs. Cross just wasn't convinced that I could succeed.

But it didn't matter to me what Mrs. Cross said or how she looked at me. My seven-year-old mind already knew that I would be going to college and that I was smart enough to do so. All of my older brothers and sisters had gone, and every Christmas they would come home from their semesters and talk about classes and professors and dorm life. I would listen to their enthusiasm over Christmas dinners of macaroni and cheese, turkey, ham, dressing, green beans, yeast bread, squash casserole, and the okra that had been frozen from the summer. Then over chocolate cake, pecan and sweet potato pie, and my mother's jelly coconut cake (my favorite), I would listen to more college stories, dream of my own, and absorb the confidence that floated through the house like the sweet smells of Christmas dinner.

I loved Christmas breaks because not only did it mean feasting and stories and laughter, it meant playing games with all my brothers and sisters. They'd smile at their little, penny-colored sister and oblige her with Old Gray Horse—one of my favorite games played with pecans, where we had to guess how many someone was holding in his cupped hands. The object was to end up with the most pecans.

I never won. I had the smallest hands.

It didn't matter, though. I just liked being around my brothers and sisters, whose college experiences were a badge of honor in our family. Now I was convinced it was Mrs. Cross who was the stupid one. We all knew that education was the only way out; otherwise, you were destined to live on a farm, share crops, or hang out at the juke houses like everyone else.

The Reeds were different.

And I knew it. Though we were never actually told, "You're as good as anyone else," we all believed it. Maybe that's why I always got along well with the white kids in my class. At least until I got older and we all began to move into the adult world of bigotry. I can't deny feeling that white people always thought they were superior to blacks. Yankees might not understand it, but white people's attitudes of superiority were just how life was in Arkansas, as commonplace as the summer heat. It's just how it was. The Reeds, though, never let it overshadow us. We knew who we were.

And so I attended classrooms filled with people who looked like I did, as well as a few who didn't. Most of the students in my public school were black—a lot of white children were sent to private, Christian schools when integration was passed—and most of the teachers were white. After Mrs. Cross, I didn't see myself again in front of the class until seventh grade.

New faces showed up. The middle-class white kids who had gone to the private elementary school in Hughes suddenly were mixing into our junior high. They were friendly enough to us and seemed "normal." But I did notice they wore better clothes: Chic or Lee jeans and Nike sneakers—things I never had. When you buy clothes for a few children, I guess you can afford brand names. But when you're from a family of fifteen, well, you shop at Wal-Mart, my favorite store.

Regardless of what we were wearing, I knew I was their intellectual counterpart and in some cases their superior. I made better grades; I did better on standardized tests. My parents never pressured us about our grades—they just expected us to do our best. And so we did. Still, no matter how many A's I got on my report card, my white peers always acted a little more confident than I did, and, ironically, we both felt there was something correct about that.

They knew their place. Just like the farmers who met my father in town did. Yes, they had a long history of *place*. Of power. Of "superiority."

My mother would show me the trees or the fields where friends of the family had been lynched. "Right out there," she would point, "is where Jimmy Ray Jones or Danny Smith was lynched. Right out there." In the telling, her face was stern, distant even. I guess she had to be. Such memories were painful lessons, and she felt her baby needed such instruction.

It wasn't until my senior year of high school that I began to realize there was something not quite right about this sense of superiority, this white confidence. It was, after all, the early 1980s, not the '50s or '60s. Things were not as obvious. I was never called nigger, for instance, or instructed to pick up someone's books. I was never ordered to sit in the back of the bus or demanded to drink out of a different water fountain.

Life was just split in two: a white culture and a "colored" culture. That's the way it is.

Two Americas.

I had no problems with most of the white kids for several years. Maybe because we kept our distance. Boys and girls liked each other inside our own circles. Ate inside our own circles. Lived inside our own circles. Hughes High School's proms were even separate. The school day was the only shared turf between black and white.

But age has a way of making life more complicated. And during the year of my high school graduation, I began to pay more attention to this issue called race.

In Mrs. Cook's American history class, I learned about the civil rights movement. In February we celebrated Black History Month, and that year, I was elected president of the Beta Club. I had lost the bid for student council president but was happy to be leader of the smart people as opposed to the popular people. The only problem was that mine was one of only three dark faces in the club.

At one meeting I was presiding over, we spent hours debating a particular policy at school. The members were divided over the issue, though it seemed a particularly trivial one to me. I listened to arguments from both sides, and when it became obvious we weren't going anywhere, I pulled rank—and in the process I also pulled what I have learned can be interpreted as a cultural faux pas: I overruled an idea by Charles Elton Wise, a white boy with glasses and Nike shoes. He turned red and looked at the ground, silent. A sharp hush dropped on the group. The meeting ended.

The next day at lunch I sat at a long table with another black girl. Anita was always a little slower, I thought, one of those black people who really believed white people were superior, and I always wondered if maybe her greasy Jehri Curl had something to do with it. I took a bite of my sandwich as I began talking about the previous club meeting. Student council wasn't doing enough for us, I said.

"I think people need to speak up and tell others what they want, assert themselves for what they think should happen," I declared to Anita and anyone else at the table.

Then I noticed that Charles Elton was eavesdropping on our conversation. He turned to a white friend sitting next to him and said loud enough for me to hear: "Listen to Elvon. She must think she's white." I knew I stood only five feet tall, but I was bold enough to challenge this middle-class pale face sitting across from me.

"What did you say, Charles Elton? What did you say about me?" I riveted. He ignored me, finished his lunch, and left.

When you confront someone and the person doesn't do anything, doesn't respond at all, you're left with an anger seething inside you.

I seethed—throughout the rest of my senior year and all the way to college. I was infuriated. Other racial incidents occurred that year—the kind you always remember—that fueled my anger and confusion.

I had known Michelle since junior high school. We had been as good of friends as white and black girls could be at that time. But I never really knew my status with her; even her white friends weren't always sure what she'd say one day or do the next. She'd toss around her long brown hair as if she owned the world.

One day after school she pushed her luck. She began teasing me in front of her white friends because of my Wal-Mart jeans. Charles Elton's comment was still boiling in me, and the last thing I needed was her stupid remark about my clothes. I had had enough. I looked right into her shallow little brown eyes and screamed, "I don't know who you think you are! What makes you think you can do something like this?"

Michelle's face turned sour, and I watched as the whiteness around her eyes turned red.

"I don't care what you think. You're just a little black girl!" With that, she tossed her head around and walked off with her friends—laughing all the way down the hall.

I burned with rage all night.

The next morning in Mrs. Cook's first-period class, I was determined to make Michelle pay. When she walked into class, I grabbed her desk, picked it up a few inches off the floor, and slammed it down so hard that everyone looked up. Terror filled her face, and I was pleased to be the cause of it.

We were both sent to the office.

The principal was white, of course, and he assured me immediately that any ill feelings toward me were not due to my race but due to other factors, like my unseemly behavior. I glared at his long skinny, head as he sat there. He wore a too-tight white short-sleeved shirt with a pale gray tie and square, brown thick glasses. He was very businesslike with both of us and listened intently to both sides of the story. Michelle assured him that she was not prejudiced; she had "lots of black friends," so this was not a "racial incident." I rolled my eyes. She gloated, her face growing whiter with each statement.

Then they both left, and I sat alone in that office, cursing the hot tears that came down my face. This was not a racial incident? They both had said it. "How would you know?" I seethed inside. It was the first of many encounters I would have where a white authority invalidated my feelings.

High school ended, and I graduated in the top of my class. That's what Reeds did. I had hoped to go away to a college out of state, but financial reality set in, and I ended up at a primarily white college campus in Jonesboro, about a hundred miles from home. I was going to study speech communication and theatre, maybe pursue teaching, maybe performing. Whichever, I was determined to start fresh and leave these disturbing racial relationships behind me. College life would surely be different than rural, segregated Arkansas.

The night I graduated from high school, one of my brothers, who had become a doctor at Yale, gave me some healthy big-brotherly advice: study two hours for every four hours of partying. So from September until I came home for Christmas vacation, I followed his advice. I was consumed with having a life. I had come to get away from home, and race consciousness was the last thing on my list.

All my friends at college were black—there were precious few of us on campus, so we had to stick together. I was a little odd to my roommate, though, because I liked rhythm and blues, "Chicago," and Bruce Springsteen all at once and listened to them on my Walkman. I can honestly say I had no white friends my freshman year of college, and frankly, I didn't want any. I believed I would be fine if I lived the rest of my life in my black world. Until I met some other black friends who were different. They didn't go out drinking or dancing all the time. They didn't fight or act out, but they weren't timid either, like Anita had been. They just had a confidence, a security, that I had never seen before, not even in my own siblings.

I decided to get involved in their group. And when I did, my whole world turned upside down.

Chapter Four
. . . In the North

I'm a direct descendent of John and Priscilla Alden, who sailed the Mayflower in 1620 and lived in Massachusetts. They believed in fierce independence, hard work, and justice for all,

Andrea

values that ran throughout our family tree: from a soldier who fought in the Revolutionary War to the famous bridge builder, John Vaughn, of the early 1800s; from my grandfather who farmed in the Massachusetts cold to my grandmother who worked alongside her pastor-husband; to my own radical parents in the 1960s, and finally to me, a thirtysomething social worker.

Mine are typical European roots—English, Scottish, French, German. I'm about as American as they come. A "mutt," I sometimes answer when someone asks me about my heritage.

But a mutt with conviction.

My supervisor in my graduate school field placement told me I was a WASP (White Anglo-Saxon Protestant), and for the next nine months she held up a mirror to confirm it. I had to admit, I hadn't thought much about my birthright.

You see, my Waspy but open-minded, liberal parents raised me with a sense of conviction and social consciousness. They were what I now call "reserved hippies," committed to social change, racial justice, and world peace. It was, after all, the 1960s, and they just could not help themselves. The pressure to "change the world" was a responsibility they couldn't ignore—if they didn't do it, who would?—and they passed on this mandate thick and heavy to my siblings and me.

But they were not the type of radicals you'd think of when remembering the turbulent American sixties. They rarely marched, carried signs, or wrote protest letters. Rather, my mom and dad were radical within the religious community—namely the mainline Methodist church—at a time when picket-fenced, "don't rock the boat" lifestyles were more the norm in white Christian families than ethnic dishes and simple living. Our first baby-sitters, for instance, were African Americans, and I can't remember many times when our dinner table wasn't full of Asian and Native American friends of my parents or European and African exchange students who had come to live with us for a semester. Even our closest friends lived this way. Cultural diversity was so typical in our home that I grew up assuming it was normal, just the responsible way to behave. These principles sunk into my head quite early in life, even if they did not take root in my heart.

My parents met in 1958 at Union Theological Seminary in New York City. My mom was working in a summer internship at the East Harlem Protestant parish for her Christian Education degree. She grew up in a liberal home with a pastor-father and a passion for mission-oriented ministry. My father, raised in a pragmatic and somewhat stoic New England farming family of Methodists, wanted desperately to change the world with the gospel. Both my parents felt a burden to minister to city dwellers. Within a year of meeting each other (and the same year my mom graduated), they got married. By 1960, my dad completed his master of divinity degree and was ordained as a Methodist minister.

They first accepted a pastorate at a church in Baltimore, Maryland, then in Boston. Five years and two sons later, they moved back to the heart of inner-city Baltimore, where I was born.

East Baltimore, to be exact, a lower middle-class, racially diverse urban neighborhood. When I was only a year old, my parents opened our home to a Cuban scholarship student. I don't remember much of Luis—he was in class or rehearsal most of the time, and I was in diapers and sandboxes—but I do know he was the first of many introductions my parents made sure I had to people who were different from me.

When I was a toddler, my parents decided we weren't living close enough to the people my father was ministering to, so we packed up and moved again. This time, though, they bought and renovated an old row house and relocated only fifteen minutes away in east Baltimore. Our neighbors were African Americans, Native Americans, and lower-income whites. We lived in a three-story row house on the busy avenue of South Broadway so we could be closer to the churches where my dad ministered and the people who needed his help. My parents hosted and helped organize many a potluck dinner and went on numerous family events with our brown-skinned neighbors. Jean and Bob Clark were not just talk.

That was an unusual posture to take if you were white and Christian in the 1960s. This was a period in American history when most "mutt" families were sitting comfortably in their suburban living rooms, watching white southern police officers hose down African-American women and children on their new color TV sets, when the U.S. Congress was still smarting over President Johnson's civil rights bill, and when most white evangelical churches were not even considering the idea of racial equality. It was 1966—a time loaded with change and tension—and my father was reaching out to black men, Indian families, and anyone else who needed support. He was intense in his focus to serve. I suppose he had to be in those days.

My radical father even helped start a community center for the Native American Lumbee tribe, a tribe whose history goes back to the lost colony of Sir Walter Raleigh in Roanoke, North Carolina. Seems the Sir returned to England and all but forgot about these English settlers he brought over. Maybe he was distracted by the Spanish war with England. To survive the new terrain, they were helped by a local friendly native tribe and disappeared into the hills of North Carolina. The two groups eventually intermarried and became a mixed race of Indians with English names. A century or so later, the U.S. government refused to acknowledge them as natives, which meant they were a people without a land or a reservation, and so they called themselves the Lumbee people after the Lumbee River in North Carolina.

The Native American Indian Center my dad helped start (still active today) was host to countless Bible studies and cultural celebrations, tutoring sessions, job training, youth programs, you name it. My parents were devoted to the people there, immensely concerned that they receive some justice and opportunity in a world that had not given them much of either. In 1967, my parents adopted a newborn baby from the Lumbee tribe, a beautiful caramel-colored girl named Emily. My brothers and I danced around the dinner table when we learned our baby sister was coming home. Emily was so beautiful.

But the excitement quickly wore off for me as I watched my new cute sister receive more and more of my parents' attention. To win back their approval, I tried keeping up with my big brothers, playing tag, king of the hill, and war. Any game they could play, I would try to play better. If being good meant putting away my toys or helping around the house when my mom asked me to, I did it without complaint. If it meant staying out of fights when the neighbor children teased me, I'd grit my teeth and smile. I would be a good girl, a perfect example of what a minister's daughter ought to be: determined, obedient, quiet, responsible.

Meanwhile, the rest of the Clark family lived under the weight of my dad's position and his intense nature every day. He had little tolerance for mistakes—including mine. We were expected to live up to his demands for perfection and righteousness. He was forever correcting us. He was a strict disciplinarian who utilized spankings and stern rebukes whenever necessary to keep his children in line. Everything in our house had its proper place, and woe to the one who didn't return something to where she had found it. I could never seem to measure up to my dad's high standards, no matter what I did, and was often told that I was, "not thinking" or "not careful."

Family dinners were for serious talk about school and other important issues. They were no time for fun, and we were told so. Smiles and laughter were rare treats with my dad (when he did smile, he was very handsome). Sometimes my brother Greg would mimic my dad as a way of breaking the tension. Dad would give in to a momentary chuckle, and for the next ten to fifteen minutes as my brother continued, we would enjoy a good belly roar. Then our dad would get serious again: "OK, stop it now, children," and we'd stifle our giggles to return to the serious business of family time.

When I turned six, my parents decided that inner-city Baltimore wasn't quite adequate enough to give my siblings and me a *real* cross-cultural experience. My dad seemed tired, restless even, but genuinely concerned that we encounter something a little more challenging, that we experience life in another part of the world. So, my dad delegated his leadership roles in the Baltimore church to men from the community and accepted a two-and-a-half-year position teaching English at a college in Nagoya, Japan. It would be the best thing for us, they told us.

For the first time in my young life, I was about to experience what it was like to be really different, to be a foreigner in a strange land. I didn't know what to expect, but I didn't want to be left out of the adventure.

I wasn't disappointed.

We arrived in Japan tired, hot, and a little apprehensive. But within weeks, we were welcomed with a warmth and sincerity I hadn't encountered in Baltimore. People gave me gifts, teachers enjoyed my obedience, and families invited us into their homes for meals of rice, sea weed, and sushi rolls. They were intrigued by this white family from America. They respected the fact that my father was a minister teaching English in their country and appreciated his desire to be immersed in Japanese culture. His children were not only smart and talented, they said, but very beautiful Americans.

I loved the attention.

I couldn't show it too much, though, because my parents saw this as a great opportunity to teach us how to behave properly, how not to embarrass them or our country. What I enjoyed most about this new experience were the little treats: I loved the hot steaming cloths they gave us after meals, the curried chicken over sticky white rice they made for us, the toys strangers would give me, and the hot wooden baths in the small Japanese hotels new friends treated us to as we traveled throughout the country. I loved being an English professor's kid at the international elementary school where I sat in first and second grade with other missionary kids and local Japanese children who thought I was . . . well, special. One teacher even told my parents I had leadership qualities.

In Japan, approval, hospitality, and kindness met me at every turn, even under the watchful eye of my parents.

One day when my father was away teaching, my mother, brother, and I visited some friends who lived close to the college. Children were quickly left out of the conversation, so my brother Greg decided to go exploring . . . on the roof. I followed. (So much for leadership qualities!) While my mother was talking and eating with the adults, we were crawling across the strange flat metal roof above them. We snickered and giggled in our discovery. We saw bare treetops and people across the street about thirty feet below; we heard the hum of my mom's voice and the laughter of children in the yard. We kept crawling a few more inches and almost ran into an inconvenient wire that ran across the roof, connected to other wires on other roofs.

My brother and I did what any children bent on exploring would do: we wrapped our little fingers around that wire to move it out of the way. That's when a high-voltage electrical shock zapped through us, short-circuiting our little bodies and causing us to convulse like snakes in a fire. The shock couldn't have lasted more than ten seconds, long enough for me to wet my pants and start sobbing at the same time.

Sometimes I hated being a minister's daughter.

I became hysterical—both from the shock and the liquid running down my legs—and I quickly found my way back to Mom. She scolded my brother, cleaned me up, and shielded me from her friends as we hurried out. I had pulled what I thought was the ultimate no-no in the Clark family: I had embarrassed a parent. When we got home, I was still shaking from the electricity, terror, and shame. I hid on my straw mat. I wasn't so sure about this cross-cultural stuff after all; it was a little too jolting for me.

I survived the remaining months in Japan until my father's teaching contract ended and we flew back to Baltimore. We quickly returned to urban life as we left it: living in the church parish house, my dad working long hours with community residents and parishioners, my mom volunteering, looking after us, and cooking meals for friends, and us children going about the business of playing and pleasing our parents.

Then my parents made another decision that would have a far-reaching impact on our growth and development: they sent us to private schools. Public schools in the 1970s were not quite adequate enough in what they offered the children of my Waspy, liberal parents, though they certainly seemed convenient and sufficient for our neighbors in inner-city Baltimore. My parents' larger vision was not about making us comfortable in the suburbs, but about exposing us to the idea of making a difference. They felt they could do that by living in the inner-city yet still providing us with the type of education those in the suburbs could afford. That meant private schools. I didn't really understand why I had to go all the way across town to the "rich" part of Baltimore just to learn math and spelling, but as an obedient child, I wasn't about to make waves. It would be the best thing for us, they told us.

Of course, my parents could not afford the luxury of private education on a minister's salary, so my mother dipped into the interest of the stock she had inherited from her mother. My grandmother's brothers had started a successful washing machine company, leaving my mother a safety net to fall back on. Though my parents always lived simply and conscientiously, instilling the same values into my siblings and me, they also knew they had something their low-income neighbors probably never would: privilege. Still, the tension to do the right thing surfaced into many, many discussions that took my parents late into the evenings. When all was said and done, though, they used the dividend income from the stock, and our tuition was paid. I spent my elementary school years with wealthy white children at Roland Park Country School.

My parents were discussing other things late into the nights too—hard, painful, personal issues that I in my twelve-year-old world had no idea were coming. It seemed that in spite of all the world-changing my father was doing, his own inner world was in chaos. He was, and probably had been since before I was born, exploring another lifestyle none of us could have imagined. Sometimes my mother would wait up wondering if her husband was coming home. He would always make it home though, just in time to see his children off in the morning and make his way to the church to serve the poor, care for the sick, and fight injustice. As if everything was fine.

All the preparation in the world, all the exposure to cultures and diversity and differences, could not have prepared my young heart for what was about to happen. There was no question my daddy loved me; he loved each of us with a firm and devoted father's love. That much was clear. He just didn't know how to keep living with us.

Everything was not fine.

We had awoken some mornings to Mom sleeping on the couch; some mornings it was Dad. Then one night our mother called us into her bedroom, and we were instructed to sit on the edge of her bed. Tonight, Dad was gone, and my mother's face was pale and serious. In her arm she held a big red textbook with the words "Sex Education" written across it. We stared at her, nervous and still. Then she opened the book to a marked page, looked down, and then looked up at us.

"I need to read you something. This might not be easy, but you need to know." With that, she proceeded to read the text's definition of a word I hadn't heard much before: *h-o-m-o-s-e-x-u-a-l-i-t-y*. Mom cleared her throat, looked at us, and then told us that our father was "a homosexual," that they were going to be divorcing soon, and that we would be moving out of the church parish and into a nearby middle-class neighborhood. She said he had struggled for years with his sexuality. The summer before, he had met an African-American man named Jay and had fallen in love with him, and now they wanted to be together.

Her eyes clouded, and she went on. She had known for some time but couldn't accept it any longer. She realized that she could no longer listen to our dad preach the gospel on Sunday mornings, knowing that he was involved in this double life, and still respect him in our home. She knew the gay rights movement was beginning to take off, that other men were "coming out of the closet" across the country. But she could not live like this.

"We've decided to divorce," Mom said. "He's decided to live his life with Jay." My brothers sat still, subdued. I was enraged.

"Why are you telling me this? I don't want to know this!" I screamed. I ran into my room, cried into my pillow, and yelled some more. What was I going to do? What had *I* done wrong? Why did this have to happen in *my* family? How was I going to make it through my teenage years with a dad who was not only gone but was also *gay?*

The next morning, when I saw my father on the staircase, I started crying. He wrapped his arms around me, held me, and listened to me asking over and over, "Why? Why?" Then he did something I had never seen him do before or since: *he* started to cry. For the next ten minutes, my world-changing, intense, firm father let down his guard.

I cried harder, confused from feeling loved and abandoned at the same time. But no amount of tears, his or mine, could change my father's mind about what he was going to do. He told me to go eat some cereal and get ready for school. Daddy was leaving. It would be the best thing for *him,* he told me.

The months that followed were a tornado of emotions and changes: My mother moved us into a house in a middle-class neighborhood that sat on the edge of some governmental housing projects; my siblings and I were sent every Wednesday night to Dad and Jay's house for dinner; my hormones started to kick in, making me completely boy crazy; and I suddenly wasn't so sure anymore what it meant to be a minister's daughter. When I would tell my friends about my father's decision to "be gay," they reacted with strange looks, shocked stares, or honest emotions: "That's really weird." Life was chaotic.

My need for approval skyrocketed during the next year when I turned thirteen, transferring especially on the opposite sex. I would do anything to get a boyfriend or to get a boy's attention. Anything. That meant never telling a boy no. If he wanted to drink Colt 45, I would. If he wanted to smoke marijuana or hash, I would. And if he wanted to have sex with me, I would. Each experience allowed me to avoid the pain I was feeling from losing my dad. Though my parents had taught me a lot about respecting others, I hadn't yet learned what it meant to respect myself.

And I certainly didn't know where to put the pain or the alienation I felt.

So I worked hard at winning attention wherever I was. Eventually life became routine again. By junior high, Mom enrolled me in a Quaker school in another upper-class neighborhood, and I was expected to take the public bus to get to this section of Baltimore. Every morning my brothers and I would leave the diversity of our neighborhood and enter the world of sculpted shrubs, trimmed houses, and fashionable classmates.

I continued to be a good girl at school and a bad girl with the boys after school. I did well in classes, joined the field hockey, basketball, and gymnastics teams and worked hard to impress my teachers and coaches. By now it was more important for me to be accepted than it was to care about the issues my parents had always seemed passionate about. Even listening to my father and Jay talk about their involvement in an organization called "Black and White Men Together" did little to pique my teenage interest in racial issues. I was merely being a dutiful daughter when I sat at the dinner table of my father and his lover; I was just trying to survive in a world that seemed to get stranger and more stressful every day.

I was especially unprepared for an encounter with racial anger.

One Friday afternoon I was coming home from school on the city bus. I was tired from athletics, boys, and school. My muscles hurt, and my mind wandered over homework assignments and chores that waited for me when I got home. I stared out the window as the bus pulled in front of the projects and slowed to my stop.

I was getting off the back of the bus with three African-American girls who seemed about my age. My mind was still a bit preoccupied, so I hardly noticed who was around me and who wasn't. I waited as the girls got off and followed. When the bus rolled away, I stared blankly at it, glanced at the projects, and started walking the two blocks to my mom's house.

Then one of the more outspoken girls began taunting me. Her thick black hair moved back and forth as she tilted her head; she looked ready to pounce. "Hey, White Girl," she raged. Was she talking to me? I stared in shock. "Hey, White Girl. What are you doing *here?*" I began to tremble, much like the time I was electrocuted in Japan. But my legs wouldn't move, and I said nothing.

The girl walked up to put her face only inches from mine, Then she heaved her thick black head back, cleared her throat, and spit on my white, Waspy cheek. The moisture stung. She and her friends had a good laugh. And as if nothing had happened, she and the other girls simply walked away. I was paralyzed.

When I realized what had taken place, when I breathed the smell of that angry girl's spit, dripping off my cheek, I felt a surge of emotions. What had I done to her? Why did she spit in *my* face? I grabbed a tissue from my pocket and scrubbed the saliva off my face until I was sure no trace was left anywhere on my skin. I choked back tears, feeling angry, afraid, and vulnerable. Then the emotion finally entered my legs, and I ran home faster than I ever had. My safe, comfortable living room never looked so good.

Where *did* I put my pain?

I did not find a place for it during the rest of my days at Friends, nor did I in high school when my mom moved us to California, to be near her elderly parents. I couldn't find it in my family, in my partying, in my boyfriends, or in any of my accomplishments in school or sports.

I didn't even know what it was for.

And though my parents always wanted to provide "the best thing for me," and usually tried, it wasn't enough. Yes, my heritage and inheritance made any dream possible, any opportunity open, any desire fulfillable. White privilege at its best. But it wasn't until years later that I would realize just what that meant.

.

Coming of Age

The Best of Times

Chapter Five

When I entered high school, I was amazed at how many other people who looked like me were roaming the shiny, marbleized halls. These young brothers and sisters were bright, well-

Pamela

dressed, well-spoken, well-read students from two-parent families (or strong single-parent families). You looked at their calm, eager, confident faces, and you just knew they woke up in nicely decorated bedrooms, watched PBS specials on late-model television sets, and ate brand-name cereal before they boarded their buses and subways to school. Their mothers and fathers found the cash for private French lessons, karate classes, tutors, and "Jack and Jill" (the black equivalent of the Junior League). There was money saved (or borrowed) to send them to this esteemed, gleaming institution of preparation.

St. Francis Prep was by no means a predominantly black school. It just seemed that way to me because I had never seen so many brown-skinned students in one place before. It was in this place that I found what I had been unknowingly longing for:

friends who were black like me. Unwittingly, these relationships transformed me. Young women who had bodies shaped like mine (and even more "ample," I might add), African features that resembled mine, and coiled hair like mine befriended me and made me feel at home in a way the MarygraceColleens never could. The idea of yearning to be like the MCs to be accepted now seemed ridiculous. Who cared? My black sisters and brothers welcomed me just as I was. Florence, Karen, Dilcia, Dawn, Henri, Tony, Keith, and Vernon, to name a few. We enjoyed our own music, our own foods, and our own laughs in the safe enclave of the "black" table (though it was never actually called this) in the corner of the cafeteria. It was an absolute blast. Yet every one of us knew how to mix and mingle with white students, many of whom were also friends. We were not prejudiced. We were just doing what we needed to for self-preservation, taking a breather from the often wearying task of living and working among white folk.

After beginning to date one of the smartest, most well-liked black student-athletes at Prep, I hardly even glanced at any of the blond-haired men walking the halls, tanned or not (and it would be years before I'd glance that way again).

Several of my white grade-school friends also chose to attend St. Francis Prep. It was a totally different experience having them say hi to me in the hallway of our new school. Now I saw them from the safer, more empowered vantage point of my newly evolving identity as a young black woman. They were less important to me now. There was no disdain or enmity, but my conversations with them between classes were only occasional. When we did chat, it was often the way one does with a family friend who calls just as your favorite television show is coming on or while your hair is wet. All of us were developing our own new friendships and were "otherwise invested."

I did develop friendships with white girls I met at Prep (many named Mary-something again, just like in grammar school). These new relationships were easy to develop because I had so much practice. It was like climbing into a second skin, if you'll pardon the pun. I knew the social habits, speech patterns, preferences, and proclivities of white girls better than I knew myself.

These new friendships were more fulfilling than before because I felt I had less to prove than I did with the Marygrace-Colleens. If I was rejected, misunderstood, or just plain tired, I was now free to go home to the "family" of brown-skinned peers. Actually, most of these white girls became good *during*-school friends but were not *after*-school friends, a typical scenario in white-black friendships. I remember them fondly, though. I might never have passed freshman Algebra if it wasn't for my friend Mary Pat's patient explanations of what x and y had to do with math. And without Mary Beth to giggle with, free periods and gym class would have been total Dullsville. Mary Ann's encouragement to enter the Miss Junior America pageant gave me the opportunity to experience the thrill of entering, becoming a finalist, and walking off the stage with a trophy.

I had found the right place to put the Marys in my life.

Finally I had a balance of black and white friends. I was hopeful that when I made the proper introductions and we got to know each other, all of us would hang out together. . . . Not.

First of all, the white girls listened to head-pounding rock, drank astounding amounts of beer, and only wanted to hang out in places that served it. The black girls would rather dance to seductive funk music in someone's basement and sneak tastes of rum and Coca Cola. One thing we all had in common was boys, but, of course, they were *different* boys who hung out in *different* places. No one wanted to cross over.

The music and drink preference ruled. Few people in either group could handle an entire evening in the others' environment. Few tried. Those black students who were known to frequent local bars with the white students were considered oddballs. And I don't remember any whites at our basement house-parties at all. The emphasis on dancing was just too embarrassing for them, many told me later. And the absence of beer kegs was more than they could bear—just as enduring an entire evening with no danceable music would have been for us. This saddened me, but I tacitly agreed that was just the way things were.

I quit trying to play middleman.

Even nestled snugly among my black brothers and sisters, I was still having hair problems, and so were they. Almost all of the girls had permed or pressed hair (straightened with a hot comb) and wore it, or attempted to wear it, in that flipped back, Farrah Fawcett style 'do that was so popular in the seventies. For all those who don't know, our hair does not "flip." It will flip only when flattened by a process of slapping a pasty, perfumed mixture of chemicals on our African roots. This procedure must be repeated every three months or so, lest the natural hair "come back." Even then, there is still no guarantee that a hairstyle will hold up in rain, heat, or humidity of any kind (as I found out the first time I tried to blow-curl my wet, relaxed hair with a roll brush the way I saw my white track and field teammates do). By lunchtime, my lovely new Farrah 'do was a fuzzy, tangled mass.

Understand, our hair angst was not just a matter of style; it was a matter of our very beings, especially as teenage girls. The intensity of the hair struggle reeked of some inherent, underlying mistake. Only whose mistake was it? The media supported the hurtful myth that our hair was unacceptable in its natural form. Few of the girls in *Seventeen* or *Glamour* magazines had black-textured hair, and if they did, it was the curly, corkscrew kind that was more acceptable to white society. "Straight," "long," and "silky" were the synonymous buzz words for American beauty. Our hair was unmanageable by these standards. And there was a whole industry of hair products that promised to "fix" us. An African friend of my cousin's said, facetiously, "I never knew I had 'problem hair' until I left Africa and came here." What a concept.

During my sophomore year, my parents sent me to London for spring break to get to know my relatives there. I loved it. Brown-skinned folk sporting English accents, drinking tea, serving crumpets and runny eggs, and loving calypso and reggae—

how cool! Seeing my brothers and sisters making it in prim-and-proper English society—among the very people whose great-grandfathers financed much of the African slave trade—made me marvel at the literal world of possibilities available to those who are young, gifted, and black.

Jacques, my high school sweetheart, was the embodiment of those three qualities. He was, as teens today would say, "da bom" (translation, "awesome"). An A student, well-built, dimpled, and sweet, Jacques was well-liked and admired by both teachers and students. He was a school record holder in the triple jump and pole vault. In these less-celebrated track and field events that others dismissed as too difficult, Jacques shined. Even as a teenager, his goal seemed to be to carve out a niche for himself, to devise ways to become a big fish in a small pond. He was the future son-in-law parents dream about. My mother trusted him to take her just-turned-sixteen only daughter out for her first "night on the town." (And if you knew my mother, you'd know this was a phenomenal step of faith.) She even had him hold the money she lent to the excursion.

But even dating a smart, well-bred, popular guy within my race didn't free me of ethnic strife. Just as everyone that speaks Spanish is lumped together and called Hispanic or Latino, so too are black people. Jacques' family was from Haiti; my family was from Grenada. The two countries are not far away, but they are worlds apart culturally. Jacques' Haitian parents never seemed to accept me. Though I had a decent grasp of French and the right-sounding last name, I was not raised with any Haitian influence. I was unaccustomed to Haitian food, music, or the rough sound of spoken Creole.

I also did not pass the paper bag test (where one is accepted or rejected based on whether he or she is lighter than the color of a brown paper bag).

Once again, I found myself trying to fit in, even within the brown-skinned world. I listened intently to the Creole that was spoken in Jacques' home and tried to mimic it when I was alone.

I pretended to understand when I really didn't, a strategy that was destined for doom. It was clear that I wasn't one of them.

Our relationship lasted about two years and had many good moments, including attending his senior prom. By the time my own prom rolled around the next May, Jacques had left me for an ivory-skinned Haitian girl who spoke Creole.

I was seventeen and broken-hearted.

I plunged into my schoolwork, got ready for the statewide Miss Teen America pageant, and wondered who I would take to the stupid prom now that I was shamefully partnerless. The only other guy I wanted to go with turned me down. I ended up going with an older guy I hardly knew.

It wasn't the best of times.

The hoopla that surrounds being in a "beauty" pageant served as a perk-up. I had done well in the city-wide competition and was preparing for the New York State pageant. This experience came complete with group dance numbers performed in red, white, and blue outfits, photo sessions in various forms of attire (no bathing suits, thank God), talent, and evening gown competitions. I rehearsed "As Time Goes By" on the piano so much that everyone within a half-mile radius of our apartment was probably humming the melody in their sleep. I smiled into the mirror and practiced clever answers to the inevitable question, "How would you change the world if you were crowned?" I also practiced waving from an imaginary float.

Though I didn't make it to the finals, I did win the Miss Community Service award (all those hours working at the hospital as a candy striper finally paid off). My pageant roommate, Saskia, a beautiful Arab girl, won Miss Congeniality and went on to win the entire pageant the next year. I was disappointed with my finish but glad to have gotten an award. I was told later by pageant officials that they didn't think my dress fit quite right. Humph.

Back at school, an annual retreat was being planned for juniors and seniors only. It was called a Christian Awakening weekend, or CA for short. I cannot say I had a deep, burning desire to go on this CA thing. But several of my friends were going, and it meant a few days away from home.

During the weekend we listened to talks about faith by students from our school and others. We played games and did something called icebreakers. We sat in small groups and talked about life, God, and other stuff. I had never been in a setting like that. And I had never, in all the years of Catholic school, felt challenged to think about my faith as a living, breathing thing. Faith wasn't personal; it was what you did, a series of rituals to perform to win points with God, right?

For example, a good Catholic girl participated in the four Cs: church, first communion, confirmation, and confession. Faith consisted of memorizing prayers, lighting candles to various saints for various things you wanted, and, above all, making sure you would never have an abortion or get divorced. And of course, being a "good person," a catch-all phrase so vast and vague that it fits almost anyone's lifestyle. I remember the CA as a warm and fuzzy experience where we "graduates" promised, in front of others, that we would change and be "better people." God was involved, but I don't recall that accepting him as personal Savior was a central part of the equation.

It wasn't until college that I was really motivated to delve deeper.

The so-called guidance counselor at my school did not guide me very much. The deep lines in Sister Agnes' brow reinforced her position of authority. I was making the obligatory visit to her office to discuss college. I had my mind somewhat set on Columbia University and was looking for encouragement and direction.

She was reticent. Actually, she balked at the suggestion. This was a no-nonsense nun, uninterested in hearing about a teenager's wide-eyed hopes (at least not mine). Panic washed over me. I was a solid B student. I had B+ or A averages in several classes, including English Literature, and was in at least three advance placement courses for which I was receiving college credits. I did well on the SATs and was well-rounded: my extracurricular activities included track and field, peer counseling, community service (plus the Miss Teen N.Y. award), and the CA. Even running down this list of achievements did not stop Sister's head from moving from side to side, her thin lips pursed and downturned. She urged me to take a prep course for the SATs and try again. And to apply to less prestigious schools.

I had strolled into this old lady's office just looking for some advice on filling out applications, and now I was allowing her and her white authority to threaten my dreams.

It worked.

I did suffer through a ten-week SAT prep course that set my parents back several hundred dollars and improved my score by one hundred points. But by then a part of my spirit had been clipped. The Columbia catalog was now mocking me, telling me I couldn't cut it. When my parents cringed at Columbia's price tag, I decided not to bother apply. I was accepted into Fordham University, which was known for its communications department. White girlfriends who got into Columbia later told me that I should definitely have applied there; they confessed that their grade point averages weren't that great either.

Humph.

If I was pleasantly surprised by all the sweet, brown faces at Prep's open house four years before, I was in total shock riding a bus to visit Fordham University's campus in 'da Bronx.' This place was an entire black universe! Everyone—the people on the subway, the bus driver, the passengers, the street merchants, the store owners, and the shoppers—was black. Only these were not the same preppy-looking, conservative black folk I encountered at St. Francis. These Bronx-ites sported their hair braided in tall, elaborate creations and wore heavy gold earrings, medallions, and sometimes teeth, spiked heels, furry Kangols (men's caps), and stretch-jeans that had zips at the bottom of each pant leg. As they dropped their fare in the metal box, the adults greeted the bus driver as if he were an old friend; he responded in kind. Little spontaneous conversations erupted here and there as one person made a comment to the person next to her about the heat, about how long she waited for the bus, or about where she was going. They were strangers, but they chatted like they understood each other innately. There was a bond between these brown passengers that I both admired and feared. By virtue of my skin color, I knew I was free to partake of it, but I wasn't sure I knew how.

The world of the actual Fordham University campus was much less colorful than the bus ride down Fordham Road. As usual, the university had a small pond of black students and a black professor or two within the ocean of white students, tenured professors, and old-guard administrators who really owned the place. This was such a contrast to the ratio that existed just outside of the campus' iron gates. We owned the streets; whites owned the institutions.

I was assigned a white roommate my freshman year. We lived in a two-by-four in the only girls' dormitory. She was nice enough, but we had little in common. The "beer drinking versus funk dancing" issue was still alive and well. I sought social refuge with the black girls in my dorm, while maintaining cordial relationships with a few white girls. The girls I recognized from Prep barely acknowledged me. They were fashioning new identities and whether it included black friends was apparently still under investigation.

We were all re-creating ourselves to some degree in college. As a new member of the African-American Studies Club, I discovered racial anger. My own. In a setting where I could discuss race-related things with people of my own hue, honestly and openly—angrily, if necessary—I was able to unleash pieces of the gnawing pain I held in my own soul all my life.

It was incredibly liberating.

I was outraged about racial oppression here in America but mostly about apartheid in South Africa, the hot issue of the time. I was speechless when I learned about the modern-day slave system there. And I was incensed when I discovered that American businesses and institutions—in fact our own school—might be tacitly supporting the oppression of my South-African brothers and sisters by refusing to divest holdings in that country. It horrified me to think that my black parents' tuition dollars, which provided me a way to get ahead, were inadvertently keeping back a whole country of people who were just like us. Was there any real "getting ahead" if others like us are always left behind? It seemed as if we were in a losing situation. At various moments I felt disgusted, thrilled, sad, fatalistic, confused, and empowered.

In college, I discovered my solidarity with all other black people everywhere. I had a responsibility to lift others as I myself climbed upward, I was told. By any means necessary.

I believed it with all my heart.

Along with other black students from the Club, I decided to picket the school in hope of pressuring it to divest any holdings it had in South Africa. I also participated in a rally in Manhattan to call for divestiture from the American business community. My friend, Tina, a bright and self-assured young woman, allowed herself to be arrested along with some others for the cause. I thought she was incredibly brave. Me, I was still checking out this activist life.

It was through these, my first political events, that I began to gain my footing as a black woman in a country run by a white power structure. Slowly, the weight of what we were up against as black people in America fell upon me. I saw everything with new eyes. I learned how my courageous ancestors survived the Middle Passage, chained together and packed like sardines for months at sea. They watched their husbands lynched, their children hosed, spat upon and denied, and their babies left to die because some southern white doctor wouldn't come. They fought their way to freedom, dodging bullets, real and implied. Now I must carry the spear of my ancestors. As I began to understand my place, my stomach churned with both excitement and fury.

Why was all this history withheld from me for the past twelve years of so-called education? While I was staying up late memorizing details about the Iroquois Indians, the Japanese, and the Jews, my ancestors must have been shifting in their graves.

I had so much more to learn and to question.

Only God could tell you how a course called "The Black Church in America" made its way into the Fordham University catalog. I'm only glad I made it into the interesting-sounding class with "space is limited" typed in italics next to its listing. I wasn't sure I could articulate what the black church was, but my mind was a sponge that wanted to sop up everything it could about the experience of blackness.

The class was taught by a good-natured, black Catholic priest from the West Indies. I marveled as I learned how the black church emerged from slavery times and how much of a mainstay of spiritual, political, and socio-economic power was. Walking out of class, I felt dazed. Why had I never had this black church experience that was such an integral part of our life in America? Again, I wondered where I had been all my life.

Not long after arriving at Fordham, I plunged headlong into a relationship with one of the biggest football players on campus. Tony was six-foot-four, had forty-six-inch shoulders, and, when not practicing with the Fordham Rams, was a bodybuilder and bouncer. I had never seen anything like him before, at least not up close. We so-called dated during my freshman year, much to the chagrin of other girls who didn't think I deserved him.

Through my association with Tony, I got involved with the sister organization to the only black fraternity on campus. The group was made up of friends and girlfriends of the guys who were pledging the frat. Our goal was to support our men as they proved their manhood, sometimes in ridiculous ways. We hid them from the "big brothers" in our tiny dormroom closets, fed them when they were being "starved," and washed their dirty pledging uniforms, wet and smelly after a variety of rituals that involved wading in seawater—in the winter.

It was a great time of bonding with other girls, having late night talks and step-dance practices, and working together to help perpetuate a black tradition on this white campus. We had fun, but we also had purpose. We even began supporting a little girl in one of those ubiquitous poor African villages after seeing a poignant advertisement (which tends to make you think that the entire continent lives in squalor). Everything an educated, socially-aware black individual did had to have a purpose greater than just yourself, I was taught. We always had to "represent" (the race). And that was sometimes a heavy burden.

I discovered the power of the pen and began writing for Fordham's alternative newspaper, *The Paper*. I wrote features about any black alumni or speaker who came to campus and whatever message the speaker had for us. I was a budding journalist, writing passionately, if not flawlessly, about the things that were important to me—to us. I was experimenting with my craft and finding my voice.

My mother was worried. Not only was I strangely unavailable to answer our dorm phone when she called at 6 A.M., but my grades were far from stellar. I showed up to my Finite Math class only occasionally, and it took wild hyenas to get me to Philosophy 1. I took comfort in the fact that I had twelve college credits from high school to play with. I could afford to take it easy, I reasoned. I was an adult.

My mom had been worried about me for awhile. In my late teen years, I boycotted going to Catholic church, or any church. She would come to my room every Sunday, dressed, and smelling of Bal á Versailles or Joy, her favorite special-occasion perfumes. Usually I was still in REM sleep from being up or out late the night before. I wasn't interested in what the church had to offer. I watched groggily as she and my father walked down the path toward the nine o'clock church service with distressed looks on their faces.

Now that I was in college learning about this wonderful thing called the black church, I wouldn't have minded going *there*. But no one I knew went to church, except for a very few who attended the Catholic service held at the Fordham chapel on campus. I went alone a number of times, but I wasn't a regular. My favorite part was when they turned off the lights, distributed lit candles, and asked everyone to gather around the altar for communion. I felt holy and peaceful watching everyone's face take on a shadowy hue in the dim candlelight as the priest spoke in hushed, pious tones.

I got my holy fix on Sunday and went on with my less-than-holy campus lifestyle on Monday. Not a bad deal.

And why not? There wasn't much challenging me to make changes. It was college; you governed yourself. That was the beauty of it. *You* were your own little god. *You* decided who you would or would not make out with, what you would or would not drink or smoke, which foul words would or would not come out of your mouth, and where you would or would not go, all according to your desires and personal discretion. Mommy and Daddy were not here, and there were no surrogates.

Furthermore, I decided that I was doing well morally. At almost twenty, I waited longer than most of my girlfriends to have sex. And I waited until I was "in luuuvvvv." Drinking never thrilled me, so I did little of it. But my mouth was getting fresher with each progressive year. I enjoyed the way I could spit out venomous curse words with emphasis and power on occasion. It was all part of being cool. And I was behind.

So, I was cute, cool, sarcastic, and free to be me (whoever that was). By sophomore year, I had a new boyfriend named Phil, a great guy whom I had become friends with during the summer between my first and second years. We were practically inseparable on campus and off. He came home to Queens with me for visits, and I did the same with him, usually to get a hug, a bag of groceries, and hopefully, some cash from our parents to make it until the next visit.

On those visits to my parents' home, my mother was glad to see us but still looked distressed. She would always remind me to pray, which I only did occasionally, and would shove a tract, a sermon tape, or small prayer book in my bag as I hurried out the door back to school. Those little gifts of love often stood untouched on some shelf in my dorm room.

Pastor Fred Price and Oral Roberts were two of my mom's favorite preacher/teachers, along with Kenneth and Gloria Copeland and Kenneth Hagin. She watched them faithfully on television from her violet bedroom on Sunday mornings. She, too, had tired of the Catholic church, though she hung in a while longer when the church began to offer a special "charismatic" service. I guess others in the parish, which was now enjoying an influx of Latinos, were itchy for a more spirited experience.

There was no way my mom's newfound excitement about faith could not spill over onto me, whether I liked it or not. I listened to a few of the tapes she planted in my luggage, more out of curiosity than out of a quest for catharsis.

Clearly though, God had other plans.

But who needs God when you have a great boyfriend? Phil was sweet, hilarious, athletic, fun, and affectionate. When I was with him, I pushed away the nagging feeling of being a misfit and embraced his high energy. Phil loved me as much as he could, but it never seemed to be enough. There was something deep inside me that wasn't being fulfilled by friends, boyfriends, boycotts, or even hours playing Centipede in the campus Ramskellar. I felt convicted by some of the moral issues brought up on the sermon tapes my mother smuggled into my life. And being unsure of where I stood with God became unsettling. My alleged "personal theology" seemed shaky compared to what was being presented so clearly on the tapes. It is one thing when you don't know any better, quite another when you *know* that you know better. When things got too heavy, my remedy was to take a vacation from the tapes.

One day my mom encouraged me to attend Fred Price's crusade that was to be held at Madison Square Garden. Not sure of what exactly went on at a "crusade," but suspecting it might be wacky, I was reluctant. But every time I watched Dr. Price's television show, I saw a converted version of Richard Pryor, sardonic humor and all, which I thought was kind of cool. A few days later, a brochure for the crusade arrived in the mail, courtesy of my praying mom. The effervescent-looking crowd shown on the front of the brochure was mostly black, which encouraged me. I decided I could handle it (Madison Square Garden was a large enough place to be anonymous) and decided to go. Phil agreed to come along.

Madison Square Garden was filled with an electricity that I couldn't explain. The crowd and even the hostesses who helped seat us had anticipation on their faces, as if something incredible was going to happen before the night was over. People who arrived late were in a mad hurry to get into their seats. I was amazed that this large crowd, of both blacks and whites, would come out for something like this. I was amazed that *I* would come out for something like this. This same famous arena had beckoned me for concerts, sporting events, and even a convention, but never for . . . church. It felt good—in a weird sort of way. I was finally going to have a sort of black church experience, and I was excited.

Phil and I held hands as we listened to the pastor's words and tried to follow along in the leather-bound, embossed King James Bible my praying aunt Elsa had given me when I was a child. We realized we didn't know John from Jeremiah as we ruffled the delicate, tissue-like pages searching for the proper place. What the pastor said seemed to be so simple and make so much sense. He spoke to us as friends, as family. He was our Uncle Fred "holding court" with us around the dinner table, telling us about ourselves, speaking the truth in love, and trying fervently to lead us into the land of milk and honey he had found.

As Fred Price's teaching built to a crescendo, the audience was on its feet, saying things like, "Preach it!" and "That's right!" and long "Haaaaalelujahs." Clusters of people would break out into an applause that became contagious. Soon all the people in the auditorium had their hands raised above their heads, some holding up their Bibles, some their wallets, as they shouted sincere-sounding prayers and praises toward the ceiling, which was covered with NBA championship flags.

We stood up too.

Suddenly, the arena became quiet, the lights dim. Dr. Price asked that every head be bowed and every eye closed. As he prayed, I knew he was talking to me, but I was afraid to go forward. I peeked out of half-closed eyes to see who else was raising a hand, indicating a desire to accept Christ. There were many hands in the air and several tear-streaked faces around me. I closed my own welling-up eyes, fully this time, and let the words sink into me. It was a free gift, he said, the only way to restore the broken relationship we had with God because of sin. As I scanned my laissez faire college life, I knew there were some big sins there that needed to be forgiven.

"Don't let this opportunity pass you by," he encouraged.

As instructed, we made our way down the long, narrow steps from the middle tier of the huge arena all the way down to the center platform. Halfway down the stairs, I had a desire to turn back, but the desire to go forward won.

My stomach was flip-flopping as I saw this larger-than-life TV-pastor making his way around the platform to me and Phil. His perfectly coifed Afro glistened in the spotlight. I saw some people falling backward when Dr. Price touched them, and it made me nervous. They were caught by ushers who followed Dr. Price, seemingly for this express function. I didn't think I wanted to fall down, but I wasn't sure if the experience would be valid if I didn't.

When Dr. Price got to me, he placed his hand on my forehead, prayed a few words over me, and concluded with " . . . in Jesus' name." I felt wobbly when he touched me, but I did not fall backward. We were then instructed to go into a separate room where we would be given a booklet and some counseling about our "new lives." In that room, we were encouraged to pray in tongues, or "in the Spirit," which consisted of opening your mouth and allowing out whatever words, in whatever unnamed language, wanted to come. We attempted a few times, but nothing much happened. Then we were dismissed.

Standing out in the Manhattan night air in front of the Garden, it seemed like I had stepped out of a wonderful play. I felt a large burden lifted; like I had finally taken care of some messy, unfinished business and could move on to the next task at hand with new confidence and security.

But the play, with all its drama, was over, and I stood costumeless on the streets of New York. What was supposed to happen now? I didn't know. Could I keep the commitment I just made to God? I wasn't sure. As I went down the steps to catch the subway back to campus, reality gripped me by the throat.

Yes, my soul was rescued from the fiery furnace, but I had a feeling my problems were just beginning.

Chapter Six
Beyond the 'Burbs

Life for Denver's suburban teenagers in 1974 was a lot like the field of poppies that Dorothy and her bound-for-Oz pals stumbled on: a sedating calm after gobs of excitement. The 1960s

were gone, the war was over, Nixon had dropped out of office, and Denver was still just a cowtown whose biggest event of the year was the National Western Stockshow.

Snooze City. Predictable. Like homogenized milk.

That's how I remember it. A land where nothing's quite like we hoped, but we weren't sure what it was supposed to be anyway. We just followed the yellow brick road adults said would lead us toward a future of station wagons, good jobs,

Jo

and basic all-American normalcy. Half sleepwalking; that's just what we did.

Unless it rained and woke us up.

Maybe that's why I said yes when these weird youth-gatherers announced they were heading to the hills, Colorado-style, for a weekend of more weirdness, fun, food, and no parents. I was ready for something different, some rain in my restive adolescent field.

Besides, my oldest brother, Jimmy, had gone to the same weekend camp the year before, and something there—mountain air maybe—had gotten to him. He didn't go to as many keggers anymore, didn't fight back with my mom and was starting to seem, well, as we said in the seventies, together.

So if it was good enough for big brother, it was good enough for me. That's how I figured it. That's how Jack and Jan, our suburban parents, saw it too. Maybe it'd be good for her, they must have said to each other. Still smarting from my ninth-grade rebellion. Still hoping their defiant daughter would learn the right things.

Maybe she would.

On Friday at dusk, the charter bus pulled into a gravel parking lot at the base of a stone lodge called Silvercliff Ranch. A five-hour trip from Denver through the Rockies—lined with blue spruces, aspens, and mountain rivers—was already working its magic on me, tugging at my dreamy emotions as I looked out the moving window. Fifty or so popular people on the bus cheered as we slowed to a stop under the lodge and a glorious peak that towered behind it; college-age counselors led us in call-and-response-like camp choruses. We were assigned our cabins and counselor, rolled out our sleeping bags on skinny bunks, and wandered into the big lodge for an evening of skits, songs, jokes, games, and some fortysomething-year-old, brown-haired guy talking about God.

The weird was getting fun.

On Saturday, under Colorado blue sky, we played games in the snow, a sort of Winter Olympics for the sake of absolute absurdity and "team-building," I guess. We jumped backward, through piles of wet snow. We built "creative" ice sculptures in record time that looked like suburbia-on-speed. No one cared if you were a fast runner or a cool jock or a total goon. Everyone was a fool. Everyone was encouraged.

Equality at its best.

That night after a feast of homemade pizza we met in the lodge again for more songs, more skits, more jokes. And more talk of God. Stories, even, about Jesus. I'd only heard his name before at softball practice or in the basketball locker room when the coach was mad or a player was frustrated.

In fact, I don't think I had heard the name of Jesus anywhere else. Not even at church. Maybe I was sleeping the few times our family attended, but I don't think our Sunday school teachers ever talked like this. And the Reverend Sweet—which really was his name—a little man with big glasses and no hair, rarely changed his tone or emotion when he lectured on Easter mornings. He could have been talking about car engines or art history as I nodded off in the pew and my mom's sharp elbow nudged me back to polite coherence.

But at Silvercliff, I paid attention. The fortysomething-year-old cool guy was making this Jesus sound hip. He told us how during his life on earth, he went about doing good, healing the sick, and feeding the hungry. Seemed he spent his whole life reaching out to people in their pain, to those who felt like outcasts (like they didn't fit in anywhere).

Nice man, I thought. *Nice like Mrs. Manning.*

Jesus, the speaker said, loved people so much that he was even willing to endure our sin and suffering so we wouldn't have to. The cross—he was getting serious now—proved Christ's love, and his resurrection from the dead proved how much he wanted a relationship with us.

I sat up straight on that one.

My eyes narrowed in on the brown-haired man's face; I was sure he was speaking directly to me, like Mr. Archebeque had done in fifth grade when he taught me about slavery. Forget about the popular people. Forget about the mountains. I was being invited into a relationship with someone who, though I didn't know a thing about him, already loved me, and that was no small thing for a suburban teenage girl in 1974.

That night I sat under a million mountain stars, my jeans pressed against a cold, huge rock, the smell of evergreens fresh around me. I sat alone in the dark, surprisingly unafraid, and talked to someone I had hardly thought of before now. I even asked him to help me cry—Kadleceks did not cry much—as if that were a sign of releasing some of the loneliness and receiving some of the belonging I had always hoped for.

The answer rolled down my cheeks, and I shivered both from the winter cold and the strange, comforting presence that now sat beside me. I wiped my eyes and wondered what would happen to me after this. It wasn't like the rock beneath me moved, nor had the night sky suddenly turned bright. A soft mountain breeze did touch my face, and I was aware that something had moved in my soul, something that would surely change things when I returned to Denver.

Now I was alone but not lonely. Spring *and* winter were stirring inside me, music *and* quiet. Exhilarating and somber and joyous.

I was waking up.

I almost ran back to the cabin to tell my counselor and friends of the conversation I had just had, of the presence I had bumped into under the stars. They listened with eager ears, familiar with the words of such an encounter.

Sunday afternoon, in our last lodge gathering, the speaker asked those of us who had met this Jesus to do something about it. He wanted us to stand where we were and show our peers our new faith, as if we were modeling a brand new outfit, spotless, unwrinkled, never-before-worn. Now it was public.

I returned to Applewood with a tiny seed of rain planted in me, one that gently began to fill the corners of my world, coming up to my ankles, then my shins, and around my knees by the time I graduated.

I think my friends and my parents wondered about me the same way I had wondered about my brother. I wasn't getting kicked out of class anymore. I didn't throw tantrums at softball practice, and I worked harder than ever during basketball season just to make the team. When I wasn't sweating in the gym, my time was filled with guitar playing, Bible studies, and work.

It's just a phase, Jan and Jack must have said, one they didn't seem to mind. It did their daughter good, this "Christian thing."

"That's good for you, honey," they'd tell me when I tried to talk about my starry encounter. "Good," as if I had just swallowed children's medicine, the cherry-flavored kind that would make me feel better but was not quite potent enough for adults.

In the midst of my high school reform, I found myself drawn to others who never quite fit the suburban mold. I was basketball buddies with the only Japanese girl on the team; I practiced speeches for the debate team with a Filipino ballet dancer; and I was friends with the only African-American guy in the entire school of two thousand.

On some Saturdays, friends and I would ride the city bus to the downtown Denver Public Library and stroll through the aisles of books just because we were curious about the diverse array of people who always gathered there. The sizes, shapes, colors, voices, and outfits of these public library users were much more interesting than anything we'd seen galaxies away in suburbia. When we'd gotten our fill inside the library, we'd wander outside and across the street through Civic Center Park to talk with or take pictures of the homeless men who lived in the shadow of the Capitol. City life, it seemed to me, was a magnetic diversion from the yellow brick road and homogenized milk of Applewood.

But there was also a growing discomfort in me as we took our urban field trips. I began to wonder why my own neighborhood was mostly white, while the city was comprised of so many colors. I wondered why city folk on the streets often seemed hungry, disheveled, or homeless, while my suburban neighbors owned so much. It wasn't quite the same shock I first felt when I learned of American slavery, but the splinter was in and starting to ache.

Christian faith did not yet provide the answers. My feet were barely wet. But my intrigue with city life was firmly lodged.

Armed with a high school diploma, a continuing desire for relationships, and a blurry sense of purpose to be—of all things—a teacher, I headed to college an hour north of Denver in a rural university town that smelled of cows and fertilizer. I joined the women's soccer team, volunteered to help with a high school youth group, and showed up for class every now and then, when it was convenient. Young adult status, with all its frivolous autonomy, was a welcome sigh of relief.

The same semester I flunked geography. But I also found myself in an elective course that was surely the remnant of Mrs. Manning's influence: African-American Literature. It was only 1977, so any sort of ethnic studies programs were still a novelty, popping up in academia as a result of the preceding decade that grew revolutionaries like the Black Panthers or Cesar Chavez, who demanded inclusion in the national perspective on college campuses. As an English minor, I needed an extra literature class, and this one seemed the obvious choice.

How was I to know I'd be the only blond in the class?

The first day of class, I wandered in sleepy and clumsy. When my eyes darted from dark faces to Afros to slick outfits, my stomach jumped a nervous, lonely number. I targeted a seat in the back of the room against the wall, certain that all the other students were staring at me. I tried hard to be invisible, to hide in my sloppy athletic shorts and soccer sweatshirt, but the young, elegant professor was not so naive. Out of the thirty or so dark faces in the class, she called on my white one to explain what I thought this course was about. The fact that there was not a wrinkle in her African-print dress, her nails perfectly shaped, and her black leather briefcase neatly filled with books and files all told me she was serious about this academic endeavor. Therefore, her manner said, we should be too. Barely looking up at her, I mumbled something about the importance of cultural understanding and Frederick Douglass. She stared at me with a heavy, silent stare, as I sank lower in my desk, moved my feet forward, then back, then forward again. Thankfully, she asked another student the same question and left me alone for the rest of the hour.

It was the first time I was a racial minority, and there was something both incredibly awkward and strangely comforting for me in that.

To be honest, I was more interested in soccer and friendships and dates that semester than I was in black literature or classwork. Nonetheless, my attendance and assignments were better in that class than in any other. African-American literature and our elegant professor seemed important to me, even if I did feel like an outsider and even if I hardly understood the instructor's passion. I earned a B- and was secretly pleased.

The summer after black literature and my first year of college, I returned to Applewood and to a mess that permeates more suburbs than people like to admit: divorce. My brothers were working at a factory in California—for the "experience"—and my mom had gone to visit them. I had long suspected something wasn't quite right in my parents' relationship—there was a cold tension that hung in the air of our suburban home—though I was hardly an expert in this arena. Apparently, though, my dad had grown increasingly unhappy in his marriage to my mom, so he decided that once she returned from California, he would pack up and find his own place. If he had waited another month, they would have had their twenty-fifth wedding anniversary.

Even with adult children, divorce is never easy. Our case was no different, and none of us knew how to handle the change. So we just didn't. Didn't talk about it, didn't extend comfort or understanding to one another. We just endured it like we had endured other changes in our predictable lives. My mom sold the only house we had ever called home; my father found an apartment in the city, went on with his work, and two years later remarried. My brothers and I continued floating through a variety of college majors, hoping to "find ourselves" in the midst of the unspoken uncertainty.

All-American independence at its best. When Thanksgiving or Christmas break came around, friends or roommates at college would ask me where I would be going for the time off, a confusing question when you're not sure where your home is. I was now officially on my own.

I was more than ready my third year of college when two friends invited me to take a semester off of school to go backpacking (via the rail system) through Europe. It was the escape I needed. I worked two waitressing jobs to save for the trip, borrowed what I hadn't raised from my dad, and spent the next three winter months exploring the cultural landscape of Switzerland, Germany's Rhine River, Italy's Florence, and England's countryside.

While we were in the French-speaking Swiss Alps—snow covered mountains as stunning as Colorado's—we wandered into "L'Abri Fellowship," a community founded by the notable theologian, Francis Schaeffer. His intentional Christian commune, comprised of about a half dozen families living in chalets throughout the small mountain village, had attracted students from around the world to come and question issues of faith and purpose. For about four weeks, I participated in daily chores, listened to Schaeffer lecture at nights (trying, with great futility, to understand his intellectualism), studied the Old Testament and the Gospels each morning, and engaged in a variety of dining room table discussions. Mostly, I contemplated all the recent events of my twenty-year-old life—divorce, family life, friendships, Christianity—as I walked through freshly fallen snow past quaint Swiss chalets, sharp icicles hanging from the roofs and fresh cold air buffeting my face.

I began to ask more questions. What was my purpose, after all? When would my family come together? Why was I still drawn to those who were different? Why did injustices bother me so much? And why had I become a Christian: because it was a cool thing to do at my high school or because it was true?

The lectures and discussions didn't help. The chores and personal studies and morning walks did. Although I left L'Abri with no clear direction about any of my inquiries, I had come to two helpful conclusions. The first was that I was more convinced than ever that I did not just want to exist throughout this journey called life; I wanted to live, really live—the way writers wrote about in biographies and novels. The way Jesus talked about life in the Gospels. Abundantly. That was what became as clear to me as the winter Alps in front of me.

The second was a simple truth, a small drop of rain that nourished my soul again much like it had in the Colorado Rockies: Jesus loves me. This I knew. Now the Bible had told me so. That seemed enough for now. So, with a European adventure behind me and a firm reminder of a faithful relationship, I returned to college and picked up my courses with new fervor. My student teaching experience two semesters before I graduated suddenly exposed me to a long overdue sense of accountability. I panicked at the revelation: I was expected to know, really know, this stuff about English in order to teach it.

Studying took on new meaning. I would be a good teacher, no matter what. For God's sake, I would make a difference, the way the Sir had, the way Mr. Archebeque had.

Abundantly.

An Iranian friend from college introduced me to a friend of his—who just happened to be the superintendent of a school district in a suburb just east of Denver, a "transitional" community comprised of a few military bases, thriving ethnic restaurants, and several new housing developments. So, only two months after I graduated from the university, I got my first job teaching English and speech to high school tenth graders, barely older than some of the students themselves and scarcely more qualified than they. I wondered what Mrs. Manning would have thought of that.

My classes were made up of African-American, Vietnamese, and white students. I was surprised at how much they reminded me of . . . me at their age: struggling for acceptance, aching for affirmation, wondering what they were supposed to be doing. I knew what they were going through and worked all the harder to try to support them. With Olympian-type zeal, I was determined to save them, to save the whole public school system if I had to. God and I could do it together.

What I hadn't anticipated was that I might need help.

I spent all my waking hours with teenagers, listening to their emotional woes, encouraging them in their talents. I often gravitated especially to my African-American students, somehow feeling the need to make up for the many disservices my white heritage had inflicted on them and their ancestors. I was even taking some of these young people to downtown Denver to serve the homeless. All good intentions aside, I did not have the wisdom, and perhaps the courage, to, as they say today, get a life. Teaching had become my god.

So, after five years of coaching, instructing, and avoiding any external help from peers at my church, I grew restless again. And tired. So tired I often made bad choices in the one thing I had always known I needed: relationships.

I pushed away friends, avoided potential dates, and ignored voices of concern from older friends or family members. I could handle it. I was, after all, a strong, capable, independent woman who came from a proud line of privileged self-sufficient entrepreneurs.

Yeah, right.

I eventually grew so uncomfortable that I did the only logical thing I could think of: I went to graduate school. In Virginia. Far away from Colorado.

And there, mercy's rain refreshed me again.

Through courses in cultural anthropology, urban studies, and cross-cultural communication, I began to really delve into the world that had winked at me from a distance all my white suburban life: African-American culture. I studied history, and for the second time in my life, was aghast at the incredible legislated injustices inflicted on so many of America's only forced immigrants. I learned of the laws white men, some of whom called themselves Christian, passed that denied the very humanity of blacks, laws that refused education to their children, that enforced an ugly elitism in the name of economics, that separated husbands from wives, that tried to destroy families and character and culture. As these shameful truths emerged in book after book, it slowly occurred to me how much the residue of such horrors had left its mark on our still segregated and unjust society.

What also emerged from those pages was an equally incredible resilience and strength—and sometimes, remarkable forgiveness—in a people denied the privileges I had always taken for granted. I read more of the literature, listened to the spirituals, and studied the sermons. A powerful perseverance and redemption sprang forth in the words and stories, born, no doubt, in the midst of atrocities I would never be able to fully understand. I saw a cultural definition deeply rooted in cohesion, a magnetic sense of belonging and community and passion, one most of us white Americans of European descent only scratch our heads at in response.

Culture no longer defines all-Americans. Second, third, and fourth generations of unrestrained privilege tend to make you forget who you are. And why not? You don't need to know who you are when everyone abides by your rules. Only those who are forced to swim upstream know what they are made of.

I couldn't study enough, especially when I discovered that Christian faith did, in fact, speak to such injustices. I stumbled onto the contemporary writings of various Christians who had confronted the same discrepancies. I read the books of a southern preacher from Mississippi, John Perkins, who defied cultural mores to confront a racist Christianity and now advocated for reconciliation; Roger Greenway's biblical mandate for urban ministry; Walter Wangerin Jr.'s gifted storytelling as a white urban pastor. Their works, as well as the lives of several local Christian friends—white and black—who relocated to a low-income neighborhood in Norfolk to live out their faith in collective ministry, finally, thankfully, began to give language to the tensions I had experienced for a long time.

They also encouraged me to reexamine the Book that had already changed different corners of my world. I re-read the Gospels and saw, as if for the first time, Jesus touching a leper, sharing water with a Samaritan woman "in the bad part of town" (John 4), and telling stories of a poor widow, a rich young ruler, and a judgment day (Matt. 25) that would separate Christians into sheep and goats because of how they responded to the hungry, the homeless, and the hurting. Radical, sacrificial, abundant living—justice and mercy married.

Through all of these new voices, I began to understand that the incarnation of Jesus Christ was about much more than a virgin birth; it was about hope personified amidst hopelessness, love demonstrated in a touch or a cup of cold water. It was an intentional presence for a people who knew only abandonment, oppression, and inequity.

I was waking up. Again.

To my surprise I graduated with honors, having written my thesis about, of all things, how to teach a course on urban ministry to white college students. I returned to a position teaching English and communication courses at a small Christian college just past Denver's city limits. City life still held a magic power over me, much like it had when I was in high school. Only now I had a language of faith to explain why. I decided to make my move.

No more homogenized milk suburbs for me.

I also began attending a small and dynamic storefront African-American church. The pastor had preached at our little white conservative college chapel and invited me to his church after we had talked about how the college could be more culturally relevant and inclusive. I showed up the next week at his church and was drawn to the pastor's insights and style, the church's friendliness, and the lively and sincere worship. I knew after the first few services that I was committed. For the next eight months, however, I was greeted warmly each Sunday by members who thanked me for visiting and hoped I could come *visit* again sometime.

It wasn't until I started teaching in the children's Sunday school class once or twice a month that people began to realize I also might be a member, even if I was the only blond in the church. I knew their children's names, slapped them five when I saw them on Sundays or Wednesday nights, and introduced myself to their moms and dads. The pastor encouraged me to offer some writing courses for college credit at the church. "Use your gifts for the church, Sister," he smiled.

For the next three months, I met with about ten ladies from the church on Saturday mornings, and we explored principles of good writing. They wrote thoughtful stories and profound sentences, and sharpened their skills in grammar, punctuation, and organizing essays. But I grew a bit frustrated at the realization that this classroom environment did not always afford me the opportunity to build friendships.

So I took action. I told them that the only way they could pass the course was to invite me to dinner or coffee in their homes. Their eyes got big when they saw I was serious about the proposal (though I assured them that their grades really were not in danger if they couldn't fit me in). Some of them laughed a nervous laugh; others got out their calendars. I figured I got the best deal out of it: a couple of wonderful home-cooked meals, lots of laughs, and the start of a few meaningful friendships.

I was no longer a visitor.

During the year of my first black church, I also began seeking opportunities to volunteer in the city. A friend of a friend told me about a housing ministry called Hope Communities, and after joining them to help in their children's after-school program, I was hooked.

Seven- and eight-year-old children have a mysterious power.

One Wednesday afternoon, Robin Waterman, the program director, asked me to pick up a few kids from the block at Thirty-first and California Streets in the historically black neighborhood known to locals as Five Points. Five Points is a multicultural, economically diverse neighborhood that at one time was considered the "Jazz Capital of the West." Like many American urban centers, though, it experienced the economic and social exit of its upper-middle-class residents to the suburbs, leaving the neighborhood to those who didn't always have the financial means to maintain it. Consequently, it became the stereotypical, overlooked, low-income neighborhood (that many organizations overlook).

Hope Communities, however, did not overlook this neighborhood, and the interracial staff opened offices in Five Points in the late 1970s to provide housing for low-income families who, as Hope's motto reads, "deserve to live in decent homes."

Out of their initial mission emerged the need for an educational program, combined with various recreational activities for the children who lived in the Hope apartments.

My task this particular Wednesday was to pick up six children who lived in Hope's Martin Luther King Jr. Homes. As I slowed to park my car, I noticed a young African-American woman about twenty-five years old sitting on the porch of one of the apartments I was told to visit. She wore short blue jean cutoffs and a Malcolm X T-shirt that read, "By Any Means Necessary." Long, blue extensions in her hair outlined her slender brown face. She was not smiling. She stood when she saw me approaching, put one hand on her hip, shifted her weight, smoked her cigarette, and stared.

Why did God have to make me so . . . blond?

As I approached her, I felt my palms sweat and reminded our Maker that I wasn't quite ready to meet him. When I got to the blue-haired, Malcolm X woman, I introduced myself to her, mumbling something about being a volunteer with Hope Communities kids' club, and wondered if her sons would join us at the recreational center that day. She blew smoke into my face, still not smiling, and glared at me with a look that I was sure asked, "What's a white girl like you doing in a place like this?"

Then two small, handsome boys appeared on her porch. Their Ninja Turtles T-shirts were tight on their tiny muscles; their jeans baggy. They seemed to know about Hope and waited with eager eyes for their mother's consent. She was still staring at me. In silence. Eyebrows now furrowed hard. I trembled.

What was I thinking, anyway? Who did I think I was coming into a black neighborhood to hang out with eight-year-olds? What could I possibly have to offer? Was it too late to hide in my car and drive off?

All of a sudden, the blue-haired head snapped back. I jumped. And as if she were coming out of a daydream, the woman said to me, "Hope? Oh, sure, they can go. That's a good Christian organization—lets the kids do all sorts of fun things. And I'm Freda by the way." With that, she extended her hand. I fumbled, wiped my sweaty hands on my pants, and then shook hers. I sighed a silent thanks for divine intervention as the boys and I hurried off to kids' club.

Amazingly, a friendship was born that day between Freda and me. For some reason, she invited me into her life—a very good thing, especially when the small renovated house next door to the MLK units opened up and I moved in. I had been visiting families on the block for a year now, so I was thrilled when I was able to secure a home right next door, already knowing my neighbors. For the next three years, Freda and her children, James, I.C., Qyanisha, and I shared many more porch conversations, kids' clubs, field trips, Christmas parties, and Easter dinners. We read books together, played football with the other kids on the block, and borrowed sugar from each other. And the one time my house got broken into, it was Freda who immediately appeared at my door, me shaking at the violation, she taking charge, grabbing a broom to sweep the broken window glass and saying, "Oh, Girl. Don't worry. This stuff happens." It was all I needed to hear.

Urban comfort. Neighborliness. Incarnation.

Another single woman named Janet Mayhue also decided to join me and share the rent. Roommates. Janet and I met at church and quickly discovered we had gone to the same college at the same time—we just didn't know each other because we lived in two different worlds. She had been a part of the Black Student Union, sang in their gospel choir, and studied business. I was on the soccer team and in education. Now almost ten years later, she had forged a successful career as a youth worker, businesswoman, and professional singer. And because she had grown up in Omaha's housing projects, the oldest from a wonderful family of seven children, Janet was quick to mentor me about "life in the 'hood." We talked long hours about race issues, about the children in the neighborhood, about music and family and men and church.

Others also helped me discover what it meant to be a neighbor, that is, a neighbor as the Bible describes it in Luke 10:25–37.

Grandma Pearl was sixty-one years old when I first met her. She didn't own a car or a house, hadn't held a job in years because of her arthritis, and relied almost entirely on government aid to pay her rent, medication, and food bills. To those of us who had grown up on the suburban side of town, Grandma Pearl was "poor."

That's just what I thought, too, as I watched her run her tiny three-bedroom home where her niece, granddaughter, and visiting relatives lived. Her adopted daughter with her seven children lived next door. I lived across the street.

I visited Grandma Pearl often and played with the grandbabies who gathered around her feet. The role of baby-sitter fell frequently on her while her adult children hunted for daily work. But she never seemed to mind. She had enough love to go around, she'd tell me, a sparkling white smile stretching over her wrinkled brown face.

"Baby," she would call to everyone who passed her porch, "my Jesus, he done good by me and I'm prayin' he be good to you too." Friends stopped often at Grandma Pearl's. If they were hungry, she would cook; if they were discouraged, she would listen. If they needed direction, she would glance at her huge family Bible, the source of her wisdom verbally dispensed in bite-size pieces of encouragement to "keep on, stay pure, Baby, and rejoice in the Lawd."

Rejoice she did, most days. In spite of her economic poverty, her failing health, and her difficult surroundings, Grandma Pearl rejoiced in Jesus. Sometimes she would wrap her soft, stiff fingers around my pale ones and pray for me: "Girls likes you can't be too careful around here," she would whisper in my ear. "You need some angels, honey."

I know now that each prayer of hers pushed back a bit of darkness on our block. And I realized that this "poor" woman personified the type of Christian neighbor I wanted to be.

When she died a few years later of heart failure, Janet and I attended her service. I was the only white person who attended, but I needed to be there: Grandma Pearl had prayed for me and taught me about giving in the midst of poverty. Once I thought I might help her family; instead, she helped me see my great need for the light of "her Jesus," a light that uncovers the poverty of a soul in need of grace.

I needed grace. It came in many faces.

I saw it in Pearl's, Janet's, Freda's, the children's, and the other neighbors on the block. They kept me rooted as I found my way through a foreign world, one that felt more like home than Applewood ever had. That's what friendships do; they anchor you.

I continued teaching at the Christian college, in suburbia west of the Mile High City. It was a strange reversal now for me to commute *from* the city out *to* the suburban campus, driving through downtown Denver past the Capitol and public library and toward the same foothills I grew up in. It was stranger still when nice white Christian colleagues would point to the Denver skyline and ask me, "How's your ministry going in the city? How are those people doing down there anyway?"

Those people? *My* ministry? *Down* there? Did I miss it?

No, Five Points was becoming home in every sense of the word, an intersection of faith and history, vocation and emotion, healing and serving.

I was not likely to leave the city. Or diversity. Or neighbors. It was who I had become.

That much was sure. Even if my career path was redirected and I found myself—with different and new eyes—encountering a strange world: white evangelical America.

Chapter Seven
Southern Roads

By 1985—the year I left Heth and entered college—most "No Niggers after Dark" signs had been brought down from the outskirts of these small southern towns. The "White Only" signs above public restrooms and water fountains were barely a memory, integrated classrooms were well over a decade old, and on university campuses black students across the country were carrying books and papers instead of protest signs and clenched fists.

Elvon

But no matter how much progress had been made, how many affirmative action programs had been started, it was clear that mainstream America still did not look much like me. Once in a while I saw a brown face on a television sitcom, a magazine cover, or in a film. Most of the time, however, I felt as if I had been waiting in line for one of those fast-spinning carnival rides, knowing I was going to get on, but hoping I wouldn't get sick at the end, especially since I wanted to ride again.

When you're black, it's never easy reconciling yourself with what seems like a spinning white world. Each time someone discounts you because of your skin color, you have to decide if you want to try it again. You wake up the next morning—and the next and the next—wondering if you'll have the strength to get on the ride another time. High school had already taught me who was running the carnival. Charles Elton, Michelle, the Wests, our principal—all confirmed *whose* world it was, and now the daily decision to keep going was before me.

Maybe college life a hundred miles away would be different, I hoped.

Eager to leave rural life and racial tensions, I entered the same state university some of my siblings attended. No restrictions, no rules, no chores—only my conscience to guide me. It wasn't a bad first semester. In fact, unlike most freshmen, I had the best academic semester of my college years. At Christmas break, I took home to my parents a 3.6 grade point average and was well on my way to getting inducted into several honor societies. My father expected at least that. My brothers and sisters had helped establish this family tradition of achievement, and I wasn't about to stray from it.

With equal tenacity, I had mastered a high-scoring social life as well. I must have dated and made out with half a dozen guys during those first five months of college independence. I went to dances and stayed out until three or four in the morning each weekend. On one fall night, I even decided to experience what it felt like to get drunk for the first time. I drank enough beer and spiked punch to severely influence my senses and discovered it wasn't all it's cracked up to be.

At Christmas break, I was now the one coming home from college with all sorts of stories, answering all my siblings' questions about dorm life, parties, course work, and professors. We'd pass around helpings of macaroni and cheese, squash casserole, and ham, while catching up on who was doing what or how college life had changed or why I should take this professor or that class. It felt good to be included in such an "adult" conversation, to discuss with my siblings the same issues I remember hearing them debate in past Christmases. Then we'd pull out the card games and the pies to celebrate the holiday—and each other. A sturdy foundation, a familial refuge.

Reed confidence. Black pride.

By January I returned to college with another healthy dose of inherited assurance. As a result, my social life picked up its pace, and I was busy with the Black Student Association and Alpha Phi Alpha's little sister sorority. If I wasn't waiting tables at the local Pizza Hut (where my customers regularly left religious tracts instead of tips), I was either discussing some campus policy and "how it affected black folk" or dancing with some brother at one of our sorority parties. General education classes were interesting enough, taught mostly by white professors and filled with a blend of white southern belles, white and black athletes, and black farm folk like me.

My boundaries were clear: I studied with black friends, dated only "brothers" (that is, African-American men), joined mostly black organizations, and ate at the "black" table in the dining hall. I liked staying in a black world, avoiding the other one as much as possible. That's just the way it was.

One cold day early in the winter semester, I was on my way to a Black Student Association meeting when I noticed a short, young white man dressed in Hawaiian shorts and a tank top. I stopped in my tracks, shivering from the February cold. Didn't this guy know it was forty degrees outside? He saw me staring and smiled as he made his way toward me.

"Bet you're wondering why I'm dressed like this, right?" he laughed as he introduced himself. "Wanted to get your attention." With that, he asked me if I could take a few minutes to fill out a survey for the religious organization he was part of. I figured the least I could do was take time for someone who was willing to go to such lengths just to get people to fill out his form. I took a pen from my bag, answered the questions without much thought, and handed the survey back to him, hoping the poor guy would put some warm clothes on.

Two weeks later, a white woman from the same Hawaiian-clad campus ministry knocked on my door. She said she had gotten my name from the survey I'd filled out and wondered if I could take a few minutes to talk with her. I agreed. (She seemed a little more normal.) As we stood in the doorway of my dormroom, she smiled as she began her rote but sincere speech: God loved me and had a wonderful plan for my life, but my sin separated me from God. Her eyes never left mine as she went on: "The good news is that Jesus came to close that gap, and if you, Elvon, accept Jesus as your Savior and Lord, you can have a relationship with God and go to heaven when you die."

I know that, I thought. *Everyone in Arkansas knows that!*

I smiled politely and nodded my head. Then she asked me how sure I was of going to heaven. I told her I was 100 percent sure. No doubt about it. As a child, I had been really afraid of going to hell—it seemed like a scary place to me, and I was sure I didn't want to end up there. So I read a lot of religious literature in high school, even memorized Scriptures about heaven as a kid, and watched my mother read the Bible. I knew the right answers to this woman's questions.

She proceeded. Next question: if I were to die tonight and stand before God and he were to ask me why he should let me into heaven, what would I say? Easy. Because I've accepted Jesus as my Savior. Period. That answer was in a tract I'd come across, maybe at Pizza Hut. I passed the test. She walked down the hallway satisfied that I was a Christian.

I was, after all, in the Bible belt of the nation. Close to the buckle—everyone here was a "Christian."

Soon after, I was invited to a meeting sponsored by the ministry this heaven-bound woman and the Hawaiian-shorts guy were part of. It was a place where students came to discuss the Christian faith. I didn't have anything else to do that Thursday night, so I decided to attend these white folk's religious gathering. I was curious that I had even been invited. But as I walked toward the event through the business building where I had been studying, I wondered why I was going. Accepting the invitation might improve my social status, I told myself.

When I walked into the room, not only did I see the two folk I'd already talked with, but I noticed about a third of the group was comprised of black students. That first meeting, I met Bryant, Tosknella, and other upperclassmen who seemed as devoted to their religion as I did my social life. After introductions, they led us in singing and prayer, and then a discussion of a Bible passage. I met other black students there too: Antrim, Eric, Alonzo, and Brad—"brothers" who told me they were serious about their faith in Christ. I was impressed that young, gracious black men were vocal in this meeting. A few were what we called "preacher types," who got everyone, white and black alike, listening as they expounded on verses in lyrical, stirring rhythms. Not only did these brothers exemplify strong leadership skills; they conveyed a deep sense of religious conviction I had not seen in anyone besides my mother. And it wasn't religion as I had known it at old St. Paul A.M.E. Church. This was just a group of black and white students who met together weekly to talk about Jesus.

For some reason, they also seemed genuinely concerned about me. They picked me up for picnics, and they called me to make sure I was coming to their meetings. When I'd ask them about music, they'd answer that they only listened to Gospel. They never read horoscopes (like I did each morning), never partied, always worked hard in their classes, and encouraged me to do the same. They interacted with a confidence that made me question my own, an assurance that caused me to wonder what, if anything besides black pride, could motivate them. And because they assumed—like the white dorm lady had—that I was already a Christian, they let me tag along with them—as if I were their little sister—to lunch on Sundays after church.

Church. My new friends introduced me to a whole new experience in church, one completely different from the African Methodist Episcopalian services I had suffered through as a child. I hadn't heard anyone talk about church with the same sincerity and enthusiasm as my new mentors did. I insisted they take me.

We pulled into the parking lot of Central Baptist, one of the largest churches in town. The outside of the huge sanctuary was painted clean white; a steeple above the steps shot high into the sky. We joked and laughed like old friends as we walked through the front doors. But once inside I gasped aloud: it was filled with *white* people! Each pew had a white family, white children, white grandmas. Everywhere. I panicked.

Had Tosk and Alonzo forgotten to tell me? Why in the world were these young African-Americans coming to a *white* church? How would they ever fit in or feel safe *here?*

Within seconds, the answer walked right up to us.

"Welcome, Brothers and Sisters!" exclaimed an energetic, tall, handsome, middle-aged white man with graying hair, hugging each of us. I felt a million white eyes staring at what I was sure must be the most bizarre exchange imaginable.

"It's good to see you. How's your week been? I'm Brother Rex," he said directly to me as he shook my hand and hugged me at the same time. "Elvon" barely squeaked out of my mouth. One of my big brothers rescued me, and introduced me to the pastor as one of his new friends in the ministry.

"Elvon hasn't yet found a church home in town so we thought we'd bring her with us," Eric said. The pastor welcomed me again, told us he'd talk with us afterward, and then made his way to the pulpit. We were ushered to our seats—in the *front* of the church. My eyes darted over the white faces seated around us. Heads were bowed, friends were catching up with one another, parents were keeping children occupied. In other words—no one had watched us after all. It was as if Brother Rex's congenial response to this group of black students was, well, normal.

It was. Seemed Brother Rex treasured having African Americans in his congregation. No matter what people said, this white man loved us. Maybe it had something to do with the fact he had been a missionary in Togo, Africa, for several years. Or maybe he knew that it wasn't always easy for black college students to find good churches away from their homes—churches, that is, that would welcome them wholeheartedly. He knew all too well that even in the 1980s there were still some white Christians who would not allow blacks into their churches. And maybe Brother Rex knew the grief my friends would receive from other black students who refused to set foot in any white church in Arkansas.

I had been one of them.

"The ground is level at the foot of the cross," he often reminded the members of his church. And he lived it out.

My initial shock about Central Baptist was soon replaced with a genuine desire to join Eric and the others each Sunday. It might have been the dozens of welcomes and friendly conversations I had with members, but really I think it was the sincerity of a few that made me want to come back each week. I was learning so much. Amazingly, I began to feel somewhat safe at this huge white church.

I listened hard to the sermons Brother Rex preached—they challenged me in ways few other pastors had. He was a preacher and teacher, not like the black preachers I had heard who emphasized in their sermons the emotion without necessarily the thinking. I always left Brother Rex's sermon intellectually stimulated, not just emotionally invigorated. My respect for him grew, and I found myself wanting to apply the lessons he taught me. Sunday school was helpful in pointing out ways I could live the faith my brothers had helped ignite. Even after Bryant, Eric, and the others graduated, I continued (as one of the only African Americans) to attend Central Baptist, so I could be around Brother Rex.

My white pastor.

I wasn't sure what was going to happen to me when my big brothers took their diplomas and their faith into the world and left our little college town. But their encouragement and affirmation instilled in me a new confidence, one significantly different from the Reed tradition of achievement. My family's had been for me a steady shield, polished and sharpened over years of reacting to and second-guessing the dominant system, that is, white folk. Alonzo, Tosk, Eric, and the others showed me an alternative: theirs was a faith that transcended even the strongest of cultural fortresses, a love that did not react to whites but instead pursued relationships with them. I saw a mysterious freedom in that, and though it meant risking a great deal, the reward, I began to learn, was far greater than any amount of social status could provide. They showed me a vision that said black and white together did not always have to translate into misunderstanding and tension, as I had mostly seen. There could be mutual acceptance and respect, even if it did seem supernatural.

Authentic Christian fellowship, on earth as it is in heaven.

I had watched it all those first few years. What I didn't really know was that the field of my soul was being tilled, watered, and prepared for harvest.

It wasn't until after graduation in May that the gospel seed finally began to bud. One day in the library, I was reading the Bible my friend Brad had given me. On the way out, I ran into a thin white man with curly blond hair. I recognized him as one of the staff members from the campus ministry my brothers and I attended. Carroll saw my new Bible and commented on how much he liked this version. "Oh, this is a great Bible. Let me show you something," he grinned as he took it from my hand. He turned to Romans 3:25 and read aloud—on the steps of the college library—how Jesus is the propitiation of our sins.

Then he looked at me, smiled again, and said, "Isn't it great that Jesus took our place?"

All I could do was stare at him. He said he'd see me later and hurried off to an appointment. I was stunned; I had heard these words hundreds of times before from dozens of people I respected. Yet, when Carroll now asked this simple question, neon lights flashed in my head. Finally. Clearly.

I walked back across campus unaware of the passing faces or buildings or trees. Words swirled around in my head as I marched home. Suddenly, I understood the question of Jesus on the cross, "My God, my God why have you forsaken me?" I had never grasped that Scripture before, but now Carroll's comment helped me see that God had to forsake Jesus *then* to accept me *now*. My mind was spinning—all the spaces were being filled in, all the Scriptures I had read for years suddenly made sense, and my heart was full and hurting and ecstatic all at the same time. I went in the house, sat at the kitchen table, put my head down in my hands, and wept.

I was overwhelmed that Jesus would take my place. On the cross. For *my* sin. I felt so sorry he had to do that. All I could say—in between my sobs—was, "God, I'm so sorry, I'm so sorry. Please forgive me."

Nothing was quite the same after that. No more pat, Bible-belt answers. I knew my need, and it was real. New life had come.

Throughout the next year I developed new friends at both Central Baptist and on campus. I was enjoying all the more the college ministry they had invited me to, Sunday school at church, and the various black organizations I had joined. I worked hard in my classes, studying speech and drama with the hope of entering either a career in teaching or performing. Before I knew it, something very strange began to happen: my social life started changing colors.

My circle of friends was turning white.

My new faith, however, was just that: new. It was also idealistic and hopeful and eager. Underneath some of my growing friendships was still a lingering separation of race, one that my brothers hadn't fully prepared me for.

At one of the Christian student events, I met Kate. She was as short as I was and as blue-eyed and blond as I was penny-colored. Besides that, she was from the north—a true Yankee, I teased. After a few minutes of conversation, we realized a kinship that was strong, especially when we learned that we both had rejected the advances of a brother who was a little too desperate for feminine attention. We laughed at the revelation, asking for the Lord to bless our brother. "Help him, Jesus," we prayed.

Kate and I began spending more and more time together; we'd plan to meet at the student center to study, work out in the gym, or walk to Bible study. Late into the nights, we'd talk about guys, assignments, Bible verses, dreams. Eventually we became roommates, a black girl and a white girl living together in a dormroom in northeast Arkansas.

We were friends. Safe friends.

That meant we rarely talked about race. No matter how much we shared, the line was clearly drawn. Without words or looks or signs. A cloud always seemed to hang over us. I knew.

By the time we graduated from college, I was the best girlfriend Kate had in Arkansas. So you can imagine my surprise when she didn't call me a few months later when she was planning her wedding. She didn't ask me for my dress size or my opinion about colors or music. She didn't describe for me how the wedding ceremony was going to go or who would be attending. She didn't for one simple reason: I was not going to be a part of the wedding, just a guest. Friends who knew how close we had been in college assumed I'd be a bridesmaid.

I brushed aside questions with easy answers about Kate getting married in her hometown up north, how she naturally would prefer family and old friends in her party, wanting it to be traditional. Then I'd change the subject and pretend it didn't bother me. But when Karen, another black friend of ours whose wedding I *was* in, asked me why I wasn't in Kate's, I didn't know what to say.

Christians. Friends. To a point.

I served punch at the reception, along with a white woman who had barely known Kate at college.

I experienced the separation of race in other ways too. One night I was watching television with my buddy, Freddy. From Batesville, Arkansas, Freddy was a white Christian rocker with long dark hair and bangs, and eager to make sense of the "race thing." He honestly didn't seem to care that I was black. Unlike Kate, Freddy took every chance he had to ask me about the ramifications of race. He wasn't afraid if he looked stupid or if we'd disagree. He just wanted to know.

As we watched television that night a commercial came on advertising *"flesh-colored* Band-Aids" shown on beautiful white people with little bitty boo-boos. I knew what the ad was saying. I held up my finger and declared to my young white friend, "What about *this* flesh?"

He sat silent.

A few days later, he told me that my comment about the Band-Aid commercial helped him understand how much of society was directed toward him and not toward people who looked like me. Many other times, Freddy would want to talk, about U.S. history or discrimination or white supremist groups. We'd discuss what it means to be black in a white world and what it means to be Christians in the midst of such societal discrepancies. Every now and then I'd even catch Freddy watching me, a sparkle in his blue eye; this sweet young white boy was developing a crush on me.

I teased him about that, and he'd blush and change the subject. We remained good friends throughout college. Whenever Freddy had a question about racial issues, I was the one he called—and still calls.

Most days I'm glad. But some days I get a little tired of being his "black" friend.

Spending time with Freddy and other white boys, though, was not always easy for me. After my big brothers graduated, some of my best buddies during college were white guys, fine Christian gentlemen who cared about me. Kenny, Todd, Danny, Mark—all had a fingerprint on my life without being intimately involved in it. But other black students on campus did not always like the fact that I spent time with these "white guys" and often threw evil looks my way. Maybe they thought I was selling out or giving up my black identity to be friends with white people (and, therefore, those in power). Maybe they thought I was trying to be white, betraying our unspoken cultural mandate that says, "Black folks stick together."

Whatever their reason for the "evil eye," I'd look back at them with a "holier than thou" stare, determined not to let their glares penetrate my new confidence.

I would not let them get to me . . . much.

Besides, it wasn't as if I had abandoned my black friends just because I attended a white church or had white friends. Many other African Americans were on the speech and debate team with me, so we'd practice together almost every day. And if I didn't see them in classes twice a week, I could count on traveling with them to tournaments throughout the south once a month, comparing briefs, preparing arguments, and strategizing about how to beat the other teams.

I wasn't in danger of losing my roots, even if my footing was shifting. But that didn't mean the struggle wasn't there. When a few white guys asked me out on dates, I wasn't sure what to do. Never in a million years had I expected to find myself in this position. Now questions surfaced in me like dust on a southern road: Was it wrong for a black girl to date a white guy, especially in a region of the country loaded with racial tension? Would my friends, both black and white, see it as betrayal? How did my new Christian faith guide me in this area?

I went to Brother Rex. I had to find out what I was supposed to do about this thing called interracial dating. As usual, my pastor got out his Bible and spent the next hour exploring with me what he thought might be the biblical response. He pointed me to the passage where God turns Miriam white because she didn't like Moses marrying a black woman from Ethiopia. He showed me Proverbs. He told me that some Christians liked to use certain passages, such as 2 Corinthians 6:14, about being unequally yoked, to show how whites and blacks shouldn't marry. But he explained that this passage does not refer to racial differences, especially if we are all equal in God's eyes. Finally, Brother Rex concluded that God does not forbid interracial marriage or dating, and he said, "The same rules apply for these marriages as for others: You need to have your parents' blessings. This will provide a haven for the child even if society may disapprove of the relationship."

I thought of my father, especially his stern discipline and heavy hand, looked at my options, and chose to believe my father was stronger than God. So I dated only black brothers for the rest of my college days.

By the time I was preparing to graduate, I knew I had to get out of Arkansas. I had traveled enough to know that a small southern town was not for me. I wanted something different, different cultures, different people, different types of people. Mostly, I wanted to know what it felt like to live in a city. My southern experiences had not given me much cultural diversity, the kind I had always seen in urban areas. Though I loved the South, I knew eventually I would take one of its roads north and discover the rest of the world.

To get there, I spent Christmas of 1987 with a few friends and attended a college convention for Christian students instead of going home for our traditional Reed celebration. The conference introduced students and graduates to opportunities for Christian ministry in different areas of the world. I strolled through the huge exhibition hall past hundreds of (mostly white) people, looking at the booths, reading pamphlets, and talking with representatives from a variety of organizations. Though it was all interesting, nothing really caught my eye.

I kept walking, wondering how God might direct me. Then I turned my head and saw a booth that read, "Summer in the City." This was different than the cushy beach projects that were held each summer for wealthy white students or blacks who could afford them. This one said, "Work with the homeless. Make a difference in a kid's life. Spend a summer serving God in New York." On the front of that brochure was a picture of the Statue of Liberty with the New York City skyline in the back. I stared at it for a few minutes, talked with the representatives, and knew this was where I should be.

By May 1990, I graduated from college with a degree in speech and theatre and began preparing to join the "Summer in the City" team.

All the participants had to read a book called *With Justice for All,* written by a black civil rights activist and evangelist named John Perkins. It dealt with the author's calling to return to his native Mississippi after he had left its tensions for California life. As his Christian faith grew, he realized he had to go back to "bring healing to a community in need." Then he described his solution for healing through three Rs: relocation—moving back to the community of need, redistribution—economically healing the community through creative uses of resources, and reconciliation—bringing different races together in the community to mirror "God's idea of harmony inside diversity."

As I read that book, I understood what I wanted to do with my life. The years I'd spent in college caught between the black and white worlds finally had meaning. This had all been and was continuing to be a foundation for the future.

I arrived in New York City zealous about bringing the healing waters of racial unity to our thirsty country. I was spiritually equipped, emotionally charged, and intellectually certain miraculous changes were about to happen.

What I didn't know, though, was just how rocky—and just how wonderful—the road would be.

Chapter Eight
Coastal Cares

If you've ever been to California, you'll know that pain hides itself well there. On the beach. In the redwoods. Through the city streets. In any of its many subcultures—druggies, CEOs, hippies, gay activists, Hollywood hopefuls, radical environmentalists, suburban families—numbing is a way of life.

Andrea

So when I started college at a northern California university, I was well on my way to anesthetizing myself with parties, pot, and picked-up guys. Though I knew my mom loved me and my dad, and his lover, cared about me from a distance, there was still a gaping wound in my adolescent soul that needed attention. It was the early 1980s, and most California teenagers I knew were trying all sorts of "socially acceptable" first aid, hoping for some relief. I was too.

Maybe that's why most of my friends were nonconformists whose hearts always seemed to beat against the mainstream. Pain has a way of giving you permission to try just about anything. It pretends you don't care what people think. It fortifies you into believing there's nothing to lose because you have nothing to begin with. I gravitated toward the "have nots" because I knew they'd accept me more than those already identified as the "beautiful ones."

Enter Emma Garcia and Traci Rodriguez, two Mexican-American college friends who were as different from each other as redwoods are from palm trees. Emma came from a huge family in Los Angeles and loved her punk rocker image. Her hair was usually a different color every time we got together, and she loved wearing "T-shirts with an attitude," black leather jackets, spiked jewelry, and lots of earrings. Traci's hair was predictably dark and wavy, and she wore blue jeans or a jumper to fade into the image of a typical college student. She was from Sacramento and didn't mind at all being conventional. They were my two closest friends those first two years in college, placing me somewhere in between punk and mainstream. Wanting to fit in but not wanting to conform.

I met Emma at registration, and Traci and I were assigned to be roommates. Immediately, the three of us were aware of all that we had in common: smoking, drinking, guys, and surviving all three. These "bonds" always seemed to eclipse any cultural or personal differences we had.

For instance, Traci loved decorating our tiny dormroom with cutesy balloons and matching bedspreads and ruffles. I'd have my lacrosse and field hockey sticks against the wall and my James Taylor and Jackson Browne records playing whenever Emma, the punker, came over with a few six packs or some tequila. We'd drink, sleep until noon the next morning, miss class, and turn around that night to find another way to have fun. We were determined to make the most of our campus life, a schedule that gave us Wednesdays off. This was great news for the likes of us because it meant that Friday, Saturday, and Tuesday were all party nights.

This schedule, of course, meant we often wrote papers the night before they were due. The three of us would stay up all night in our little cutesy dormroom, smoke pot to stay awake, and finish our papers just in time. (No one on Earth knows what those papers said!) Because I had declared psychology as my major, I was always trying to analyze things, even when I was high. I would look at my Hispanic friends and say, "Why are we hanging out? Here's Emma, the punk rocker, and Andrea, the good girl gone bad, and Traci out in la-la land!" We'd laugh at the weird trio. And think we were crazy.

It was one big party. Barely getting by with Cs.

One day we decided to do another crazy thing: we were going to join the crew team. Rowing in a boat. On the water. With seven other women. Though we'd barely even heard of this sport until now, we figured it would surely add another dimension to our athletic careers and deepen our self-imposed, counter-cultural mandate. It meant we'd have to "cool it on the drinking" as our coach told us. Especially before races. We were as headstrong and enthusiastic about this new recreation as we were our partying adventures. Besides, now we also had to be responsible to our team.

That seemed important. Even "losers" can be loyal.

So off we went, the three of us strange young college friends, rowing faithfully and working hard at a sport we knew little about. Emma quickly earned the position of coxswain, which meant she was the one who yelled and commanded the rest of us as we rowed. With her green or blue or pink hair and spikes, she'd sit in the front of the boat and work her vocal chords while we worked our arms. I was in relatively good shape from high school basketball and lacrosse, so the coach placed me as the "stroke" or eight (wo)man. I had to set the pace for the other women, to be consistent and smooth as each stroke hit the water, and keep count. In other words, each member of the boat followed my stroke in a steady rhythm; technique and leadership were everything. Others *had* to pay attention to me.

I loved the spot.

Behind me as "seven woman" was a tough, short-haired blond named Karen. Because she was competitive like I was, she and I began joking about rowing in the 1988 Olympics. We were serious, and both felt the other had the ability to get there. After practices, she'd join me and my friends for our dorm-room parties or now-limited drinking sprees. Soon the joking subsided into serious conversations. Karen started to talk openly with me about her struggle to fit in, to live out what she thought she might be: a lesbian. Karen, an only child whose parents always lavished her with love, was horrified to think how they might respond to her if she explored a homosexual lifestyle.

It didn't horrify me; I was still numb from the last time someone close to me chose to enter the gay life. So I listened to Karen for two reasons only: we had connected as athletes on crew, and I needed people to like me.

At least for the season.

After crew ended that year, Emma, Traci, and I returned to our usual superficial gatherings. They never told me anything about their Hispanic heritage. In fact, we never had one conversation about racial issues at all. Though Karen had talked openly about her struggle with her sexual identity, my two closest friends never did tell me about their cultural identity. And I didn't ask, even though my parents had certainly instilled in me a sensitivity to various cultures. Blame it on our youthful foolishness, but it seemed that Emma, Traci, and I could only talk about beer, boys, or boats.

Maybe we just didn't want to risk losing our friendship over a topic that might make us squirm. Or think. Shallow exchanges were safer, to be sure. Or maybe my Latina friends never felt completely comfortable talking about it with me, a Waspy, privileged girl whose dad was gay and whose skin was as pale as the cigarette paper we used to roll our joints. I can't assume.

Do most minorities feel comfortable talking with white friends about their culture or the discrimination they experience? Did Emma and Traci trust me enough to divulge that?

Maybe we thought our bottled, inebriating fun would deaden our troubled emotions, hoping it would be some magic healer. But the perpetual "morning after" always came.

Whatever the reason, I had all but forgotten the religious, socially conscious life my parents introduced me to as a child and was well into this familiar way of life, one I had set in place in high school while dating a guy who had little on his mind but drinking and sex. In fact, he was one of the motivations I had for staying in northern California for college. I wanted to be close to Eddie: the skinny, white cowboy who told me he loved me, who carried an old rifle in the window of his pick-up truck, whose parents were from the South, and who always talked about wanting to go back to Alabama.

I learned from him what *redneck* means.

Eddie loved hunting, beer, and sex. Usually in that order and regardless of who got in his way. If we were driving to a party and someone would cut him off on the highway, he'd speed up just to yell, "Crazy Chink!" If he saw someone walking down the street who happened to be Hispanic, he'd swear at the person from his window, "Stupid greaser!" or "Wetback go home!" Nobody in Eddie's world could do anything right—including me—and so I submitted to his demands, hoping his anger and manipulation were a protective affection for me. If I stayed with him, if I gave in, and mostly, if I did not challenge him, I was sure he would not abandon me.

Like my dad did.

So I pretended this lanky seventeen-year-old loner cared about me. That made me believe I could talk with him about anything. When I told Eddie about my dad's decision to leave our family—for another man—he took a gulp of Budweiser, looked out the window of his truck, and with eerie dullness, responded, "Oh, Andrea. That's unnatural, sick. He's crazy." With that, he stared at me with a look that seemed to tell me not to mention my father again.

Eddie never met my father.

Eddie's parents thought I was good for him because I was from a family who went to church each Sunday. They were nice people who worried about their son. What they didn't know was the double life I was living: church girl *and* party addict. But since Eddie and I met at a church youth group gathering, I convinced myself that the way he treated me was OK. With a piercing remark or a series of hard kisses, he let me know who was in control and who wasn't. And for the next three years, every time I challenged him or tried to break up with him, he would persuade me that he was only thinking of me, that I was his girl, and his only. The attention was all I needed.

Pain sometimes blurs your vision.

When graduation came, I listened as the commencement speaker talked of change, of entering a new phase in our lives. Something in me told me I deserved more. I faced the fact that I was being controlled by Eddie and no matter how much I, or his parents, wanted to change him, I could not. Change only comes for those who know they need it. Eddie did not. The nagging wound within me, however, wouldn't leave me alone; it forced me to move on, to look to college as a new opportunity of focus. Maybe to earn someone else's affection. Maybe to be free to date other guys. So right before the semester began, I told my redneck boyfriend that we were through. Over. This time for good.

As usual, his anger found a string of ugly expletives to throw my way. I held my ground. He groped for something else: he would kill himself if I left him, he told me. But I knew there wasn't anything good for me with Eddie. And somehow I knew Eddie could survive without me. He did.

If dating a guy like him spoke volumes about how I felt about myself then, having the resolve to end the relationship reflected a hunger that was far greater than me.

College life gave me a chance to start over. And after two years of starting over . . . and over and over, of constantly trying to look my best so I could catch a new guy, of wearing down my body with alcohol, one-night stands, and marijuana, I was tired, aching, restless, empty, and damaged.

I was in crisis mode. No purpose.

There had to be more to life than partying, sex, and sports.

I did what most twenty-year-old college girls would do in a crisis: I went home to see my mom. But miles before I pulled in her driveway, I fell apart. Right there on Route 280, I sobbed and yelled and broke. And dared the Almighty. I could hardly see the road as I drove. I screamed to the God my mom had told me about as a child, the one my dad had preached about before he changed careers: "What's this about, God? Why do I feel so miserable? Why is my life so pointless and my friendships so . . . empty?"

Silence. A wall. Nothing.

Raw agony.

My mom and I decided a move would do me good. Somewhere far. Somewhere soothing. She mentioned New York, knowing it was the only place in the world that could draw a smile from me. She was right. Again.

Almost every summer as a kid, I went with my mom and my siblings to beautiful Lake George in upstate New York, about two hundred miles north of Manhattan. It was a guaranteed delight for us, a family tradition (though my dad rarely joined us there before or after the divorce), one we could hardly wait for every spring when school let out. My mom would pack us in the car, drive up from Baltimore, and move us into the small cottage that would be our home for four happy weeks. We stayed about a mile or so from the Silver Bay Association YMCA conference center, and each day we'd walk through the woods past the lake to the center. I learned to swim at Silver Bay, and when I wasn't swimming or hiking, I was making bracelets, leather belts, or pottery in the arts and crafts cabin, playing shuffleboard or tennis, basketball or volleyball, or having hot fudge sundaes in the Silver Bay Store with my mom. The best fudge you've ever had, the employees would tell me. I'd giggle and savor the smooth rich chocolate, the attention of my mom and these other adults, and the carefree life of summers at Lake George.

I loved that place so much I worked there the summers between my freshmen, sophomore, and breaking years of college. As a child, I imagined the fun of scooping ice cream in the store or teaching swimming lessons or answering the phones at the Silver Bay front desk. My brothers had both gone to work there, and I just had to follow each June, July, and August as a college student.

So when I broke down after two years of body abuse from college life, and my mom encouraged me to go to New York, I did smile. I called my friend Laura, a fellow employee I had met at Silver Bay the summer before. She was a kindergarten teacher in Queens, New York City, and when she heard the distress in my voice on the phone, she agreed to pick me up from LaGuardia Airport and to let me crash in her apartment for as long as I needed.

Just after New Year's Eve of 1986, I boarded a plane and headed east, gladly leaving my California college days behind me. I was tired, eager for a rest. For the next six months, I concentrated on getting better, which meant I didn't drink as much and scheduled time for myself. I tolerated the busy, crowded city, talked with Laura, or worked part time in the nursery of her school. My interest in psychology led me to some "transpersonal psychology" seminars. My intrigue with spiritual matters led me to services and singles' groups at a Dutch Reformed church in Manhattan, and my search for guys led me to both.

That summer Laura encouraged me to go back to work at Silver Bay. The first week I was there I met Ji Lim, a tall, thin Asian musician who wore thick glasses and whose soft brown eyes communicated a purity and kindness I hadn't seen before. I was drawn to him, not in the way I had been attracted to other guys. His passion for life, his honesty with his struggles, his love for music and people and God gave him an intensity and confidence I could not ignore. He was broken yet sure, serious yet joyful. I was not interested in picking him up; I was interested in his life. I had to pay attention.

Ji was different from the other employees at Silver Bay. He did not go out barhopping after hours with the rest of us. He did not try to get women in bed with him. He always talked about wanting to do the right thing, wanting to play his music the best he could, wanting mostly to be a good friend to people who might need one. Like me.

Ji spent time with another employee named Adelle Engle. Adelle had the same mysterious brokenness and confidence Ji had. Her kind face was full of freckles, and her rich full smile was always warm and inviting. I watched her too. Especially after she told me how once she had been so distraught over some sin in her life that she stayed up all night on her knees praying and crying before God.

She might as well have been speaking to me in Russian. I did not understand her language. I loved to sleep, so I didn't have any idea how anyone would want to stay up all night because of some little mistake she had made. And how could she speak about it now with such energy and certainty?

Adelle and Ji noticed my wonder of them—and my longing for what they had—and went to work. They invited me to look at the Bible with them, a completely different experience from my years of Sunday school and Vacation Bible School at my dad's church or the Quaker school. These words they showed me looked different, alive, even applicable to me. And they began to explain to me ideas like grace and forgiveness and newness. Though we were all about the same age—in our early twenties—I soon realized these two people conveyed a depth and maturity that showed me how young I really was.

One night toward the end of June, I joined some other employees for our routine of barhopping, pool, darts, and drinking games. Only this night I went a little too far, gulped too much beer and too much Southern Comfort. The combination slapped reality in my face. I stumbled to my dormroom, angry, confused, and really miserable. As I sat on the edge of my bed, alone, I took inventory: I was still as unhappy as I had been with Eddie, as I had been at college in California, as I was that night I drove home to my mom's. I was sick and tired of drinking. Of going to bars. Of picking up guys. Moving across the country to another state had not solved the problem and, I realized, probably never would.

Adelle and Ji's faces came to mind. They seemed to know a way out. I knew they were Christians who loved me and cared about me. I could tell they loved God, though I hardly understood it. Ji would even go off on what he called *solitude trips,* where he would take long walks just to be alone with God. I thought that was really weird. But I watched. It was as if he and Adelle had this personal thing going with God, where they talked to him during the day and sometimes stayed up all night praying to him.

And I still ached.

"OK. I give up. I'm ready to give you control of my life, God. If you want it, take it." I had had it. That June night at Lake George, I think I finally understood that being a Christian wasn't about trying to be a good girl, but recognizing simply that I was not.

I quit drinking. I told Adelle and Ji that I was ready to make some changes. I even started going to a Bible study with one of the conference chaplains. We'd gather on the dock or the porch of the inn or in the auditorium, and we'd study one of the epistles of Paul. The Scriptures became intriguing, practical, helpful.

And comforting. A balm for the wound.

The summer ended, and I'm not even sure Adelle and Ji knew how much they had done for me, how their lives had helped redirect mine. By August, I knew I needed to go back to college to finish my psychology degree. A reputable university in upstate New York accepted me, offered a good psychology and liberal arts program, and that seemed good enough for me.

Alone, but with a new sense of security, I drove to Syracuse, about two hundred miles southwest from Lake George, ready to pick up my course work where I had left off in California. And ready to grow in my young knowledge of this thing called Christianity.

The heavenly silence was lifting.

When I arrived at the end of August, I was surprised to learn I had been assigned a roommate whom I had known years before at the Quaker school in Baltimore. Of all the dorms on this campus, we both had chosen the one with a community focus. It was the most different, the brochure had read, the most radical, the one where you had to be involved with others. We both had to apply for this particular dorm to learn "how to be more than just another college dorm"; we'd be one with a purpose. With causes and agendas.

While I was standing in line at registration, someone from a Christian organization handed me a survey. It was a long line, so I had time to fill it out. In it were questions, like do you ever think about God? Do you think there's a heaven? Do you want to be a part of a Bible study that investigates the claims of Christ, and if so, write down your address and phone number so we can contact you.

I did, and they did.

I went to the group's ice cream social in September. About fifty or seventy-five people were there as we scooped vanilla ice cream. Eunice, a dark-haired, middle-class white woman in her late twenties, walked right up to me and introduced herself. I was obviously wet behind the ears, looking for community, approval, and acceptance and trying to make sense of this Christian thing. Though I was saying yes to all their invitations for coffee or Bible studies, I wasn't quite sure what they were about. But Eunice was reaching out to *me,* seeing some potential in me, and so I was eager to attend her Bible studies.

We met weekly at the student center or the cafeteria or my dormroom or outside in the quad. She and I would go through a lesson from the Bible study she led for me and a few other women my age. Then she'd meet individually with each of us to see how we were doing and to answer any questions we had. And she'd make sure we were understanding what it meant to walk with Christ and that we were praying and having what she called "quiet times."

Naturally, I met a new boyfriend at the ice cream social, and Andy and I started attending an Assembly of God Pentecostal church on Sundays, a lively service with clapping and dancing and loud music. But on Thursday nights we'd go to the campus ministry meetings and sing quaint praise songs, sit with our hands folded in our laps, and whisper. White conservative evangelicalism.

My mom was worried that this group might be a cult since she did not see much action or justice efforts coming from its ministry.

That was going a little too far, I told her, but something did bother me.

Christianity seemed a good thing, I told Eunice. It seemed like it was drawing all these people together on this campus and helping a lot of us experience significant changes. But, I wanted to know, why were there so many denominations? Why the divisions? Why were there movements of charismatic churches and noncharismatic churches where both professed faith in Christ but lived it out in completely different ways? Why had someone even asked me, "How can you be a Christian and not be a Republican?"

Could this just be a slice of the gospel and not the whole thing?

I looked at both groups and noticed I was seeing diversity among Christians in a new way, a way that was nothing like the cultural variety I saw in my dad's churches. They were not unified over basic theological issues, so how, I wondered, could they be unified over more complicated issues, like race or justice, like the issues my father had always raised in his congregations?

Eunice heard my questions. She listened patiently, explaining them away as best she could. Questions did not sit well with the leaders of this ministry; they wanted us to stay in line and have a nice neat belief system that they'd pass on to us in their neat tidy system. And though my perspective of God was getting deeper, I was confused about the tensions I was seeing in the church.

The foundation was being laid.

While attending these Bible studies and churches outside of class, I also studied psychology for the next two years because I thought I was a people helper, that I should study to become a counselor. I tended to give advice as friends came to me. I knew I could listen, and I always enjoyed analyzing problems and working with people to find solutions. Besides, I wanted to understand my own family troubles, and the study of psychology could help me to do so. I studied courses such as abnormal psychology, experimental psychology, family therapy, and geriatrics. Each gave me little clues about what had happened during my childhood. But my desire to help people, and now especially in the context of my Christian faith, kept me in psychology.

I knew about pain.

One day I was on my way home from class. I went to the mailbox and found a letter with a Baltimore postmark. A letter from my dad. I fumbled as I walked up the stairs to my house, hoping one of my Christian roommates would be home. Just in case. Communication had slowed significantly with my dad over the years; his life was filled with his lover and their new life together. Mine was full of my own lovers and changes.

I tore the envelope slowly and pulled out a copy of a letter he had sent to my siblings and me. I sat down. He started with the usual greetings but then avoided the small talk that often accompanied his letters. I braced myself as I read my father's words: he was writing because he wanted us to know what was happening in his life. After having a low-grade temperature, he had gone to see the doctor. The doctor decided to give both Jay and him a special test, and, it turns out, those test results were positive. They had been lovers almost nine years, devoted and committed to one another that whole time, he said. Still, "Doctors diagnosed us both as being HIV positive. We're going to get treatment and work toward staying as healthy as possible for as long as possible. So don't worry. We'll talk soon. Love, Dad."

My father had AIDS. My dad who had taught me about religion, about being responsible, who had taken me to Japan, and read stories to me. My dad who had cared for homeless people and left me when I was only twelve years old. My dad who was kind and disciplined and gay—he had AIDS.

I starting crying. So did two of my roommates, as they came in and listened to me read my father's letter. We cried and hugged and prayed.

Fog settled over me for several days after that. But it wasn't as dark as it had been in California; the Scriptures told me that even in *this,* I would not be abandoned. I hung on.

A week later I called my dad, and we talked about it. About their plan, about my feelings, about our faith. And we decided we all had to learn to live with this horrible disease called AIDS. Somehow, with God's help, somehow.

My dad also told me he was proud of me when I described to him an internship I was about to take at a local rescue mission. Chip off the old block. Specifically, I would be a counselor in training in a residential long-term drug and alcohol treatment center for women. Christ-centered. Work-on-your-life type of place. I found it in the yellow pages.

I knew I needed to see if I could do this "counseling thing," so I called the mission—the largest in the country—and they referred me to the women's treatment center. I wanted some hands-on experience that would also earn me college credit for the internship. The clients at the center were mostly African-American women who had been referred to us from throughout the state and the court system. My job was to teach a Bible study there and to sit in on group and individual counseling sessions and staff meetings. I was even assigned a few clients of my own. I was thriving.

When I graduated the next year, the women's center hired me, and I began to merge faith and vocation as a full-time counselor. I was responsible for a full case load, running therapy groups, leading Bible studies. My boss, an older woman who commanded a lot of respect, ran a strict regime with tight rules, and the clients knew they had to obey. I did too. I saw in her and the other staff members a living gospel. The campus ministry taught me intellectually about Christianity and the Bible, but the rescue mission started to show it to me in the lives of the women who worked there.

Finally, I did not just see deed and action, like my father showed me in his early social justice efforts. Nor did I just hear word and faith, like the college ministry was so adept at. At the women's center, both word and deed, faith and action, tried to merge. There was hope for evangelicalism.

I was twenty-two years old when I held my first job there, counseling women ten, fifteen, and twenty years older than I was, women who told me they liked my "youthful zeal" because, according to them, I was "on fire for God." I laughed, knowing the distance I had come. Some of the clients even told me they stayed in the program because they knew I believed in them; I had confidence in them. I wouldn't let them get away with much because I genuinely wanted them to kick their habits. The difference between self-destruction and personal healing was a familiar sight to me, and they knew it.

It's amazing how your own pain can be useful for others. Redemption at its best.

Life at the women's center continued to anchor me in my faith and stretch me in my professional growth. Still, I wasn't quite prepared when some of the Alcoholics Anonymous women started asking why we took them to a white suburban church rather than a black church on Sundays. They didn't like having to go there, even though they knew staff policy: whoever was on duty Sunday mornings could attend her home church and take the clients with her. Since all the staff members who worked at the center were white and committed to predominately white evangelical churches, we naturally assumed it would be good for any of the clients to go to our Bible-believing services. So week after week, we'd attend a nice white Baptist church or a non-denominational Bible church. And our clients would be handed a hymnal, welcomed as the "ladies from the center," and invited for coffee after the service.

When they began to challenge us, however, we were surprised. Though it made me uncomfortable, I did want to understand. They felt discriminated against, they told us, and frustrated by the worship of white conservative churches. They wanted to go to churches where people could identify with them, where members treated them as equals and not as strange visitors who were politely tolerated. They wanted to shout during the worship, "amen" a preacher's melodic words, and clap with the organ and choir.

The disease of alcoholism or drug addiction can make you find every and any excuse not to look at your life and addiction(s). So we would counsel these black women to believe that they were using the "church thing" as a deflection. We'd tell them that they knew they couldn't use drugs or drink responsibly, that they'd have to face that fact. Any focusing off of their treatment, including where they went to church, was to us merely an excuse to avoid confronting their addictions.

If they brought up any type of trauma or racism, we would try to deal with it—that is, as best as white women who do not understand what it is like to be discriminated against because of our skin color can. Race stayed in their court, not ours. As far as we were concerned, they were there to get clean, to get sober, and to find Christ. Period. Racial justice and cultural healing were part of the curriculum.

We were more empathic with other forms of abuses since we sincerely cared about these clients. In one meeting, our boss—whom I respected a great deal as my mentor—even looked straight into the brown eyes of our clients and said, "Ladies, we're color blind here. Color does not matter in the body of Christ."

But it *did* matter. My childhood taught me at least that. Now, how would my Christian faith respond to these African-American women who spoke with such pain and passion? I had been attending a white conservative suburban church and wasn't seeing how I fit into this new spiritualized world of Bible bags and bumper stickers, this subculture of American Christianity. Something *was* missing for me. I didn't see my church—and others like it—grappling with justice issues, like the kind I had seen in liberal congregations as a child. They had at least taught me that justice and cultural inclusion were a part of the Christian mandate, but in these white Republican churches, I only heard sermons or seminars or discussions on prayer, marriage, overseas missions, or discipleship. Never on race, never on equality. Never, ever on justice.

Besides the "color-blind" approach, the staff at our center responded to the women's racial concerns by hiring an African-American counselor who took them to her church on Sundays. But the interaction with our clients left its mark on me—I could no longer ignore the reality and pain racism inflicted on others.

My mind was full of these issues as I drove the long trip to Baltimore. My dad was dying. Of AIDS. Months earlier I had visited him and Jay, and though they were serious and hopeful, we all knew it was just a matter of time before the disease took its full toll. Now my dad's health had gone from bad to worse, so I was trying to visit him in the hospital as much as possible. My brother and sister had flown in from California. Together, we stood in the room and stared at this shriveled, skinny body who was our father—the same father who scolded us when we were bad, who corrected us when we failed, and who loved us in all of it.

He looked much older than his fifty-three years should have shown. I'm not sure he even knew I was there, but he was coherent enough to let me hold his hand and pray out loud with him. Then he grunted. Was this his last chastisement? Or a final encouragement to stay the course? I wasn't sure. I was sure God had heard my prayer for my dad.

A week later, I sat in a pew next to my mom, brothers, and sister for my father's memorial service. Many people came to pay their last respects to a man who had always stood for justice; some even came from the parishes where he had ministered when I was a child.

It is a strange thing to be at your father's funeral. Stranger still to know he died of AIDS. Part of me cried that his death was premature and unfair. Part of me struggled with the tension that I knew was both true and awkward: if he had made different choices he'd still be alive. Part of me was sad, just sad, that he left me—again. I would never hear his voice again or see him smile or read a letter he wrote.

But you go on. And you hope that you can still make him proud.

Two years later, I was asked to start another drug treatment center, only this one was through the local probation department. We took drug felons—many of whom were young African Americans—and put them into our Christ-centered program at the mission instead of jail. It was an alternative for change and for a healthy future. I was convinced that what we provided these people was better than life on the streets or behind bars. My continued growth in Bible study and church activities confirmed my conviction and brought more and more healing for my own wounds. At the age of twenty-six, I was a responsible, capable director of this new Christian program for drug offenders, advancing in the field in ways I had hoped for.

It was what young white urban professionals did. My dad would have been pleased.

In running this program, I couldn't help but intersect with a variety of cultures. I often thought of my clients at the women's center, my friends in college, even the strangers my parents would invite over for dinner when we were growing up. And I realized that I did not know how to respond to them. No Christian leaders had helped me, no books had given me answers, and I certainly hadn't heard any sermons on race issues at the churches I attended. So I decided that graduate school might begin to address what I knew needed to be resolved.

By the fall of 1992, I returned to New York City to earn a master's degree in social work. I felt that if I was to go further in the field—and in this recurring issue of culture—I needed more training. Sure enough, it seemed that every class I took and every lecture I heard dealt with cultural diversity, racial equality, and ethnic sensitivity. With over one hundred cultures and languages in the Big Apple, diversity was inevitable.

The seeds were being watered.

Then my supervisor in graduate school field placement told me I was a WASP and held up a mirror to confirm it. The pieces of my life were about to come together.

Section Three
Coming Together

Chapter Nine

A Bittersweet Embrace

Whoever said that breaking up is hard to do was right.

Here I was in a good relationship with a great guy who seemed to share my new faith in God and who wanted to marry me. For some girls, achieving this goal was the main reason they went to college in the first place. You always imagine yourself getting an education, getting a job, getting married, and getting babies, right?

Pamela

Well, during our senior year, Phil and I broke up. He didn't want to be with a woman who still had feelings for her high-school sweetheart. I had blown it by going out with Jacques over the summer—and having too good a time.

I spent what was supposed to be the most exciting year of college in my two-by-four dormroom, either sulking or crying. I fed rolls of quarters into campus video game machines, hoping the time would pass more quickly.

One of my best friends had also just broken up with her man, so we grieved together. And, as women sometimes do, we rehashed the reasons for our breakups over and over again, talking for hours into the night, devising ways to get even though we knew we never would. Against a backdrop of empty pizza boxes and Sade on the stereo, we created imaginary scenarios full of assumptions that suited our desired endings.

It's a good thing neither of us drank, or we would have been full-fledged members of Alcoholics Anonymous by the end of the semester. "My name is Pam, and I am a brokenhearted alcoholic," I'd announce, tears streaming down my cheeks. The crowd would reply, "Welcome, Pam!"

But a funny thing had happened to me on the way to graduation. In the midst of despair about my confused state and my lost love, I had found comfort in God. There wasn't much else to find comfort in. So I played those sermon tapes until I practically knew the words by heart. They made me sob harder, but they also reminded me of the Man who was with me in all my sorrows, the Man who said he would never leave nor forsake me, no matter what silly mistakes I made.

I began to shed the clothes marked "Wallowing," which were dingy, gray, and tear-streaked by now, and began to walk taller in my new coat called "Expectancy." And that new coat made me strong. *Finally, be strong in the Lord and in his mighty power. Put on the full armor of God . . . .*

Shortly after graduation Phil had a change of heart about me. I don't know if he realized how much he really loved me, or if he knew I was getting over the pain of our breakup. He missed me, he said, arriving at my front door one summer evening, unannounced. Could we go somewhere and talk? I said yes. Phil was like old, comfortable shoes: every time you wore them, you remembered how nice they were, even though it might be time for another pair (or time to go entirely barefoot). We talked, and, sitting in the red, pre-owned Honda I had just gotten as a graduation gift, Phil asked me to marry him.

I was flattered the way any young woman would be about a proposal of marriage. But there was a dis-ease in my spirit, which I had just discovered was alive and kicking. I was not at peace. We didn't seem to agree on how this "Christian life" we received should be lived out. Should we or shouldn't we join a church? If so, which one? Do we want to attend a weekly Bible study? And what about our physical relationship until the wedding? Discussions about these things were tense. We were on different pages. He questioned the importance of so much church involvement—and so much change. Mentally and emotionally, I felt myself letting go of the relationship, question by question (or argument by argument), though the other part of me was afraid to leave what was safe, comfortable, and good.

After some more tears, prayers, and a talk with my newly acquired pastor, Phil and I parted. We kept in touch off and on in the ensuing years. He was a good guy.

I had begun attending a small, start-up church with my mother not long before the break-up. This was quite a feat of the Holy Spirit because I never attached the word *start-up* with anything but a business and really didn't understand the concept of "new" churches. (Weren't they all old?) But this white minister felt called to this area and began to offer a Bible study at the local hospital where my mom was a head nurse. The study, which was held during the lunch hour, soon became standing room only. My mom would speak enthusiastically and often about this man and his Bible study and mentioned that he wanted to plant a church, and did I want to visit with her one Sunday? I allowed her to talk me into going.

Whoever heard of a church meeting in a school classroom? With attendees squeezing into small desk-chair ensembles and announcements written in chalk on the blackboard (next to the leftover homework assignment). This was *not* church as I understood it. Fordham's chapel had grand architecture, elaborate organs, stained-glass windows, plush carpet, and a fancy altar. I held in my shock as I shook hands with the infamous minister who wore a simple short-sleeved shirt, tie, and Gap-like trousers (no priestly collar, ministerial robe, or even a suit jacket). There were only fifteen or so people there, and just about everyone was white, Hispanic, or Filipino. The only woman there who looked my age was with her husband. What was I getting into? I wondered.

As we sang simple songs of praise, accompanied by the minister's guitar strumming, my skepticism began to melt. I had never sung songs like these, songs I didn't have to look up in a hymn book. These words were so meaningful, so appropriate. I felt them deep in my soul. For the first time, I understood why people lift their hands in praise. It is the body's response to the presence of an awesome God.

Maybe this bizarre, church-in-a-schoolhouse would be just the thing I needed.

It must have been because I stayed at New Life Fellowship for the next eight years. My mother and I are credited with being two of the pioneers of the church, which grew steadily from fifteen to five hundred.

I met a milieu of people at New Life, mostly young singles, newly-marrieds, and young families. After the schoolhouse, New Life found a home renting the main floor of a small church in a low-income, mostly-Hispanic neighborhood called Corona. We breathed life into the host church, which was comprised of a handful of retirees. We learned to sing praise songs in both English and Spanish, shaking tambourines and playing bongos too loud for the sedate members of the church upstairs. Whites, Asians, and an increasing number of blacks who attended began to build relationships with the Hispanics in the surrounding neighborhood. Together we developed a love for them and devised creative ways to serve them and encourage them to join us at church. Free car washes, concerts, plays, park outreaches, children's camps, and English classes were all offered as part of our desire to meet the needs of our neighbors—physical, emotional, and spiritual, just like Jesus did.

It was a powerful image, those colors working side by side. For the first few years of the church's development, I had been more of a visitor than an active member. I still hadn't given in to the church-every-Sunday routine. I went when I wanted to, and I often felt guilty when I did. The other people there seemed so dedicated, so involved, as if the church was their entire world, the thing that marked their identity. My identity, on the other hand, was wrapped up in my career as an editor at *Essence* magazine. I put in long hours doing a job that I loved, surrounded by sharp, well-schooled black women and men. My position was the envy of many of my friends, most of whom were slugging it out in white corporate America. I had achieved greatness among my peers, and it took a lot to maintain that image, especially on a magazine editor's meager starting salary.

By the weekends, I was exhilarated and exhausted. Exhausted and unavailable might be a better description.

I was especially unavailable for church programs on weekend nights. I was much too cool to spend my free time hanging around a church when there was this restaurant or that party to attend. Besides, most of the "churched" singles—white, Asian, and a few black ones—seemed corny and sheltered. They rarely went to movies unless they were rated G or PG and seemed to know nothing about the latest celebrity gossip or the goings-on in Manhattan, where many worked but seldom played. On top of that, it didn't look like anyone was dating, or even knew how. These folk were all nice enough; they just didn't seem "together." We couldn't hang.

Or maybe *I* couldn't hang.

Ever since I had become a Christian, I continued to have the same friends and therefore the same influences. I wanted to take part in the things of Christianity, but I also wanted to keep one foot in the old, comfortable shoe called "worldliness." Surely, I didn't have to make a choice.

So the choice began to make *me*. I did not know how to be "*in* the world but not *of* the world," as the Bible warns. Pangs of guilt would hit me when I encountered and participated in various morally bending situations at work and in social settings, mostly around the issue of sex or sexuality. A married friend wanted my approval (and my collusion) over her impending affair with a charming, handsome client. There were photo shoots with half-naked models, homosexual artists, celebrity pandering, and the constant sexual innuendo that hovered like a fog. And most of my friends and colleagues treated sleeping with (if not *living* with) their boy- or girlfriends as the rule rather than the exception. Foul language was the lingua-franca for many. Drinking and schmoozing was Friday-night fun. Experimenting with cocaine or smoking a few joints and club dancing until dawn constituted a hot Saturday night.

I was not up to the task of breaking away. I held onto that life the way a woman on the edge of a roof claws for her very life. I didn't know that God's arms would be the safety net to catch me if I let go and that letting go was just the thing I needed to do to move my life along. I definitely didn't believe that any plan God had for me would be better than my own. I imagined that God would want me to leave all this fun and become corny like the other single Christians I had encountered, who responded to everything by saying, "Praise the Lord!" I didn't want to look at that blueprint, so I let my noisy life block it out. I just wanted to be an ordinary Christian, practicing my faith quietly in the confines of my heart.

Sometime in the midst of this inner conflict, my mother invited me to go on a bus trip to New Jersey with her friends to attend a deliverance service. Now, if there was ever a sentence that wholly described the antithesis of what I wanted to do, it would have the words, "bus trip," "New Jersey," and "deliverance service" in it.

I wasn't going for it. Have a nice time. No way. No.

As I sat slumped in the minivan on the way to New Jersey, I reminded myself of the possible dangers that might befall me if I tried to hitchhike back home to New York. Just because my mother prayed me into going on this trip didn't mean I was going to like it. In fact, I was determined *not* to like it, no matter how good it was for me, like a child made to eat broccoli smothered in Velveeta.

My mother and her friends were happy as larks during the drive, chatting as they sang songs and nudged me to join in. They neglected to tell me that there were two services, one in the afternoon and one in the evening. The day service was nice enough, the preacher rousing and the crowd exuberant. But I was more than ready to go home. I insisted I had had enough and caught a bus home, much to their chagrin.

The truth was, I was afraid. I wasn't like those people who had to go up front to writhe and wail and spit up green stuff as they got their demons cast out. I had done some bad things in my life, but not *that* bad. I knew my so-called demons and promised God that I would deal with them, privately.

He kept me to that promise (as God does). Not long after that New Jersey trip, I accompanied my mother to a local church where a visiting pastor was preaching. The word *deliverance* was not on the marquee, so I felt it was safe. At that service, the pastor simply asked for those who had accepted Christ but weren't fully committed (that would be me) to come forward. I went up willingly, received prayer from the pastor without fanfare and sat back down.

That was the real beginning of my Christian life.

I soon discovered that church *was* the place to be after-hours. There was so much to learn about God and so little time. I was open to everything, as long as it wasn't too way out. I went to Bible studies and even helped lead a few. I coordinated a fun singles' night at New Life that folk still talk about today. I volunteered in the nursery, ushered, and wrote announcements. Now, when I was absent from church people wondered if I was sick or on vacation. I entered into the lifeblood of this body of believers, and I was loving it. I constantly sought ways to use my talents and abilities to serve. In the five years since college graduation, I had left *Essence,* pursued a start-up magazine venture, worked as a reporter, went back to *Essence,* and then started a marginally successful public relations business out of my apartment in Brooklyn. When New Life's leadership team invited me to join the ministry staff as communications manager, I was excited. I had passed the test; I was accepted in the upper echelons of evangelical Christendom.

My whole world was changing rapidly, but I was confident in the Man at the wheel. It was a nice, protected feeling.

Membership in New Life's inner circle had its privileges. I sat in meetings with the all-white, mostly male leadership and was privy to the behind-the-scenes workings of the church. I was proud to be an insider. In that capacity, I got to meet and greet most of the important speakers who came to visit at New Life; some I even hosted.

One of them was named Dr. John Perkins. It was the rare black pastor who got to grace the pulpit at New Life. Dr. Perkins, grandfather of the Christian community development and racial reconciliation movements in the evangelical world, was one of them. His messages on both subjects were targeted mainly to whites in the church.

Dr. Perkins challenged both church leaders and churchgoers to take up the cause of bringing about racial reconciliation in their spheres of influence. He had a powerful testimony, which included being severely beaten by a group of white police officers and other instances of horrid racism in his home state of Mississippi. He had forgiven these cops—believing God's love had to transcend race—and now he was at peace on the issue. Thirty years later, he led a growing national ministry to promote racial unity.

He worked with us to devise a model for doing community development within our home-group-based philosophy. It was no easy job. People came from many different New York neighborhoods to attend New Life. How could one rally such a diverse and divergent group of people around the needs of one particular area? Dr. Perkins's message was not to go into a poor community and do a few charitable events. He was talking about *years* of commitment, maybe even for *life,* with members of the church slowly relocating for the sake of development—for the sake of the gospel. He was putting forth some radical stuff. We listened.

I had never heard such a message. He was taking white people to task about their faith when it came to racism and serving the oppressed. I began to look at my white church leaders with new eyes. Hopeful eyes. Excited eyes. We were now going to take this message and run with it. We hosted Dr. Perkins at New Life a number of times, as well as Reverend Raleigh Washington, another African-American racial reconciliation advocate, whose book, *Breaking Down Walls,* was becoming required reading among the staff. I took all this as clear signs that we were going full throttle on these important issues. I became a student of the cause and prayed about what role I was to play in this new thing God was doing.

When I got the vision to initiate a ministry of racial reconciliation at New Life, I figured I'd better have a meeting with my friend Elvon Reed before I started. I had met Elvon at a Shakespeare in the Park event held in Central Park. Ironically, we were both feeling sad and lonely that day (no boyfriends, no money). We chatted about life and about future possibilities.

Elvon was attending and was on the staff of a very white church (if mine was "mostly," hers was "very") called Redeemer Presbyterian in Manhattan. The folk at her church were well educated, well heeled, and successful; many were affluent. Yuppies. The thriving church, once featured in the *Wall Street Journal,* was quite successful in reaching its target group. Elvon was the only black person on the church's twenty-plus member staff, just like I had been. And the only person on the staff with a vision for a ministry of racial reconciliation. Just like me.

Something was wrong with that picture.

Elvon's approach was to devise a series of sessions in which multiethnic groups of church members got together for intentional evenings she called "Crossing Barriers." She wanted to hear what was on the hearts of people regarding this issue and wanted them to hear one another. In fact, she included a segment on "Empathic Listening" to facilitate that very thing. Then the group would explore what the Bible had to say on this tough subject and the floor would be open for discussion. Elvon got the sanction from her pastor and invited anyone who was interested to attend the sessions.

I was impressed with Elvon. She didn't seem to have any illusions that just because she was creating an environment where a few people got together to talk and pray about race issues, she could make all the pain go away (like I did). Her approach was practical, her notes organized, and her discussion clear. In about forty-eight hours she trained me to start a similar ministry at New Life. She was wonderful, freely sharing with me everything that the Father had "made known to [her]" (John 15:15).

Elvon's "partner in crime," a woman named Andrea Clark, was equally supportive. She faxed me helpful articles and outlines and offered encouragement. I was sold on this woman the day I met her in person a few months later. Andrea attended some of the same ministry meetings I did, which were held to discuss the community development concept locally. When she heard that a young, African-American woman from our church was hoping to attend a national conference for the Christian Community Development Association (CCDA) in another state, Andrea approached her after the meeting to offer her own plane ticket.

I had never, *ever* witnessed such generosity, especially on the part of a white woman toward a black young person. Usually, whites wanted to talk about such things (until the cows came home) but weren't quick to "do." Her unflinching, giving spirit sent chills down my spine. If we could just clone this woman, I thought, we would have economic justice in no time. Clearly, Andrea was a diamond in the rough.

Armed with my gathered information, I felt a clear direction from God to start the ministry at our church from the top down, with the involvement of my pastor, associate pastors, and lay leaders first, then filtering through the congregation. A conversation with Spencer Perkins, Dr. Perkins's eldest son, at a CCDA conference, confirmed the wisdom of this direction. I felt burdened to pray continually as I proceeded though I didn't know why, until later. My pastors weren't racists, after all. They brought in John Perkins and others to guide us toward reconciliation, didn't they? This wasn't going to be a tough issue for us. We were already a model of racial harmony: Hispanics, Asians, whites, blacks, all in one room. Surely, my pastors would be on board of anything that helped us model the message of reconciliation.

I had the utmost confidence in them.

These were the men who had helped me mature in Christ, the men who modeled Christian manhood, husbandhood, and fatherhood for me, some from up close, others from afar. I had meals in their homes, held their children, and prayed beside them. They "talked the talk and walked the walk" in many other areas of their lives and certainly would on this one too. After a few Crossing Barriers sessions, I reasoned, all the leaders would be on board, and we could carry the torch to the rest of the congregation. To me, it was a simple, neat, righteous package.

The pain-filled lesson I learned over this issue sometimes brings tears to my eyes and anger to my heart. *"There is nothing concealed that will not be disclosed, or hidden that will not be made known"* (Matt. 10:26).

Several of our church leaders attended the first Crossing Barriers sessions held in my home. My pastor, however, declined the invitation, citing that he "didn't feel he needed it." I was terribly disheartened and affronted. I knew how important it was that racial reconciliation be modeled from the top down. And he knew that too.

How could he say he didn't *need* it? Didn't we all need to understand more about each other's pain? Especially in the polarized, American evangelical church? And if he was already so racially reconciled, where was his personal involvement in the dilemmas of the black Christians in his congregation? How could

I believe in the sincerity of any white Christian who says we are all one in Christ when my own pastor wouldn't even come to my home to discuss *our* race issues?

So, the sessions went on without him. African-American Christians who attended marveled at how shocked many of their white brothers and sisters in Christ were to hear that they still experienced things like being called nigger as they crossed the street (yes, in the middle of New York City in the 1990s), along with more subtle racism in housing, employment, or just walking into a department store and being followed by security officers. When everyone was asked to describe a time of discrimination in their lives, the whites' stories, save one, were tame by comparison. The room would often fall silent. Then that heavy, necessary silence would be filled with words.

Through the sessions, it also became clear that most of the African Americans who attended New Life Fellowship were well assimilated into the white Christian subculture. In some regard, they were being practical. Why waste energy trying to buck the system by being the distinct person God made you to be? I, too, committed this sin. The problem was, I just couldn't live with that. I had a vision of a brighter day, one in which we *contributed* our uniqueness rather than assimilated into the dominant culture.

We had done this somewhat successfully with our Hispanic contingent. No one seemed to expect them to assimilate. The validity of their culture was upheld in many ways, from our pastor learning fluent Spanish to the songs we sang, struggling to pronounce the rolling Spanish lyrics. *That* was OK, so why not embrace black culture as well?

Naively, I expected that the carefully chosen Scriptures about Christ's heart for unity would pierce the souls of those attending the sessions and propel them into action, right away. I was truly shocked and duly dismayed when months later I saw little change in my fellow Christians and leaders. My only comfort came from the few folk whose hearts really seemed to break over this excruciating issue of racism in the church. Etched in my soul is the image of one dear, white couple who held hands throughout the session and were on the verge of tears as they realized the magnitude of our racial sin. God bless them. But you can't confront the residue of a nation's painful history with only a few tender hearts, though it's a starting place, for sure.

I was rocking the boat, but the crew wasn't ready.

I began to see what it meant to be a black Christian woman in a white Christian environment, and it was a disturbing picture of lopsided compromise. I felt very sad and alone. Now that I was asking hard questions about race and faith, my popularity waned. I was no longer one of the safe, smiling black folk that the church leaders seem to prefer. Looking back, I saw the string of African Americans who had left the church, one after another. I looked at our monochrome leadership team, wondering why in almost ten years no black brother (or sister) rubbed elbows with these men in a position of authority. Where was the evidence of the professed belief in racial equality? Faith without works, the Bible said, is dead as a doornail.

The shiny, pie-in-the-sky image of my beloved church was falling apart as I discovered that roaches were living well in the closets and under the rugs. It was time to sail on.

"I'm amazed you've stayed as long as you have," said an exasperated Jo Kadlecek when I told her of my situation. This was a curiously evolved response from a white woman, I thought. But I was warned that Jo was no ordinary blond. And she isn't.

I first met Jo on the phone—she was in Mississippi, and I was in New York. She came highly recommended as the perfect person to coauthor a book on racial reconciliation with me, so I chatted with her for over an hour. I was impressed with her background and her humility. She seemed honored to be chosen for this possible project. That made me chuckle inside. This woman—who had written a book with revered bigwigs like Dr. Perkins and authored award-winning articles—was *honored* to write a book on race and faith and friendship with this disenchanted black woman who was leaving her church.

God really does have a sense of humor.

At the time I called Jo, I was living in an experimental situation called a "discipleship apartment." This was the brainchild of the interracial couple who directed a ministry to mostly black and Hispanic teens in foster care and was attached to New Life. Two mature, single women were to live with one girl who had "aged-out" of her group foster care home (you age-out at about nineteen), and give her one year of life-skills training. I thought it was an excellent idea, though I was scared to death about whether I would be able to relate to a troubled teen. I did know that I had to be part of the incarnational gospel.

New Life had underwritten the program by providing a small rent subsidy to our apartment. I was again hopeful at this show of commitment to social issues that, in this particular area, affected African-American youth. This program was spurred on by my then-boyfriend, James, who had just been hired as the community development pastor. James was white-Italian and had a tremendous heart for the poor. I learned so much from him about Jesus' heart for the oppressed, and I watched it lived out in his ministry to the homeless. Together, we fed, clothed, and prayed with thieves, hoodlums, and prostitutes. One particular woman, a newly converted prostitute, and her family won such a place in my heart I would have done anything legal to help them make it. James and I visited her meager apartment, played with her small sons, made brownies with her daughter, bought shoes for her first job as a waitress, encouraged her when she was in tears, paid her bus fare to our Bible study, and shared whatever we had.

We ministered to a number of others, all of whom were "handicapped" in some way emotionally, physically, or socially. Through James' leading, I saw clearly that the mere poverty of the poor causes their downfall, as the Bible noted, not their lack of talent or potential.

I was in love again. With a white Italian man who had just spent four years doing volunteer work in the bowels of Bangladesh, loving the people there, teaching them job skills, and being loved by them in return.

Even though I had slow doses of black culture over the years and had developed an identity as a black woman, my church environment was still so white. And where does a Christian woman look for a mate? In her church, right? Exactly. James' broken heart captured my own, and we began a relationship. He was one of my pastor's best college buddies.

It was a rocky road.

The problem was that as our relationship progressed, so did my race consciousness. Initially, James had a nice, black girlfriend who was sweet and assimilated. But he ended up with a raving lunatic by our one-year "anniversary." An exaggeration, maybe, but I was continually annoyed about one thing or another not being fair or right or sensitively handled with regard to the church and African Americans.

For instance, the injustice in the lives of those foster care kids and the fact that we were doing little about it practically caused me physical pain. These young people were supposedly "part" of our church, but after years, few of them even knew the names of the leaders, far less had a decent conversation with one of them. Weren't there any Andreas here? These children, abandoned by their parents for one reason or another, seemed invisible in the body of Christ. The insistent denial that there was any division between "church kids" and "foster kids" just made me more incensed.

I brought my angst home to James. But it wasn't his fault.

He was having challenges of his own re-adjusting to American life. To him, New Yorkers seemed extravagant and spoiled. He took one look at my spending budget and commenced to whipping it into shape. Before you could say "mutual fund," my whole financial life was on a computerized program. I kept track of every little expense, including gum and newspapers, in a little notebook similar to the one James had kept for years. Eventually, I had savings, aggressive IRA and stock portfolios, and even a budget for spontaneous gifts. Any sense of financial savvy I have today is credited to James.

He shared his knowledge freely, and I was bettered because of it. In my mind, *this* is racial reconciliation personified.

Other areas in our relationship were not such a quick fix. Though James never showed any sense of shame about being with me, his relatives were less than pleased about his brown-skinned choice. "Why do you always have to do things the hard way?" one remarked when James told her about me. "Don't you see those interracial couples on 'Oprah'?" James spent the rest of the conversation assuring her that we would not end up on the talk-show circuit. We prayed that the situation would improve.

It didn't. And, for other reasons, including our personality differences and his phobia about the word *marriage* (to anyone), our relationship unraveled.

I was devastated. What was really going on here? I wondered. He probably knew all along that he wasn't going to marry a black woman, anyway, I decided, angrily. What a sham! What a show! Sitting in the front seats at church showing off our racially reconciled relationship to everyone. Now I felt like the joke was on me.

I felt betrayed, robbed of my opportunity to model a successful black-white marriage to the unbelieving world. I wanted to fight, struggle, and win this race battle. Together we would challenge conventional thinking, walk boldly hand-in-hand through forbidden Samaria, defy stereotypes with our very presence, and restore the entire world to its original sinless state.

I guess God had other fish for me to fry. Or rather, other ways for me to fry fish. Between this breakup and the growing dis-ease I was feeling at New Life, a cynicism fell over my sprit. I was weary, and I wanted to leave, but I didn't feel fully released in my spirit to do so. The year-long wait was painful but wise. I needed to go somewhere where I could rest.

Meanwhile, Jo had now moved to New York and was anxious to talk more about the book I'd proposed to her on racial reconciliation. Oh, uh, yeah, right, I sighed. I managed to work up enough energy to keep the phone pressed to my ear. Jo's enthusiasm made up for my weariness. At least I could say with conviction that there were lots of folk who needed a reconciliation manual, that was sure.

We met at a race forum held in the home of a black ob/gyn during Black History Month. This year, lucky for me, she decided to dedicate the entire forum to race relations. I was invited to be one of four speakers, two white, two black, including Elvon and Andrea. Relunctantly, I agreed.

I am not sure how many people have the experience of talking about something that is piercing their souls while having to keep a smile plastered on their faces at the same time. The black moderator of a race discussion with white Christians cannot get mad. Or so I thought. You had to hold it in until you were alone or when you could cry through the phone with a sympathetic black friend.

These events, which I was being invited to participate in more and more, were incredibly taxing. There was always some redheaded teenager from the Midwest, or some facsimile thereof, whose reason for existence seemed to be to deny that racism existed. "How do you know the people in that all-white neighborhood were looking at you funny because you were black?" they would ask.

Ho hum.

Thankfully, I don't think people in the audience could see the veins in my neck beginning to bulge. Rushing to deny the validity of a person of color's account of a racial incident is mistake number one. As if a black person doesn't know an admiring look from a disdainful, fearful one, where the person's eyes avert and the corners of their mouth turn downward. Please. I have seen that look *all my life.* From passersby, from shopkeepers, from out-of-towners and from so-called neighbors, from butchers, bakers, and candlestick makers; *that look* was very real. Who were these sheltered white people to tell me otherwise? Nonetheless, I responded calmly, rehearsing deep-breathing techniques in my head. I emphasized the importance of validation in the racial reconciliation process and moved along.

But Jo wasn't through yet.

We were doing a speaking engagement together for the first time. I had been nervous about how it would go. Jo was prepared and cool. She had relevant historical references in her notes, enhanced by her extensive teaching background. She had lived in poor, black neighborhoods—in the South. She had done a book with Dr. John Perkins, for crying out loud. And she knew how to stand at a slanted podium and keep her papers from sliding off. She was a white authority on the subject of racial reconciliation. Who was I? Just someone black and willing and righteously angry.

Seeing my agitation with the redhead, Jo jumped in quickly to support me. Sometimes Jo is so passionate about this issue that it flabbergasts the whites in the audience. It also forces them out of their complacency. Now *that's* fun to watch. She is direct and matter-of-fact in a way that I cannot be, at least not as effectively with a white crowd. Without hesitation, Jo pointed out that whites *must* be willing to take ownership of their part of the sin in our race history and that this was one of the major problems in obtaining racial unity, the first of many crucial steps "we must take" to facilitate meaningful dialogue across the color barrier.

Jo uses the word *we* in ways that I cannot. And she would say the same about me. The beauty of how each of our unique abilities (yours too) submitted to godly influence can work together for good is astounding.

We pour out our little jars of oil, and it shames the wise.

Elvon, as a strong, southern black woman who grew up in an environment where everyone accepted the racial divide, today brings a fresh perspective as a partner in an interracial marriage, raising biracial children. Andrea, taught practically from birth to embrace other cultures, can explain how important—and sometimes how *un*important—that was to her personal journey toward racial sensitivity. Jo brings her knowledge, experience, and a heart broken for the oppressed. I just babble and tell stories (but it works out).

I am in good company.

There were no tearful good-byes when I left my church. No party, no wish-you-well letter from the pastor, no bulletin announcement. I did take with me a few close friendships and a lot of good memories, even amid my discouragement. Friendships with wonderful women of God—like Vicki, Lori, Maria, and Holly—that have stood up under the weight of time and the challenge of racial differences, give my heart hope.

Still I felt called to sow some seeds in a church that celebrates my culture, both the West Indian and black American sides of me. Oh, it's a joyful time when I am swaying and praising to a calypso beat at Christian Life Centre in Brooklyn or clapping my hands to a deep bass or jazzy improvisations that transport me heavenward. Or watching a visiting Ugandan worship team minister mightily in an awesome new way I've never experienced before. Or ministering alongside talented men and women of color and character. Or just sitting back admiringly as I watch my beautiful brown brothers and sisters teach, preach, announce, sing, dance, act, and, best of all, give their lives to Jesus. A tear streams down my face at almost every altar call. Each black man redeemed is another black *family* redeemed, I think, as I watch them make their way forward each week. And it is a special feeling when I see white men and women touched by the message, moved to surrender their lives to the Lord.

I consider the awesome privilege God has extended to me when I hear my pastor, Dr. A. R. Bernard, speak words into me, words that penetrate more deeply because of the relevant context in which they are presented. The anecdotes, the sermon illustrations, the loving rebukes, the many humorous notes, and the unique perspective offered by the preaching staff all plant custom-made seeds in my thirsty brown spirit. Like a dress that fits you just right—you always feel beautiful when you wear it. Thank you, Melinda, for taking me shopping.

As a people, we are being liberated, celebrated, esteemed, encouraged, and, most of all, *empowered* to succeed, things we rarely receive in the world or, unfortunately, the church. This same message stirs the hearts of black, white, red, and yellow peoples, as evidenced by the incredible response to Dr. Bernard's teachings at national Promise Keeper rallies, Christian Men's Network events, and at other venues around the nation and the world.

From this privileged place I am learning to admire the true beauty of God's multihued creations.

And I am richer for the view.

Chapter Ten
Habits of Companionship

I used to hate the word *lonely*.

Where I came from, to say you were lonely was to admit weakness—a horrible faux pas for those emerging from strong-willed suburban families with self-sufficient European roots that survived the depression of the 1930s and conquered the American dream by the 1960s. To talk about being lonely was to lay bare for all the world the center of your pain. It was to risk being misunderstood—what right, after all, did I have to be lonely when I had everything society endorsed, from blond hair and blue eyes to athletic ability, a suburban upbringing, college degrees, and opportunities? Even to utter the word was to confess vulnerability. You were exposed, out of control. And maybe a little incompetent. God forbid a white, educated, middle-class woman from the great American West should be incompetent.

Jo

I could not let the word *lonely* squeak past my lips for years. In my teens, it wasn't included in my vocabulary in any way, shape, or form. In my twenties, it stirred in my soul like a bad memory I didn't dare confront. In my thirties, it was a word I felt "mature" enough to use in describing others who seemed broken and aloof from the rest of us "together" people. Now at forty, I know that to say the word *lonely* is simply honest.

I need people. Honest.

Truth is, I am not self-sufficient, though I used to think so. I am not Thelma or Louise, though I've admittedly wanted to pop a man or two along the way. In other words, I am not able to handle life alone. Never have, never will.

All-American independence is a myth. And a sin.

What is real, I've learned, is that we've been created with an inherent need to have flesh, bones, and language surrounding us in breathing, feeling containers scientists call homosapiens. I have other, more recognizable names for them: friends, spouses, neighbors, sisters, peers, colleagues, grandmas, allies, pastors, brothers, bosses, coaches, teachers, nieces, and so on. They come in little, big, wide, or thin sizes and are brown, pale, dark, gray, or yellow on the outside. As long as there's red blood running through them and a heart that's pumping it from head to toe, they qualify. Human beings. Friends. People. Community. God's masterpiece. I need them. It's the plain and simple truth.

Puritan writer Nathaniel Hawthorne said it as if he knew me: "It contributes greatly towards a [wo]man's moral and intellectual health, to be brought into habits of companionship with individuals unlike himself, who care little of his pursuits, and whose sphere and abilities he must go out of himself to appreciate."

And so I got out of suburbia's grip, the one that often mistakes space, grass, and big houses for "the good life" and went searching for other "spheres and abilities." Maybe I'd find them in the city. What drove me out of comfort-land, out of *sub*-urban life, wasn't any noble cause or radical agenda as much as it was a personal ache for relationships. I suppose my journey has always been marked by this "habit of companionship," expressed initially in lonely adolescence, then given meaning and direction in a book that shaped my thinking—and living—more than any other, the Bible, and finally finding connection in the "individuals unlike myself" I met in northern America's urban mosaic.

Besides the fact that I had always loved being in the city, I moved into Denver's inner-city neighborhood for two reasons: I genuinely wanted to be closer to James and Freda's family and the other children I met through Hope Communities' children's program. It made life simpler if we lived next door to each other; that way, I wouldn't have to spend so much time traveling in my car to visit them.

The second motivation came after I realized I had a bad memory. In other words, when I was really honest with myself, I knew that if I did not see low income housing projects, homeless families, or boarded-up buildings on a daily basis, I would easily forget that two-thirds of the world's population lives in economic poverty, primarily in urban areas. I felt that if I ignored or overlooked their plight, my Christian faith would seem irrelevant, selfish almost. Why bother believing in an incarnational God who cared for the poor and outcasts, and whose Son modeled such compassion, if I wasn't willing to do the same?

Not that I was the Great White Hope. That was abundantly clear when I realized I had no idea what I was doing moving into Five Points in 1989. No plans to organize the people, no strategies for economic development, no husband to share a vision with, not even a roommate (Janet would move in a month or so after I did), and no talents—that I knew of—to offer the community. I was just a suburban college English teacher who liked working with kids. The only thing I knew for sure was how I wanted to perform some praiseworthy act of Christian charity in the midst of this urban turmoil.

I had a lot to learn.

And lest I entertain any hint of superiority because of my background, my very first living experience in the city provided me a healthy dose of humble pie. When I moved into the old house I would call home for the next three and a half years, it was still being renovated by my Greek landlord and his two workers. The place had been abandoned for over twenty years, so any current work was like an archaeologist on a dig. That meant mice were crawling around my closet—a frightening thing for suburbanites—and there was no hot water or heat yet; the pipeline wouldn't be connected to the main source for at least three more weeks. It was October. In Denver. I had no choice but to knock on my neighbor Cheri's door each morning, look at the ground, and ask if I could use her shower before I left for the college where I was teaching.

"Of course, Girl, that's no big deal," Cheri would say. Then this strikingly beautiful, thirtysomething African-American woman would show me to the only bathroom she and her three children shared in their Hope apartment. For the next twenty-one days, my gracious neighbor never seemed to mind helping her new, sorry-looking blond neighbor.

Human need is a great equalizer.

When Janet moved in as my roommate, some of our neighbors weren't sure what to make of it. Here was a professional, college-educated black woman with no children, sharing a house with a white woman who was a college instructor at some religious suburban campus. Were they gay? Were they nuts? Why in the world would these two live together in *this* neighborhood?

I didn't care what they thought (though I have to admit I was glad when Janet started dating a great guy from church); I was just thankful to have a roommate, someone to process things with and pray with. Janet ignored the "meddlin'" about us and continued serving as a consistent role model for many of the youth around us and at church.

One night Janet invited me to join her for a political rally and fundraising dinner where she was the featured singer. When I arrived at the ballroom of the huge suburban hotel, I noticed that 99 percent of the thousand or so people who had come this night were white. (Living in a diverse community makes a room full of sameness stand out.) Red, white, and blue balloons hovered over miniature flags on each table of the banquet room. This was one of those meetings where white evangelicals were seeking to "restore America to her original purpose." It was fall of 1992, and this particular conservative Christian political group was just starting to recruit support from around the country.

As the rally began, we were asked to pledge allegiance to the enormous striped symbol that hung behind the podium. Then Janet led us in a few "America the Beautiful" tunes. We were served a dinner of meat and potatoes and then listened to the evening's guest speaker.

My program read that he was a "nationally acclaimed historian and evangelist." Tonight his mission was to teach us of our country's Christian roots and to walk us through several history lessons that confirmed this. He cited the Battle of Valley Forge as a heroic symbol of loyalty in founding this country, the techniques of early American educators who used the Bible to teach children the ABCs, and, of course, the righteous faith of our founding fathers. And though it was a fiery sermon with an ardent appeal, it stirred an uneasy reaction in my gut and raised several questions in my head. I suddenly felt anything but patriotic.

Janet saw me struggling; she smiled and reminded me that these were, in fact, "brothers and sisters in Christ." She always was more gracious than I.

I wondered how this "acclaimed historian" could be so culturally selective in describing America's past. How did the handful of people of color listening that night feel, hearing only half the truth of our country's noble and horrible heritage? For instance, why hadn't the speaker told us that the conditions slaves (and other "minorities") endured were far worse for far longer than what those brave soldiers who *chose* to be at Valley Forge endured? Why hadn't he told of the shameful laws that forbade black children from learning to read *at all* while their white counterparts were learning from the Bible? Why hadn't he revealed the truth that many of our "righteous" founding fathers, committed to liberty and justice for all, *owned* other human beings and called them slaves?

Why hadn't this speaker told *all* the truth?

"Girl, they never do," Janet told me. "You get used to it. And you keep challenging it by loving them."

When I got back to our urban home, I couldn't sleep. Not because of city noise—it was a welcome lull compared to what I had just heard. In fact, the only enjoyable aspect of the evening was hearing Janet sing. I wrote a letter to the speaker, asking him these same questions, encouraging him to take advantage of his opportunities to speak to predominately white audiences. Maybe, I said, this could be an exciting time to discuss racial reconciliation in the church, to give a more balanced view of our country's history to white Christians who had long overlooked it. I dropped it in the mail the next day.

About a month later, I received a personal response from this renowned speaker. He thanked me for writing and raising these issues. However, he said, he did not have "sufficient time to talk about the attitudes of our founding fathers toward slavery" or the history of slavery in America. Besides, his historical expertise and personal calling uniquely qualified him to work toward restoring our original vision as a "Christian nation," not to discuss "black/white relations" in this country. And he had to take issue with me that there were not "two Americas" as I had claimed in my letter: "It is rather naive," he wrote, "to expect that these social sins will not be present in every society on the face of the earth. . . . Historically, ethnic groups that have come to America have slowly assimilated themselves into the American culture."

He ended his letter with another astonishing statement: "I could understand how you as an African-American woman would feel deeply about these issues, but I must be faithful to what God's called me to. Let me recommend some books that might help you understand." I read it again. This man assumed I was black because I had encouraged him to discuss the racial history of our country! Even with a Czech name like mine, he presumed my concern was based on my own experiences as a woman of color!

I had to write him back.

I assured him I was as European American as they came. "True, racial reconciliation and unity in the Body of Christ is unique to most Anglos but I don't believe these issues ought to be," I wrote. "Wasn't Christ about crossing cultures by identifying with societal 'outcasts' and regarding all people with dignity? The Bible confirms for me that Christians should allow God's love to transcend cultures while at the same time affirming the individuality of each."

As to the idea of two Americas, I admitted that "perhaps I am more sensitive to racial issues because I live in an urban community where I have seen first hand many black friends denied jobs or harassed by the police simply because of their skin color. And I have seen our community denied economic development because major retail corporations refuse to build their stores in our neighborhood. That's why I try to encourage Christians, the only true agents of change, to realize the reality and manifestations of racism and to take intentional steps to affirm the qualities and contributions of all of God's children in our wonderfully diverse country." I recommended some books (especially the books of John Perkins) to help him understand and mailed my letter.

I never heard from this speaker again.

Did most white evangelicals really think that only people of color cared about racial justice? This was a new kind of loneliness for me.

As soon as I joined the ranks of urban diversity, the word *lonely* took on a new identity. Suddenly, I was very obviously a minority, though I was rarely treated that way in our neighborhood. But as an urban resident on a Christian suburban campus, I began to feel a little odd. I tried to raise the issues of racial inclusion and diversity to our all-white faculty. So what if we were recruiting urban black basketball players, I challenged. Many of these same students often felt so ostracized and alienated that they'd leave when the season was over. We offered them no black studies courses, not even a black literature class like the one I had taken in undergraduate school.

Maybe the closest we came was when I used Maya Angelou's autobiography, *I Know Why the Caged Bird Sings,* in my freshmen composition classes. (One redhead nineteen-year-old student of mine told me that she had gotten so engrossed in the narrator's life that she actually was surprised when she looked in the mirror and saw a white face!) Or when I taught a new course called Cross-Cultural Communication. This was one way I could require my students—most of whom were white suburban or rural Christians—to participate in some cross-cultural endeavor throughout the semester. Some tutored neighbor children of mine, some volunteered at a homeless shelter or an after-school recreational program, some attended traditional African-American church services or befriended international students on campus. Many were admittedly uncomfortable and stretched; some were resistant or afraid at first. But as the months progressed and the friendships developed, attitudes began to change.

To my amazement, some students continued volunteering long after the class was over. Authentic relationships had gotten into their blood. It seemed to me that these young people were more open to risking their emotional safety for an opportunity to experience life from a different perspective than their elders at the college. While many of my colleagues rarely ventured out of their suburban neighborhoods, these Generation X students wanted to learn how to build bridges in the city.

Even before I had moved into the city, I noticed that some of the children in Five Points did not have the opportunities to play during the summers as I had always been given in the suburbs. It bothered me that there were parks and tennis courts nearby, the mountains only an hour's drive away, and yet the children's parents didn't usually have the transportation means to get them there. It bothered me, too, that the local swimming pool cost only fifty cents, yet many of my neighbors—whom I knew loved to swim—would sit on their porches or play on the sidewalk all day long. Fifty cents was hard to come by.

One spring day in 1990, I was talking with a few of my students in the campus center about this reality. Like me, they, too, had been given youthful summers to play, and they, too, were troubled that these urban kids didn't have the same opportunities. They were eager to commit when someone came up with the idea of organizing a week-long summer day camp for the children on my block. We would make sure each child had a Bible, a T-shirt, a lunch, and a fun camp experience. In the mornings, we'd play games and teach Bible lessons in the gym of a church. In the afternoons, we'd pile into whatever cars we had and take a field trip to the zoo or a mountain lake or an amusement park.

One week. Thirty-five children between the ages of four and fourteen who lived on or close to our block. Seven or so college-age counselors (including some basketball players), a few adults, and moms like Freda (thankfully!), and me.

Our summer J.A.M. (Jesus and Me) camps were a surprising testimony to the Almighty's provision. We asked churches to donate money for camp T-shirts, women's groups to make lunches, business clubs to pay for our field trips, and congregations to donate Bibles. We recruited children we already knew and asked their parents to register them, pay a $2.00 camp fee, and join us if they could for a week of camp fun and organized chaos. JAM Camps never grew to more than forty children living on or nearby our block. We weren't interested in building numbers but relationships. So, for the next seven years, the same African-American and Latino children and many of the same white and black college students spent a week of each summer together at day camp.

Throughout the rest of the years, many of the same college students would come to our neighborhood each Wednesday for what became known as JAM Club, or Kids' Club. The time they gave to teach a Bible lesson, toss a football, or sing songs became an important exchange. They'd help throw special parties with our young neighbors—Back to School, Pumpkin Carving, Christmas, or Jesus Loves You parties—and even joined us as we'd march each January in the Colorado cold for Martin Luther King Jr. Day.

One of these white college students in particular was deeply affected by the friendships she built with some of the children and their mothers. Kathy had grown up much the same way I did—blond, suburban, athletic, churchgoing—but developed a growing restlessness in her early college years. She had heard from other students that I lived in the city, so she tracked me down to see how she could get involved.

"What makes you think you have anything to offer these kids?" I asked her the first time we talked. It was a hard question, insensitive now that I think about it, but one I struggled with often. What made any of us think we could "do" anything for anyone? The last thing I wanted was for white college students to feel sorry for or think they were better than their urban neighbors.

"I have no idea. But I want to learn," Kathy responded. With that, she helped plan JAM camps and became one of our first counselors during a summer when she was working two jobs to earn tuition for the fall. During the days of that first camp, Kathy taught Bible lessons during the day (though she barely knew the stories herself) and waitressed late each night.

And she became friends with seven-year-old Freddy Mae. One day while we were at the zoo, Kathy and Freddy Mae walked hand in hand past the lions, zebras, and elephants. They laughed and talked and pointed at the different shapes, sizes, and colors of each animal. Then all of a sudden, Freddy stopped, looked up into the white face of her camp counselor, and said, "Kathy, isn't it neat how God made all these animals different? He's pretty amazing, huh?"

Kathy could only nod her head at the truth of this child's observation, but Freddy's comment stayed with her the rest of the day. She couldn't shake it that night either when she went home. She had been given the night off of work, and now she knew why: to get right with God. Kathy cried on her bed and asked God to give her faith like Freddy had shown her.

Every JAM camp after that and every Wednesday during Kids' Club, Kathy faithfully offered her friendship to Freddy and the other children. Two years later, she rented an apartment a block away from us, began an elementary teaching career at a local school, eventually bought a home around the corner from where we first began JAM camp, and grew out of the role of student and into the role of friend for me. She's taken numerous trips to India and Mexico to work with children and remains active in her urban church and neighborhood to this day.

I was never quite sure who really benefited more from these urban/suburban friendships—the children who had special big brothers or sisters or the college students who had entered another world and discovered how much they had in common with their neighbors across town.

Or me. I got to watch the whole transaction.

And I got to be around children like James, Freddy, Jennifer, and Michelle. They knocked on our door almost every day to see if they could come in to play or talk or help me cook dinner. Or they would holler high-pitched greetings of "Hiiiii Jooooo!" whenever they'd see me riding my bicycle through the neighborhood. Or we'd plant flowers in our yard during the summer or build snowmen in the winter. They taught me more about love and acceptance and play than any book, college course, or relationship I had.

Accepting. Eager. Forgiving. No wonder Jesus said in Matthew 18:3, "I tell you the truth, unless you change and become like little children, you will never enter the kingdom of heaven."

I was changing. And Lonely was seeming a long time ago.

By now I had taught writing and speech courses full time for ten years, and I wondered if I could make it as a writer. I loved the interaction and the schedule of college teaching, but I wanted to stay in the city and explore writing. I took a leave of absence from the college, attended a few writers' conferences, and went to work.

One of the first places I applied was a multicultural monthly newspaper whose office was six blocks from our house. A friend from church told me they were looking for an editor there and was willing to introduce me to the publisher. But when I walked in, the publisher (a short African-American woman), had her doubts. She had started the paper on her own ten years before, fought hard to sustain it, and wanted to make sure it would always be a voice for people of color throughout Denver. How could I reflect that voice? she asked in the interview.

I tried hard to impress her: I lived in the neighborhood, had a master's degree in cross-cultural communication, had taught English for ten years, and had done some writing for a local business newspaper profiling black-owned businesses in Five Points. I was committed to this neighborhood, I said. In it for the long haul.

She didn't blink. I was an outsider. How could I know her people's history or literature or contemporary issues?

Good question. I struggled with it myself, I said. What *did* I think I was doing living here or applying to work as an editor at a black newspaper, when I was really just another white woman with a few wacky ideas about justice and diversity? I tried to tell her that we weren't all bad. There was, after all, Justice John Marshall Harlan, who in 1896 was the only dissenting supreme court judge in the famous Plessy vs. Ferguson case, which called for "separate but equal" railway cars. Justice Harlan claimed the "Constitution was color-blind" and that the law of the land could not discriminate on the basis of race or class, though he knew quite well (like we all did) that separate was *not* equal.

The publisher asked when I could start.

So, for the next year I earned three hundred dollars a month working three days a week as the editor of this monthly news-paper, covering events, editing and assigning stories, and writing an editor's column in each issue. Although I was one of two white woman on the small multicultural staff and the first face people saw as they walked into the office, only a few visitors wondered if they were lost. Or if I was.

Most of the time, though, I was grateful for this opportunity to hone my skills, learn from my publisher, engage in interesting discussions about race with others "unlike me," and find out more of what was happening in Five Points. But it was hard to live on three hundred dollars a month. I was using most of my savings from teaching, while sending out so many query letters to editors or résumés for reporting jobs that I eventually lost track. (It didn't help that I was getting the same number of rejec-tion letters from editors as letters I sent.)

One day I got a call at my office (my dad had given me a lit-tle room for my writing in the old house he had converted for his real estate business). It was the CEO of a company that pub-lished a biweekly news publication called the *National and International Religion Report* (NIRR). Was I interested in report-ing for them? Part time? They needed a Colorado correspondent because of all the international evangelical ministries whose headquarters were located in Colorado Springs.

I drove the sixty or so miles from Denver to the Springs two weeks later to meet with Steve Wike and his wife. I liked them immediately, was impressed with their integrity, vision, and pro-fessionalism, and hoped they would hire me for the job. Four days later, they did.

Four months later I left the newspaper. It was a mutual deci-sion. Several months before, I had written an editorial express-ing my concern about the rising gay rights movement. Those living homosexual lives were actively campaigning in our city for the same civil rights as people of color. I cautioned our read-ers not to confuse sexual identity issues with what I considered legitimate civil rights protection based on race, ethnicity, or class. I had warned my publisher early on that this column might not go over very well, but she felt confident running it. We received dozens of ongoing letters over the issue raised in my editorial and many more advertisements—the stuff that keeps small newspapers alive. Still, over lunch at a soulfood restaurant, the business manager told me they'd have to let me go. The column had been too much.

Interesting timing, I told him, since the NIRR was requiring more commitment. We parted on good terms, and I began traveling across the country to cover evangelical Christian conferences and events. From denominational meetings to missions or association conventions, from Orlando and Los Angeles to Minneapolis or Chicago, I spent January of 1993 to August of 1994 writing daily news pieces for the NIRR.

Every time I covered one of these meetings, I wondered why they were attended by predominately white men. Why were there so few people of color in these Baptist or Presbyterian denominations and even fewer in missions agencies or parachurch ministries? And almost nil in positions of leadership? Surely the body of Christ in North America reflected more than white suburban evangelicals, didn't it?

My own experience said it did. But as one black seminary professor explained to me, I was witnessing America's great "spiritual apartheid."

This selective and dominant white Christian subculture was confusing to me as I read the Scriptures, and as I continued to interact with neighbors in our urban community. It seemed to me that many Old Testament passages, the ministry of Jesus, and the Book of Acts all reflected to me God's desire for unity—not separatism—in the church. Jews and Gentiles in all regions of the world in the early church days seemed to reflect a culturally diverse church.

Not a red, *white,* and blue one.

I read the apostle Peter's speech as he repented of his racism in Acts 10:34–35: "I now realize how true it is that God does not show favoritism but accepts men from every nation who fear him and do what is right." I knew the men and women I interviewed at these conferences would never claim to be racist, nor discriminatory. They believed that race and color weren't important, they'd tell me. I wondered, though, why I rarely saw people of color at these conventions, meetings, and conferences, or in leadership roles.

I also wondered why the predominately white evangelical subculture in this country, that is, the leaders of many international ministries, the publishers and editors of many Christian publications and publishing houses, and the pastors of megachurches had done so little to work toward racial justice. Why had there been no evangelical voice in the 1960's civil rights movement? Why had this not been placed on the agenda? And why, now in the 1990s, were so many of the headquarters of these evangelical organizations located in homogenous suburban areas like Wheaton, Illinois, Colorado Springs, or Grand Rapids, Michigan, away from even the possibility of diversity? Why did they have so few people of color on their staffs, telling me that they would hire African Americans—"Ours is a color-blind employment policy"—but *they* "just haven't applied"?

Who goes where they know they're not welcomed?

Being comfortable is easier than justice.

The phone rang again one day. It was an editor for a magazine called *Urban Family*. I knew of *Urban Family* because I had joined the Christian Community Development Association, a national network of urban ministries begun by one of my favorite authors and heroes, black evangelist Dr. John Perkins. His eldest son, Spencer, was running this unique magazine in their hometown of Jackson, Mississippi, which tried to bridge the cultural gap among Christians. He and his white ministry partner, Chris Rice, had heard of my editorial about the gay rights movement and asked if they could reprint it.

I hoped they wouldn't lose readers over it, I teased.

For the next few years, I wrote other articles for *Urban Family* and for several Christian magazines about cross-cultural ministries, urban issues, and racial reconciliation efforts happening among evangelicals. Editors recognized that I was concentrating my freelance writing efforts on these issues and began assigning me stories. This encouraged me that maybe we were getting somewhere after all in regard to race relations; still, I knew we had a long way to go.

Especially when a white managing editor from a major Christian women's magazine called me and asked me to write a piece for them about race relations in the church.

"But let's be real," she said to me, suddenly whispering as if someone had just bugged the phone, "there's not a race problem anymore in this country, is there?"

I tried to "be real" as I told her stories: of an African-American teacher friend of mine confronted by two older white women in one of Denver's suburban malls for being in the "wrong" place and how they missed "the good old days when niggers knew their place"; of my roommate's fiancé, a thirty-year-old business manager who refused to drive through some wealthy, white parts of town any time of the day because he has been pulled over so many times by white police officers for "looking suspicious"; of an African woman attending a Christian conference and asked repeatedly during the fellowship time in the hotel's lobby for "more coffee"; of a young black couple, both with high-paying jobs, who were told by white realtors that no houses were available in the new suburban housing development where they wanted to buy, even though they saw eight "for sale" signs as they drove through the community.

Yes, I said to this editor's silence, I think there's still a race problem in our country.

Though I was glad to have the opportunity to raise awareness in the white Christian subculture, my checkbook told me that I better start thinking of some other ways to pay the rent. (Religious magazine writing is not exactly lucrative.) The NIRR was also feeling the financial crunch and had to lay off their correspondents. So I decided to teach part time at a state college in downtown Denver. Between freelance writing, adjunct teaching, and simple living, I could make ends meet, yet still very much aware that I was earning more than most of our neighbors.

Then the path started changing directions.

Janet and I learned that our landlord would be selling the house, I began attending a new church called Church in the City where most of the white and Hispanic pastors had intentionally relocated to our neighborhood, and many of our college students who helped with kids' club had graduated.

By the summer of 1994, I had moved to a small apartment a block away from where Janet and I had lived. She took a job at a six-thousand-member white suburban church as an administrator and moved to an apartment closer to her new job and her fiancé. Kathy, Daniel (another former student who had moved to the neighborhood), and I recruited friends from Church in the City to help with that summer's JAM camp, and at the end of one long hot fun day of Bible stories and swimming, I came home to my little apartment and heard a message on my phone machine that would literally change my life.

It was John Perkins. Calling *me*.

He wanted to know if I was interested in writing a book with him, one that told the stories of twelve churches across the country committed to the three principles of his ministry: reconciliation, relocation, and redistribution. He'd be in Denver the next week for the Christian Booksellers Association convention and would be meeting with his publishers about the project. If I wanted to be a part of it, I was to call him soon.

Interested? To work with the man whom many called the pioneer of urban ministry? Oh, let me think about it, Dr. Perkins.

I arrived at the convention and was a little overwhelmed at the hundreds and hundreds of booths with mostly white representatives selling anything from "Air Jesus" T-shirts and gospel CDs to Bible bags and paperback books. When I found the booth where I was to meet Dr. Perkins, my nerves were calmed as soon as I saw the broad smile of my short, energetic, African-American, sixtysomething-year-old hero.

"Hey, our girl from Denver," mused Dr. Perkins, as he motioned me to sit down next to him, across from his publishers and editor. He'd been at this "table" for years, building bridges with white evangelicals for almost thirty years and authoring books to challenge Christians to consider urban ministry. I was an indirect result of his ministry.

I was honored to sit beside him.

We discussed the scope of the project; this book would be written in John's voice from his perspective, and my role would be to gather research from the different churches and ministers involved. The purpose was to show how the church was, in fact, responding to the needs of the urban poor while simultaneously confronting racism. Could I write in the voice of a black southern man, they wanted to know? How did I feel about interviewing and researching? I hoped to do my best with both, I responded, listening to them describe my role as a "ghostwriter."

"I want Jo's name on the book with mine," Dr. Perkins said. "Let's help her career."

I tried not to let him see my eyes well up. *Be composed, professional,* I told myself.

I spent the next seven months traveling to the specific churches we would profile, seeing firsthand how black, white, Asian, and Hispanic Christians were coming together to help bring positive changes to their urban neighborhoods. From Dr. Perkins's church in Pasadena and my own Church in the City in Denver, to his son's in Jackson, and a few in New York City, I interviewed, wrote, researched, and shaped the book that became *Resurrecting Hope: Powerful Stories of How God Is Moving to Reach Our Cities.*

Community was becoming a more frequent word in my vocabulary than *lonely.*

While I was in Jackson visiting Spencer and Chris to profile their church for the book, we began talking about *Urban Family* magazine and the need to bring changes to it. I knew their own story of struggle and ministry from reading their book, *More Than Equals*. They told me they were looking to move the three-year-old magazine to "the next level," but they knew they'd need help and experience with that.

Was I willing to leave Denver? they asked.

That really meant, could I leave James, Freddy, and their families, leave Kathy, Daniel, church friends, and my other neighbors to take on a new position as editorial director for *Urban Family?* I never planned on moving from Denver. I hoped someday to watch James and the other kids walk across the stage to receive their high school diplomas. Yet now, an opportunity to merge my desire for racial justice, urban living, and writing was set before me.

But Mississippi? "Lawdhamercy!" I could just hear Grandma Pearl.

Janet volunteered to help me make the move south if we could go by way of Omaha for her family reunion. Still, I needed another driving companion, so she, another friend, and I traded turns at the wheel in a small borrowed truck and my car.

We arrived in Omaha in time for chicken, barbecued ribs, potato salad, and a whole lot of fun. The Mayhues had come out in full force to enjoy one another—almost a hundred. What, then, was this blond friend of Janet's doing here? they must have wondered. I was admittedly a bit uneasy as an outsider at someone else's family reunion—at least for the first thirty seconds. Then, cousins, sisters, uncles, and nieces (some of whom I knew from visits they made to our house in Denver) offered me chicken and conversation and invited me into games and photographs. They welcomed me as part of the family. Even when we attended the church Janet grew up in and the minister asked the Mayhue Family Reunion to stand up and be recognized, Janet's mother motioned me to stand up too.

I liked being a Mayhue. If only for a day.

Work at *Urban Family* started out with a few challenges that June of 1995. Mississippi was experiencing a record-breaking heat wave, the magazine faced financial problems, and I wasn't sure how to fit in with this tight-knit interracial team who had worked together since the magazine began, especially since I had worked independently for the past few years as a freelancer. Still, I moved into a small apartment a few blocks away from the office in the low-income, black section known as West Jackson, hopeful I could be a neighbor while helping the magazine grow.

We survived the financial pressures—including two pay cuts—and the temperatures of the summer, but by September the road took an unexpected twist. Spencer and Chris asked to come to my house where I was working on an article. Without warning or previous appraisal, Spencer let loose a bomb: "We like your work and your writing, Jo, but there's a personality style conflict. It's not working having you at the office."

I was being fired.

I was a mess. My black and white bosses sat in silence for a long awkward hour while I cried and blubbered and argued (so much for professionalism). When they left, I paced the tiny floor of my apartment, confused, angry, hurt, and . . . alone. Again. I was in shock, questions darting through my head like bullets: After only four hard months, how could they give up on me so soon? What had I done wrong if they liked my work? Where was their commitment to reconciliation? I had uprooted my life in Denver for *this?* Would they have fired me if I had been a man or an African American? Why, God, why?

I didn't have time to let loneliness sink in.

The phone rang. It was my friend, Clarence Shuler, an African-American pastor who worked in Colorado for a huge white parachurch ministry. He was in Jackson for a conference, and someone had told him the news of my termination (word travels fast in the South). He insisted we have a cup of coffee, so he could pray for me. He wanted me to make sure I knew, "Men don't always know how to deal with strong, competent women. Sometimes we get it wrong, Jo, really wrong." With that, he reaffirmed my gifts by asking me to be on his ministry board, prayed a pastoral prayer for me to endure this difficult time with integrity, and officially established his place as big brother/good friend for the rest of my life.

Gifts of grace relieve the sting of rejection.

Clarence's confidence helped me recover my landing. So did a fellow journalist/friend named Andres Tapia, whose phone calls from his Chicago home bolstered me to pick up freelancing again. And another blond friend I had met in west Jackson named Jody Byler made sure I had enough bicycling, good southern food, and laughter to sustain me through this transition. I knew how to freelance and teach, so I started both again within a few weeks of what I now refer to as, "The Great Canning." Though I never did understand Spencer's decision to fire me, divine mercy helped me find my way through the anger, confusion, and hurt. When I was really honest with myself, I knew Spencer well enough to know that he did what he genuinely thought was best for everyone involved. His ministry, work with Chris, and devotion to his family challenged and influenced many Christians for racial reconciliation.

Because redemption's plans are never far behind difficult challenges or unexpected turns, I soon discovered one of the reasons I was to move on from *Urban Family:* her name was Pamela.

She called me one day because a mutual friend had told her I was experienced in writing about race relations, and, um, well, a little more available these days. Was I interested in writing a book with her on how to develop interracial friendships? We talked all of ten minutes about the book idea—I assured her I was interested—and another hour about life, writing, careers, books, and New York City (where she happened to live). Pam had an enthusiasm and a vigor I immediately enjoyed; her vision for race relations and her determination with her writing made me glad to connect with another freelance writer. Even if she didn't live close by . . . yet.

I knew I did not want to stay in Mississippi much longer. Though I enjoyed my weekend adventures exploring the back roads of the South, visiting Faulkner's Oxford, the Quarters of New Orleans, and the beaches of Mobile. I had to admit that I missed city life. Jackson is not exactly a sprawling metropolis; in fact, Mississippi's entire population is still less than the city of Brooklyn alone.

Instead of returning to Denver, I decided to pursue a lifelong love affair I'd had with New York City, the city of all cities. I would move to the Big Apple, the capital of the world and the mecca of the publishing world. (If this didn't work, I knew I could always go back to Denver.) I had kept in touch with one of my contacts from *Resurrecting Hope,* Yvonne Dodd, who directed the mercy ministry arm of Redeemer Presbyterian Church in Manhattan, a church I immediately felt drawn to when I visited. I called her one November day to ask if she knew of any housing situations there.

"As a matter of fact, Jo, *I* need a roommate," Yvonne said.

By February of 1996, I packed up another truck and recruited Jody to help me drive east. The view of the New York skyline from the George Washington Bridge stirred a strange excitement in me, as if I were coming . . . home. When we pulled in front of Yvonne's apartment building, I was surprised to find a team of new friends from Redeemer ready to help me unload the truck, one of whom was a tall white guy named Butch, who told me his wife wanted to meet me when she returned from a family visit in Arkansas. They had read *Resurrecting Hope* and were interested in talking about it. That first night in the city, my new roommate threw a "Welcome to New York" potluck party for me, and I suddenly understood a little more of God's redemptive purposes.

The next week I met Butch's wife, a short, athletic African-American woman named Elvon. We lived in the same building in a neighborhood called Washington Heights, and I was thankful that I had "instant" neighbors—again. When she invited me over to play cards and talk, I realized this woman's vision for unity sounded pleasantly familiar. She told me about the racial reconciliation ministry at Redeemer and about her work on staff there.

Soon after we met, Elvon invited me to join her and some other women for an evening of racial dialogue in Brooklyn. I also called Pam to let her know I had made the move to New York and hoped we could get together soon. When she told me she would be speaking at a meeting in Brooklyn on race relations, I quickly asked if she knew Elvon.

"Elvon? That's who I'm speaking with at the dialogue in Brooklyn!" I heard a deep respect in Pam's voice as she talked about Elvon's friendship and the persistent example she modeled to Pam for working toward reconciliation. If it weren't for Elvon's support, Pam said, she might have abandoned her own ministry long ago at the predominately white church she was attending in Queens. Sometimes it was just too hard being the only one to bring up racial justice issues. Sometimes, when no one seemed to hear you, you didn't want to keep going, and you wouldn't if it weren't for good friends who encouraged you.

Her sentences were familiar, soothing even. The stuff of connection and community.

I finally met Pam in person while I was on the subway with Elvon. We were headed toward Brooklyn with a group of white and black women; I was both intimidated by this underground world of F trains and token booths and excited to be with these new friends. I stayed close to Pam and Elvon, partly because I was afraid of getting swallowed up by this eerie subway confusion, partly because their comfortableness with one another was an inviting shelter for this former suburban, partly southern white girl.

Pam and Elvon presented their stories and cases for racial reconciliation that night, along with two white friends of theirs. The room was crowded with a mix of white, Asian, and black women and men eager to discuss the principles and points Elvon and her team brought up. When a black woman raised a concern about how to continue on this road, others chimed in with equal passion. She continued by telling us of a recent time when she visited her college-age son in upstate New York one weekend.

She took him to a church there, wanting him to find spiritual support during his college days, but when they walked into the sanctuary, the white usher asked whether she and her son were in the "wrong church."

The woman's story slugged me in the stomach. Hurt so bad I couldn't help but cry.

How long, oh Lord?

I put down my head, trying not to let my shoulders shake. The discussion continued all around me as I tried to dry my face. Then I felt a gentle hand on my back, stroking it like a mother does a sad child. Elvon had made her way through that crowd of people, sat behind me, and without saying a word, touched my ache with dignity and understanding.

I knew why Pam called this woman Friend.

I eventually conquered the subway system, picked up some writing projects, and settled into church life in a city known more for its "rude New Yawker" stereotypes than the kindness I was encountering. By Easter, I was invited to a potluck at a friend's apartment down the street, where I ran into one of the white women who had spoken with Pam and Elvon that night in Brooklyn. I couldn't help but notice how she interacted with the various people there; her gentle eyes focused, head nodding in support, questions coming from her heart as if that person she was talking with was the only—and therefore the most important—human being on the planet.

I wondered if this wasn't what Jesus would have looked like when he listened to his friends.

After ham and vegetable casserole, I approached Elvon and Pam's friend and asked if we could talk about what she had shared that night in Brooklyn. We exchanged phone numbers, and she encouraged me to call her at her office.

Her name was Andrea.

I took the bus to meet Andrea for lunch near her office in the South Bronx. Elvon and Pam both greatly respected and appreciated her; I knew they had talked through some hard issues together. Besides, it wasn't often I encountered white Christian women who seemed to care so deeply about people of color or racial issues, so I was curious about what motivated this woman. She told me about growing up in Baltimore with parents who always made sure she was exposed to people from different cultures, even though she struggled much of her life with her dad's decision to leave her family for a homosexual lifestyle. Now, her faith in Christ led her to explore these problems and challenges as an adult; her friendship with Elvon had personalized many of them for her, and both had given her a deep sense of gratitude and empathy.

I wasn't sure if it was the spicy Spanish food or the conversation that made tears roll down Andrea's cheek then. She took off her glasses, rubbed her eyes, and apologized, "I'm sorry. Sometimes I just can't believe how much God has done in my life."

The beauty of a broken, tender heart is an engaging thing.

That first conversation grew into many, many more—we went to street fairs, restaurants, and church events together. We played tennis with Pam and another friend of hers. We traveled on cheap vacations together, exchanged books and insights about what we were learning, and tore up floors and laid roofing on a week-long mission project with Habitat for Humanity in Baltimore. We talked often about how we could challenge our other white friends at Redeemer to continue Elvon's work in what was now called the Racial Unity Ministry, and soon we began a home fellowship group to help build the kind of cross-cultural relationships we knew the gospel required.

When Andrea told me she was thinking about relocating into a low-income neighborhood, either Harlem or the South Bronx, I asked her why she wanted to do that. Like me, she had been affected by John Perkins's philosophy of ministry and relocation, by her study of Scriptures, and by her conversations with others. Consequently, she was feeling more and more drawn to live among the people with whom she worked. I was missing life in a neighborhood (as opposed to a big apartment building) and asked if I could join her search for a new home.

We talked many hours about what it would mean for two white women to move into a black neighborhood—how could we communicate our desire for reconciliation without appearing patronizing or offending the community? How could we become neighbors without coming across as privileged or arrogant? How could we keep the door and the conversations opened when there was so much "racial residue" to confront?

How in the world could two Waspy Christian women find a home in Harlem?

Only through other friends, that's how.

Pam introduced us to a woman who owned a brownstone apartment in central Harlem nine blocks north of Central Park. Though by now Elvon and Butch had moved to Pasadena to work in a Christian community development ministry, they, too, encouraged us to move in and build relationships in the community. Another African-American Christian woman, Melinda Weeks, who was becoming a close friend and also lived in Harlem, challenged me to consider the amazing possibilities of living in this neighborhood. Andrea's roommate, Melissa, decided to join us as well, so the combined support—along with the direction of the Almighty—made it easier to move. Again. I was ready to stop moving and get rooted.

Denver was a suburb compared to Harlem. Though it was a community I had long admired from the literary pages of the Harlem Renaissance, I have to admit, I struggled with moving into this predominately African-American section of Manhattan; I was intimidated by its reputation and density. Was I ready to return to minority status for the sake of interracial dialogue in this intense world of concrete high-rises and brownstone houses?

Harlem. A place loaded with historic romance and contemporary rage, a place where working and middle-class families live next door to crack houses, where Japanese and German tourists pay big bucks to attend black church services, while youth centers struggle to pay their staff. Harlem is what sociologists call a study in despair, what politicians call a symbol of urban decay and territorial tensions, and what television reporters call a crime-infested area. By their accounts, you'd think no real human beings lived here.

But they do, of course. In Harlem, West Jackson, and Denver's Five Points. Mothers raise their children in inner city America. And Harlem, I discovered the day I moved in, is a personal neighborhood in the midst of an often impersonal city. It is full of individual human beings who struggle and laugh and hope and bleed—like I do.

Could I go back to living as one of the few white women on the block, knowing the stares and questions and wonderful tradeoffs there would be? Could I handle the crowded dirty streets, boarded buildings, and the rich African cultures that had migrated to central Harlem much like southern blacks of the 1920s did? I'd see a group of African-American teenagers laughing and joking, rapping to each other and dancing to some hip-hop—safe just to be teenagers in one of the greatest black communities in the country. Would my white skin dampen their spirits and invade their heritage?

We could be neighbors, Andrea, Elvon, and Pam reminded me, chastising my guilt, helping me remember how much I needed these young people in my life, needed their unique talents and perspectives, needed to encourage them to succeed. I knew that learning and growing is never one-sided. It's always reciprocal.

So maybe these teenagers would see in me one white woman who didn't clutch her purse in fear and hurry by when she passed them on the street. In Harlem.

I met Maurice, Dewayne, and Junior that first day we moved, three eight-year-old neighbors who stood by watching us carrying boxes, clothes, and lamps. I shook their hands, introduced myself to them, and asked if they lived close by since I was going to be their new neighbor. Down the street, they told me, pointing with proud arms and eager eyes. They mumbled that they'd see me later, that they were going to the store for their mom. An hour later, when I was carrying another box, I heard a joyous sound I hadn't heard since I left Denver: "Hiiiii Jooooo! Can we help?" Maurice and Junior smiled at the door.

And I was home.

Chapter Eleven
Chances Are

I first heard the term "double jeopardy" in college when an African-American woman professor looked straight at me one day and said, "You do know that black women are in double

Elvon

jeopardy, right?" She might as well have slapped me across the face. My two liabilities—race and gender—made me part one of the lowest group in society's hierarchy.

My chances of making it were slim. Or so it seemed.

"If the sexists don't have it in for me, the racists do. I can't get a break!" I'd tell friends, half seriously, half facetiously. I knew this much was true: many black women had suffered before me, unable to reach their potential, never given the opportunities to use their gifts to make their unique contribution to the world. Double jeopardy meant they—and everyone else—lost.

I decided then and there to see my gender and race as an asset. If anything, such knowledge made me more determined just to be me. I would not be labeled or boxed in. True enough, I sometimes felt like a tiny human dot in a huge universe, but I had never been forced to endure genocides, famines, abuse, or personal violence as so many others before me have. I was a black Christian woman—a Reed—and God's hand on my life had led me this far. I didn't think he would change his mind.

When I graduated from high school, I wrote in my memory book, "Some people go down a worn path; I will go where there is no path and I will leave a trail." Almost fifteen years after writing that, I know that being a trailblazer intimately connects you with pain. Clearing away bushes, rocks, and trees can bruise and scratch your exposed skin and make your muscles ache. It can make you bone tired. Maybe that's why my older sister Faye had the wisdom to write in my memory book, "Penny, congratulations. Be careful and tough." I have followed her advice, but through the years have reinterpreted her meaning of the word *tough*. Tough to me as a black Christian woman now is to reflect the same meekness I see in the Lord Jesus. It is power—harnessed and correctly used. Sometimes it looks as hard as nails and sometimes it looks like Cool Whip. It does not let double jeopardy keep you down; rather, it recognizes your assets and blazes a trail—for Christ's sake.

And it receives help along the way from all sorts of other human beings. After all, who makes it in this world without a hand from someone else, without a friend, a word of encouragement, or a push from behind?

My first advisor in my small Arkansas college was a tall, thin northern white man named Dr. Hoeper. When I went to see him, hoping to change my major from English to speech communication, Dr. Hoeper affirmed my decision and advised me to consider changing to journalism and broadcasting.

"That's the direction the industry is going, Elvon, and it's really opening up to African-American women." I was the only black woman in Dr. Hoeper's Honors English class, and he saw that I was serious about my education. Here was a white man telling me that who I was as a black woman could be a strength, not a defect, in planning a career.

Dr. Hoeper was one of five white male professors over the course of my college years who encouraged me, saw my gifts, and nurtured them. It was as if they would not allow double jeopardy in their academic world. These professors believed in my abilities and often recommended me for honors classes or special awards, cheering me on, wanting me to succeed.

I tried to internalize their positive support and shrug off the negative interactions I'd had with principals or peers. It helped steer me away from prejudging people, away from the evil of prejudice toward white people.

That came in handy. Especially the summer after I graduated and joined forty-five mostly white students for a two-month mission project in New York City. We were divided into teams of six and seven. My team had three guys and four women—all white—and our team leader was a nineteen-year-old boy from Georgia. Though I had just turned twenty-three—the oldest in our group—I was assigned to be his assistant, which meant I was supposed to support him in his decision making and leadership. Most days, I just tolerated him. I did a lot of nodding and praying the rest of the summer, just to endure.

The summer ended, and I decided to stay in New York. My mother used to say, "You have a life to live, a death to die, and a soul to save." In New York City, I felt as if I was living life; there was something about the busyness and the people that always stirred me. I remembered a friend told me once that he often needed to get away to sort things through, and he "could only do that by going to the mountains . . . or to the city." The city, with all its cultures, faces, and history was—and remains—very much of a haven for me.

That fall, I began a job at a Christian academy teaching junior high and high school English, the only black teacher on the staff. My students were mainly Dominican and Puerto Rican, and this was another step on the ladder of cultural awareness for me. Often, I'd walk down the hall of this urban school and hear Puerto Rican boys call each other "nigga." Where I came from, this term was anything but cool, especially if nonblacks were using it. Eventually, I had to ask these tough Spanish teenagers to stop using the *n* word in my presence.

White teachers had challenges too. Mark was a young, enthusiastic white teacher and coach at the same school. Unfortunately, he had a limited understanding of God's design for diversity. He did understand that as a white male surrounded by minorities, he was privileged. He understood that when he took his brown players to soccer or basketball games where the opposing team was white, the white referees often ruled in favor of the opposing team. He knew every Sunday during our adult singles' class at the church that he had the pick of women he wanted, no matter what color they were. He knew from growing up in America that privilege was his way of life.

Once when Mark gave his students an assignment that seemed unrealistic to them, some of the students looked at their white teacher and said, "Nigga, you must be crazy." Red-faced and obviously taken aback, he responded, "First of all, I am not a nigga. Secondly, I am not crazy." Mark meant well and cared about his students; but when the kids told me about that incident, I knew that Mark, like so many other whites in interracial situations, still had not "relocated" in his heart. He had a home in upstate New York he could go back to, white girlfriends he could marry, and the skin to take him out of a place like New York City and anywhere he wanted to go. But his students did not. *Even though he taught at that school for four or five more years after I did,* I'm not sure he ever understood what life in America was really like for nonwhites.

Being at that school and its church was a giant step for me. Our pastor there was Greek. The congregation was comprised mostly of Hispanics, then whites, and "other"—I was included in that tiny group. My Sunday school class of young adults, though, was a mixture. And I loved it. For two years, we ate, prayed, retreated, and served together. For the first time in my life I was actually a part of an interracial group whose members believed in and supported one another. Regardless of race, class, or power.

But it lasted only a moment. We were all in our early or mid-twenties, just starting our careers in one of the most transient cities in the world. Friends eventually got married, moved away, or attended elsewhere. Still, the taste of unity and support from that group never left me, making me hungry and hopeful for it to happen again.

I finished the 1992 school year and decided not to return to teaching. Instead, I wanted to join the staff of the same college ministry that had first reached out to me in Arkansas. This ministry had begun an urban-focus, and I was eager to be a part of it. By January of 1993, I left for Florida as part of the national five-week training for new staff. Sixty other twentysomethings came ready to learn how to take on their cities and campuses for Christ.

Fifty-nine of them were white. The one black woman was me.

Me. Alone. Again. Sharing a dormroom with three white women for five weeks while we trained to go on staff. One was from Texas (oh, no, help me!). One was from Iowa (are there any black people there?). And one came from South Dakota (is that in America?). I didn't really connect with anyone those first few weeks. No girlfriend to walk to the cafeteria with, no buddy to sit beside during the lectures.

Sometimes trailblazing can be a quiet endeavor.

Week three, I got an infection and found myself in the emergency room of a nearby hospital with no insurance. I had no idea what I would do. Since I hadn't made any real friends there, I was getting a little worried. But I was surprised to see a real, genuine concern suddenly pour in. I received anonymous envelopes filled with money and get-well cards from people with the ministry. Every day for that first week back, I got three or four envelopes with money. At the end of the five weeks, the ministry leaders presented me with a check to pay my hospital bill.

The generosity of these white Christians forced me to ask myself some hard questions: Was I feeling rejected because I was black or because, as a friend once told me, I had "a knack for staying aloof"? Did I keep them at a distance because of our cultural differences? Why did they offer care and friendship to me only when I had an obvious need? Or had it been there all the time and I just didn't see it?

My answers came sooner than later. Every staff training group is invited to tour the international headquarters of the ministry and meet the founders and other leaders. By this time, I felt strongly that God put it on my heart to host an "Interracial Forum" for the new staff. I asked the right people and got permission to do so. Along with some friends I had known from our "Summer in the City" project, we laid out a format for the discussion and began inviting other staff people to come and talk about how racial issues related to our ministry. I even tried out a mini race discussion with my dorm roommates beforehand: "Do blacks come to the weekly ministry meetings at your colleges?" I asked.

"No, they have their groups, and we have ours," Iowa replied with a shrug.

"I don't look at race at all," South Dakota said.

Texas pleaded the Fifth.

I hoped the actual forum would be a little more interactive. It was. From the roomful of folk who came sincerely wanting to confront this issue, I became convinced that dialogue—real heart-to-heart dialogue—was the only key in building racial awareness among Christians. Theology alone was not doing the job of bringing blacks and whites together in the church. I recognized that the only hope we have for breaking down the racial barriers in our congregations—and in this country—is to simply talk honestly with one another about it in mutual relationships.

Conversation and friendship, I began to see, are the only strategies for change.

But then I got sidetracked. Back in Arkansas temporarily, I got reacquainted with an old boyfriend. Rob was a thin, dark-skinned brother who wore glasses and was planning on becoming a preacher in the Church of God in Christ denomination. I met him in college at a speech and debate tournament we were both competing in. At most tournaments, we often met each other in the finals of the persuasive speaking category—as the only two black students competing. My teammates called me "the persuader" because I always seemed to do well with either my anti-rock and roll speech or my speech about the evils of soft porn. Strange topics for a young African-American woman to be speaking on, I know, but in those days, and largely because of the predominately white evangelical campus ministry I was a part of, I was pretty conservative. As one girlfriend told me, "Elvon, you are so far right, you're about to fall off the face of the earth!"

Rob and I wrote to one another during college and soon started dating. When I left for New York City after graduating, though, I broke it off. Now, after a few years of being the only black woman at both the Christian academy and the campus ministry, I was hungry for emotional support. Rob lavished it upon me.

When I moved back to raise support in Arkansas for my ministry position, we quickly picked up where we left off as boyfriend/girlfriend. Soon he began talking about marriage—again. I told this young black man I would marry him in two years, after I finished working for the college ministry.

When I flew to New York City three months later for a weekend meeting, I learned about the marriage policy: your spouse also had to be on staff. Fundraising hadn't gone so well anyway, so I decided to forgo the ministry opportunity, wrap up the work I had started in New York, and return to Rob.

During that time in Arkansas, I lived with my sister Bea (who became the first black female optometrist in the state of Arkansas in *1990!)* and her family in Little Rock. One afternoon, she and I were looking through my photo album. There was her little sister, surrounded by a lot of white people in a strange urban metropolis.

"Penny," she said to me puzzled, "you sure have a lot of white friends." She got up from the couch, pulled out her photo album, and showed me pictures of herself at her baby shower. Several white women were in the pictures.

"You see, I have white friends too," Bea said to me. "But I'll tell you something. No matter how close you become as friends, they will still think they're superior to you."

I did not want to believe her.

I returned to New York City eager to complete my work. What I didn't expect was that the city would give me perspective again. I realized I just could not be a preacher's wife. Just being back in the city seemed to clear my head and to help me realize why I had reignited the relationship: Rob had encouraged me at a time when I needed emotional support. I wasn't so sure that he was the one I wanted to spend my life with. I *was* sure I should stay in the city—long term.

When I called him from my little apartment in "duh Bronx" to end the relationship and to say I was not coming back to Arkansas, he reacted as anyone would who had a bomb dropped on him. But I knew my decision was right, and I hoped he would be OK.

So here I was at the end of a long hot summer in New York City. No boyfriend, no job, no church, no direction. To avoid the pain, one night I gathered a few friends to see Shakespeare in Central Park. Watching *All's Well That Ends Well* lifted my spirits, but I was still feeling the bruises of the last few years. Maybe that's why I got into a conversation with another black woman who had joined us at the park.

Pamela was a friend of a friend, and after the play, as we walked to the subway, we started talking about the recent presidential election. I laughed when she told me she had voted for "the guy with the big ears." We compared Clinton with Bush and decided Clinton would be a better advocate for the poor and downtrodden. Of course, we were dogging all three candidates;

I told her I still found it strange that the governor of the state I had grown up in now was president.

In New York City—with more than eight million people—it's common to meet people, enjoy brief conversation, and never see them again. I hoped that wouldn't be true of Pam.

Because my job plans had shifted, this small-town southern woman suddenly found herself in a classic New York situation: temporary office work. One of my assignments was telemarketing at a Jewish fundraising organization where I practiced my Jewish accent over the phone: "Hello, I'm calling for National Jewish such-and-such. As you know, the plight of our people in foreign lands remains intense. . . . "

"Temping" gave me plenty of time to do other things while I worked. I'd browse in bookstores during every lunch hour and often before getting on the subway to go home. One book, *In My Place,* by Charlayne Hunter-Gault, got me thinking about racial issues again. It chronicled this woman's story as one of the first black students at the University of Georgia in the sixties. I was drawn to it because Mrs. Hunter-Gault had come to my college to speak when I was a freshman. She talked about her civil rights experiences as well as her travels to South Africa, which at that time was still under apartheid, and I never forgot her fascinating story.

God began (again) turning my heart toward the need for open dialogue between blacks and whites in this country. I devoured books by John Perkins, Cornel West, and Jack E. White, reread some Maya Angelou and discovered Nathan McCall's *Makes Me Wanna Holler.* By Christmas, I was also reading a magazine I discovered through Dr. Perkins and the organization he started, which was called Christian Community Development Association (CCDA). *Urban Family* included articles and editorials by and about Christians committed to the principles Dr. Perkins outlined in his books. I was impressed that the magazine was helping the race dialogue I knew God wanted his people to begin. One day, as I flipped through the pages, I even read an editorial about civil rights and the growing gay rights movement. The author, a blond woman from Colorado, was pictured. Seeing her photograph in that magazine was like seeing a white person on the cover of *Ebony* magazine. It was weird. A white woman writing this way about race?

One night, while I was lying in bed, I began sobbing over America's race predicament. *How, Lord, how can we change this? What can I do?*

As if in response, I landed another job—this one was full time—as the only black in an office of twenty-five white Christians on Madison Avenue. I was hired as a receptionist at Redeemer Presbyterian Church—a church in the center of bustling Manhattan with recently converted yuppies whose circles did not include people of too many other hues.

Maybe this would be different.

But before long, my fears were reconfirmed. I was the only black person at their parties. I was often being set up for dates with the only black men my white women coworkers knew. I'd "accidentally" overhear negative racial comments around the office and was once introduced as "Elvon—she works for us, uh, I mean *with* us." When I tried to tell the pastor, thoughts of my high school principal returned; it was the second time in my life a fortysomething white male told me, "I doubt it's racism, Elvon; maybe you're just sensitive."

As if he would know.

I quickly discovered two of God's reasons for having me at Redeemer. One, of course, was to continue the work he'd begun in me on the steps of that college library some eight years ago. Another was to bring to bear upon my new church the reality of the second part of the gospel—Christ coming to earth not only to reconcile God to man, but *man to man*—as Jesus prayed in the seventeenth chapter of John's Gospel. Jesus said that our love for one another and unity on this earth should mirror the unity that Jesus and God had. I certainly had never seen such togetherness between black and white Christians growing up in

Arkansas. I wondered seriously if it were even possible. I was about to find out.

I recognized that the goals Redeemer had for reaching the city were probably not going to happen if we continued to ignore the city's and the country's racial problems. I remembered the interracial forum I helped lead with the campus ministry, prayed a lot, and approached a white friend to help me.

I began meeting with Robin Van derWerf, whose heart, too, had been directed toward the need for open dialogue between different races. One night, as we sat on the living room floor of her apartment, she told me a story she'd told no one else. Robin had been invited to a women's conference several months before. Not knowing that all the other participants would be African-American, she accepted and found herself, to put it mildly, very uncomfortable. Some of the women, she told me, were very kind to her. Others pretended she wasn't there. But she experienced this overwhelming inhibition: the fear of saying or doing something that would offend those around her. As a result, she felt she had to walk on eggshells for the entire retreat.

I knew how she felt, of course. I shared some of my own experiences as a black woman at Redeemer, *our* church. Both in the staff office and in the dating scene, I was well aware of my "double jeopardy" status. I told Robin that a few white guys from the church openly flirted with me. Then I watched the wheels turning in their heads, wondering how they'd get out of this one. If I weren't black, they would probably have asked me out. Another white guy in college told me that "if I weren't black" he'd be interested in dating me.

If I weren't black.

Robin seemed to understand. That night, we tentatively mapped out a plan for Christians at our church—black, white, Asian, Hispanic, and other—that we hoped would allow us to talk to one another. We created two ongoing rules for the ministry: we had to agree not to intentionally offend and not to be easily offended. We talked about what it would mean for

Christians to really reach across racial lines—to cross those racial barriers and to be able to talk about any issue without being easily offended. That became the foundation for what we later called "Crossing Barriers Sessions," where we'd gather a small group of culturally diverse Christians for three to four nights over a two-week period of honest discussion, Bible study, prayer, and personal storytelling. Those sessions eventually turned into a ministry at the church known as "Do Justice, Love Mercy." Unfortunately, my friend Robin moved to another city a few months later, but I continued to run (or perhaps *crawl* would be a better word) with our vision.

I started asking God to send me a black girlfriend who knew what I was up against, who knew where I was coming from, someone with whom I didn't have to explain things.

Soon I was promoted at Redeemer to help coordinate small group leaders. During the next year, as I'd attend local CCDA seminars and hear Dr. John Perkins speak, I'd run into Pam again. I began telling her more about what we were going to try to do at Redeemer. She'd tell me stories of similar efforts she was coordinating at her mostly white church in Queens. We, as two black women trying to promote racial dialogue at predominately white churches, agreed to keep in touch and support each other in our goals. It was nice to know another black friend was on the same path.

Pam was the answer to my prayer.

Shortly before we were to officially start "Do Justice, Love Mercy," I got a call at the church office. I had been talking with members from the church, trying to recruit people and raise awareness about the issues Robin and I had discussed. This phone call was like many others: a white woman who attended Redeemer and worked at the church counseling office was interested in talking about this ministry. Could we have lunch? she asked. I agreed.

I met Andrea at a little French cafe a few blocks from the office. After listening to some of her struggles with her "Waspy" identity as both a social worker and a Christian counselor, I gave her the same speech I had given a dozen people that spring: Redeemer's vision was to be a church *for* the city, but when you look at the city, it's a rainbow of cultures and colors. If our church wants to be *for* the city, it should look *like* the city. That's what we were going to try to accomplish with this new "race" ministry, I told her.

Because Andrea worked at the office, it was easy for me to bounce things off of her from then on. We'd often wander into each other's office and talk about this issue or that event in the news. Though I knew her vocation had prepared her to interact with people, I became so impressed with her ability to listen, and listen well, that I began to open up to her more. She never dismissed my feelings or ideas. I was surprised when she would ask me questions, nod her head, look me in the eye, and encourage me to keep going.

Talking with Andrea was in some ways similar to how I had always viewed swimming. Learning how to swim was never easy for me. I'd always been afraid of the water: it was unfamiliar, and the power of what it could do to me was frightening. When I met Andrea, it was as if she helped me not be so afraid of getting into the water. She helped take the fear out of "swimming" because she didn't invalidate my feelings of apprehension.

"You're worth listening to, and what you have to say is important," her actions told me. In the process, she made me want to learn how to do the same. Andrea was another person God sent along to make the water more comfortable.

I soon asked her to be my prayer partner. It wasn't easy for me to ask her to pray with me each week; it felt like I was asking for help. But when I really thought about it, I had to admit that I needed Andrea. I needed this white woman in my life.

We met Thursdays at lunch for the next year and a half, until Andrea took another job in the South Bronx leading a social agency. We'd talk about work, the men who were (or weren't) in our lives, and the lessons we were learning from both. And then we would pray for the ministry, for our jobs, for relationships.

That summer, I decided to serve on a Habitat for Humanity team to inner-city Baltimore. I'd heard a lot about Habitat, and it sounded like something I wanted to do: helping people in a very practical way. What could be better than building homes for your neighbors?

The Habitat team met for several weeks before the trip to build unity. While waiting for one meeting to begin one night, I was reading the latest Grisham novel. A tall, brown-haired white man sat down beside me and asked me what I was reading. I told him and asked if he liked reading. "Oh yeah, theology books, Francis Schaeffer lately," he told me. "My name's Butch Borst by the way," he said, as he held out his hand.

My eyebrow went up. Hmm, a man who reads theology.

At the next meeting, I told a few friends I had decided to interview a cross section of the church population, including many of the thirtysomething white males. I asked the "Francis Schaeffer book guy" if I could interview him. He agreed.

"Have you ever had racist thoughts?" I asked, expecting the usual dance-around-the-issue response. Without hesitating, he said, "Yes. Of course." I put my pencil down and looked straight into his green eyes. Hmm, an honest answer, I thought to myself, *and* a cute guy. I asked him another question, and another, and soon realized I was no longer interviewing this guy because of my noble ministry purposes. There was something else happening between us.

Of all the dozens of white people at Redeemer I interviewed for our new race ministry, Butch was the only one who readily admitted to his sin of racism.

We started dating in June. By August we had had many conversations on books, racial issues, growing up in Arkansas or Long Island, and our Christian faith. We'd go out to plays or dinner, spend time with friends or see a movie. We both knew we were not interested in casual dating—we had gone down that awkward road before and didn't want to do it again. We decided we wanted a relationship that would lead toward marriage. In September we attended Redeemer's premarital seminar and wrestled with personality issues, quirks, and visions. I never had to convince Butch we lived in a racist society; he already knew. Or that we might get stares in our relationship; he recognized that too. When he confessed that he had had racist thoughts, that single statement told me he already knew of the gulf that exists between blacks and whites. And still he was willing to see me, to love me for who I was as a black Christian woman.

Things were getting serious.

One cold Saturday night in November, strolling on the Brooklyn Promenade—a beautiful walkway on the East River with a brilliant view of the Manhattan skyline behind it—Butch suddenly stopped, turned his face to mine, and said, "Elvon, I want to ask you to marry me."

"Go ahead," I said (always the smart alec).

He smiled, took a ring from his pocket, and said, "Elvon, will you marry me?"

"Of course," I responded as I put the ring on my finger. It was too big, but it didn't matter. I was going to marry this handsome, honest man.

"Now can we go? I'm freezing!" I told my new fiancé.

Even in a huge city like New York, word travels fast. The next morning at church, friends and people I barely knew came over to congratulate us on our engagement. It was exciting to share such news with this group of Christians, people who supported our decision. But then another question began to challenge me: How was I going to tell my parents that I was getting married to a white man?

Butch and I talked it through and prayed together about it. I decided to write my mom and dad a letter, explaining how we met, what our plans were, and when we'd be married. I tried to give them the same introduction to Butch as if I were bringing him home to the farm to meet them. Then I put a picture of Butch and me together in the envelope.

The next time I talked with them, they listened to our plans. They heard the excitement in my voice as I told them more about this man I was going to spend my life with. Though they didn't mention the interracial aspect of our relationship, I knew my father didn't necessarily approve. He seemed neutral, whereas my mom was supportive. I guess they had gotten used to the "strange" things I'd been doing—I had, after all, moved to New York City for this "ministry thing" and now worked at a white church. Marrying Butch seemed consistent with the other "odd" choices I had made.

When Butch finally met my father, he told him how much he appreciated how my mother and father had raised me. "Well, I don't have a problem with y'all being married," my proud dad said to my new husband. "I'm biracial myself, you know. Half Cherokee."

People sometimes ask us if the racial "stuff" makes our marriage more difficult. To be honest, I'm not exactly sure; most of the time I think our conflicts arise not from our different cultural backgrounds, but from our gender differences. Butch and I talked through so much while we were dating that I think we were as prepared for the racial issue as we could be. For instance, one day shortly before we were married, I asked Butch over the phone how he would feel about having black children. There was a short silence on the other end. Then he answered, "What do you mean? They would be *my* children." We chatted a little more and then hung up. Two minutes later, he called me back: "How would *you* feel about having Irish children?" Touché.

A month after we got married, "Do Justice, Love Mercy" sponsored a retreat for anyone from Redeemer interested in the racial dialogue. The ministry had been met with expected smiles by some white folk, but others told their white friends, "I don't see why we need this." The biggest surprise, however, came from a forty-year-old black woman. Karen had a short salt-and-pepper Afro that was always meticulously cut. She was tall, accomplished, and commanded attention whenever she walked into a room. When I asked her for her thoughts on the ministry, she gave me kudos for the attempt, then said, "In the end we're all going to go back to our own corners of the world, Elvon. But you can try."

We later held a day-long leadership training for the pastoral staff and church officers at Redeemer. After covering some practical aspects of race in America, we explored biblical examples of race, such as John 4, where Jesus engages the Samaritan woman, or the Book of Acts. Then we got down to basics: How do you build relationships with people different from you: at work, at church, at the gym?

Answer: the same way you build relationships with people like you, only a little more slowly. You go out for coffee, a dinner, a movie. You find out what interests them; you have them over for dinner; you inquire about their families, their histories, their lives. And you do it with respect and validation—even if their views are different from your own. Leadership began to see the importance of building these cross-cultural relationships.

By the fall, "Do Justice, Love Mercy" was progressing in a positive way, and Butch and I were adjusting well to married life. But I soon realized the trail was a little too demanding to blaze. I called Pam a lot. As the only black person on the church office staff, I was enduring a lot of pain. Was I oversensitive? Or did I bring on this anguish due to my own lack of mercy toward these Christian folk whom I did not yet trust?

Double jeopardy didn't help. I was also the low woman in the organizational structure, and it became important to me to know if it was that or my race that brought mistreatment. On one occasion, I wrote a letter to my boss, the senior pastor. I reviewed some incidents that had occurred where I thought prejudice might be a factor. Again, I found myself in the presence of a middle-aged white male authority, telling me my fears were groundless, my doubts fallacious. I left that corner office, with its beautiful oak desk and leather chairs, feeling worse and yet knowing, all the more now, that my fears were substantiated.

Included in my short list of charges was a piece of information I had accidentally discovered: another woman (white) in the office doing a similar job was making six thousand dollars more a year than I was. Then I began to question. Is her job more difficult than mine? Does hers require more intelligence? Does she have a higher degree, which would validate a higher salary? On the walk back to our apartment the same answers came back to me . . . "No." "No." And "no."

What was I going to do about this? I prayed. I talked to Butch. I talked to Andrea. I called Pam. Then I wrote a memo to the associate pastor in charge of finances and went to his office to talk about it. I was abruptly dismissed.

"No money in the budget for raises now," he said, straightening papers on his desk. I looked down, got up, and walked out of his office. I was confused and angry. The distrust that had been diminishing was now finding new momentum.

I went back to the senior pastor. He listened intently, and then began, unknowingly, to tear down all the confidence it had taken for me to ask for that meeting in the first place. "It's probably your past following you here. I don't think any one of these incidents is necessarily due to prejudice." He also explained that it was possible the pay discrepancy was an oversight since there were other mistakes in the budget.

I went home and cried. Not because I wasn't getting a raise but because my feelings had been totally dismissed by a man I deeply respected and honored. Though I took my charge no further (I could have gone to the board of elders), a few weeks later at personnel reviews, I received the normal annual pay raise plus an additional raise that added up to six thousand dollars.

A rock had been cleared from the road.

It was one of many obstacles that most African Americans face when they work for white organizations. I'd fight those battles, keep my head above water, and repeatedly ask myself, "OK, what is the biblical response to those who make me feel inferior, to those who didn't care about me because I was black? What does God require of me in this situation?" Two and half years of me vacillating between, "I hate these people" and "I'm going to be a servant and do more than I'm asked."

I was getting tired. Bone tired.

As the ministry grew and evolved now into the Racial Unity Ministry (R.U.M.), I became convinced that the best person to lead it was a person representative of the majority, a white person. It became increasingly difficult for me keep the race ministry separate from the work I did as the only black person on staff. Our committee had gone through some changes, but the four who began were still committed. Andrea was the only one I felt could take on the leadership role.

But she was still processing much of this, and I wasn't really certain of where she was with race relations. I asked her once or twice to take over the ministry, and both times she said no. I persisted.

During Black History Month 1996, Andrea, Pam, and I were asked to lead a variation of a Crossing Barriers Session at the home of a prominent African-American doctor in Brooklyn. I was really excited that one of my white friends, Suzanne, had arranged for the four of us to speak at this predominantly black gathering. After two years of talking primarily to white Christians about racial reconciliation, challenging them to do justice, now I had the opportunity to encourage *my* people to love mercy.

I began preparing for my presentation and inviting as many interested friends as I could find. Butch had told me about a new neighbor in our apartment building who happened to have written John Perkins's latest book with him, *Resurrecting Hope*. She might be interested in the discussion in Brooklyn. I invited Jo over for tea one night but wasn't sure what to make of her. Sometimes, as she'd throw down a card, this white woman with long blond hair would start "jiving," or speaking in black vernacular, reminding me of those clueless white caricatures on the 1970s black sitcom television show, "The Jeffersons." They'd come over to the Jeffersons' home and look completely inept as they tried "to slap me five." I knew Jo had lived in urban areas, but, really, this was strange. I wondered if she could help it or if it was just who she was. It took me a while to realize she did that with other people—white or black—not just with me because I was black.

I discovered, despite her quirkiness, she could be a good friend. Through gin rummy, bike riding, movies, or hanging out at each other's apartments, my friendship with Jo became stronger. It was nice having a relationship with a white woman who had had black women friends before; her familiarity with black culture made me more at ease with her.

Regardless of her strange quirks (or maybe because of them), I invited Jo to our Brooklyn race dialogue. After Andrea, Pam, and Suzanne shared their stories, I gave my talk, challenging black people to build relationships with whites, regardless of the pain they may have experienced. It was a biblical mandate, and if we were going to call ourselves Christians, I shared, we had to love mercy. I ended by citing Revelation 7:9–10a, "I looked and there before me was a great multitude that no one could count, from every nation, tribe, people and language, standing before the throne and in front of the Lamb. They were wearing white robes and were holding palm branches in their hands. And they cried out in a loud voice, 'Salvation belongs to our God, who sits on the throne, and to the Lamb.'"

Then we opened up the floor for comments. One woman told us the subtle and horrible story when she and her college-age son were escorted out of a church by a white usher who told them "you must be in the wrong place." As a black person, all I could do was shake my head in acknowledgment. I could give witness.

As others chimed into the discussion, I looked across the room at my new neighbor. She was genuinely responding to this woman's story. She was nodding her head; tears even rolled down her face. Then Jo did a strange thing: She looked right at this woman and said, "I am so sorry that happened to you. We white people can be so dumb sometimes."

I was struck by her sincerity, but I was also struck by her shame. I suddenly knew that if she were looking at that usher at that moment, she would have confronted him, asking how in the world he could do that to another human being. And I realized then how important it is for white Christians to understand that racism, particularly in the church, deserves shame. Racism, discrimination, and prejudice are exactly the opposite of why Christ came. He came so we could be in relationship one with another. That part of the trail has always been clear.

By July of 1996, Butch and I decided to take a leave of absence from New York and move to Pasadena, California. Butch wanted to attend seminary there, though we always knew we'd eventually be back in the Big Apple. When we arrived, we decided to tap into the local CCDA ministry known as the Harambee Center, another inner-city ministry John Perkins had started. (*Harambee* is Swahili for "Let's get together and push.") We moved a block away from the center and down the street from the intentional community house that some of the staff had built. Daily we watched neighborhood interactions and relational growth in a community known more by its negative statistics than by its friendships. We were grateful for the opportunity to be there. Though it wasn't easy, the move itself strengthened our marriage, forcing us to rely more on each other as we were away from the support systems we'd developed in New York.

Our original plans got redirected during the next two years, and Butch never did enter a formal seminary education. We did, however, receive some very practical insights about being in community with others, urban community development, and inner-city churches. We learned a new definition for *community* from committed brothers and sisters as they tried to plant a church: "Your benefit at my expense." We learned that community development takes a long time and requires patience and sustaining vision. Dr. Perkins had started this ministry twenty years ago, and there were still drug deals happening across the street. But there were also kids who grew up in the ministry and have attended college because of their involvement with Harambee staff. And we learned that church should not be about you, but about others.

When our son, Jordan Reed Borst, was born that first year in California, Andrea, Pam, and Jo were some of the first people we called. Pam came and visited us in Pasadena; so did Andrea.

Then two years and *almost* two children later (I was pregnant with our second child), we moved back to New York City without knowing where we'd live. We stayed with Andrea and Jo at their home in Harlem for a few weeks. Why did we return? Simple: New York has always been our home. We wanted our children to be around our family and good friends, for them to know Auntie Pam, Auntie Andrea, and Auntie Jo. We're committed to raising our children in the city, so we can expose them to a variety of cultures. The suburbs lately haven't provided the safety they had in the past—daily headlines have shown that. We love the city.

Besides, the older I get the more I realize that relationships are what life is about. You can't blaze a trail alone. If we don't have solid relationships in our lives, there's not much meaning. And there's not much meaning unless Christ is at the center— with our spouses, children, family, and good friends.

The long and the short of it is this: When I was engaged, I was given a surprise bridal shower from my friends in New York. The woman who hosted it invited one of my older sisters, Mary, who lives in New Jersey. Mary's always been supportive of me but suspicious of whites.

My bridal shower looked more like the United Nations than a typical shower: there were women who were Korean, Chinese, Mexican, Irish, African American, and European American. Halfway through the shower, my sister leaned over and whispered in my ear, "Penny, you have the rainbow coalition here!" "Well, Mary, I guess I do." Though we laughed about it, I considered it a great compliment.

Chapter Twelve
Mirror, Mirror

I never thought I'd live in New York City again. A short visit in high school had overwhelmed me: crowded streets, buildings jammed together, noise bouncing off every corner. Really, nature's

beauty had always captured my affections much more than urban life: I loved the redwoods and beaches in California, the farm country just outside of Baltimore, and the hiking trails and lakes in upstate New York. So coming to the most populated city in the country—and making it my home—was the last thing I expected to do. Even if the graduate school I was attending did boast one of the best reputations around for its social work program.

Andrea

But I have to confess, higher education and career advances weren't the only reasons I chose to move to the city.

Love—or what I thought was love—played a part.

Andy was an energetic New Yorker who loved getting a group of people together to go dancing or out to dinner or to his home for games and hors d'oeuvres. When I first saw him at a ministry meeting, it wasn't so much his looks that got my attention. It was his personality, his love for life, and his ability to laugh that drew me to him. My dad had always been very intense—life was serious business to him, so I didn't grow up really knowing how to play or have fun. Andy brought that out in me.

His mother was Italian Catholic and his father was Jewish, so he had a built-in appreciation for diversity. As a boy, Andy was encouraged to choose one of the two religions. He decided to be confirmed in a Catholic church, and later in college, his faith took on new meaning in evangelical Protestant churches. When he wasn't volunteering somewhere or studying for his classes in social work, he was entertaining people in his apartment, making them feel at home with his original stuffed mushrooms, punch, or crazy sense of humor.

Andy and I dated off and on for four years, first in Syracuse, then in New York. But the summer before he graduated, he wandered off to New York City to join a team of Christian college students for two months of mission work in a program called, "Summer in the City." With about forty peers, he helped low-income families, shared the gospel with homeless men, and worked in a camp for inner-city children. He loved the black community, listened to gospel music, attended a black church, and always developed black friendships.

"I think my soul is secretly black," he used to tell me, smiling, half serious.

When the summer program was over, Andy was convinced that he would eventually make a permanent move to the Big Apple, not far from where he had grown up. Sure enough, after he completed his undergraduate degree, he took a job as a social worker in Brooklyn. I stayed at the rescue mission's women's center in Syracuse. And with the same amount of passion with which he approached the rest of his life, Andy soon began to talk about why Christians needed to live in the city.

It was the first time I heard a positive evangelical spin on urban living. My father had shown me a liberal social gospel as he reached out to our neighbors in inner-city Baltimore. And my mom had argued with me for years about the need to just "live your faith." But a social gospel didn't have much meaning for me personally. That was my parents' thing, not mine.

One weekend, I made the five-hour drive from Syracuse to visit Andy. He took me to a nice restaurant in Brooklyn, and he talked. I listened. Over pasta and Chardonnay, he shared with me his rationale for city life, pointing out that the majority of the country's population actually lived in cities, that Jesus often entered cities and encountered the people most religious folk wanted to ignore. His face lit up. His hands emphasized each point. "Christians ought to be in cities . . . with the rest of the world!" he laughed. "There's diversity, culture, the arts—you can find everything in the city, Andrea." True enough, Andy saw the city as his playground; he was in love with it.

His infatuation was contagious.

Andy went on to show me passages in the Bible that supported this call to urban living. He led me to the twenty-fifth chapter of Matthew, where Jesus commends his followers for caring for the hungry, the thirsty, the naked, and the sick as if they were caring for the Son of God himself. A lot of city residents fit this description, Andy said, and so we ought to be here serving the poor and bringing them the good news of God's love. Besides, he drove home his point like a preacher does a sermon; the harvest was plentiful, the laborers few.

Andy's enthusiasm for the city was compelling and convicting. I had already interacted with homeless families, drug addicts, and low-income parents as I worked at the rescue mission; growing up, my parents always made sure I was around others who were culturally different from me. And my own struggles had always led me to those who also struggled, to those who didn't always feel like they fit in.

The groundwork had been laid.

Largely because of Andy, I decided to apply to graduate school in New York and move to the city. Shortly after I was accepted and knew I'd be making the move, however, things got rocky with Andy. We had a lot of fun together, but we weren't able to nurture an emotional connection in a way either of us wanted. Maybe we were too different from each other, maybe we just weren't ready for a serious relationship. So we decided to break up.

Once I arrived, though, Andy and I decided to try one more time. Like a skilled tour guide, he introduced me to different parts of the city, giving me tips on how *not* to look like a tourist, how to fit in quickly, and how to find the best deals in a city that is considered one of the most expensive in the country to live in. I was thankful for his insights, help, and support as I adjusted to urban living, but when we were really honest with ourselves, we both knew we made better friends than we did a couple. After four months of living in the same city, we agreed—again—to end our dating relationship.

Another broken relationship. This time, though, I knew where to put the pain. A greater love sustained me.

I'm thankful that I'm still friends with Andy, especially since it was his perspective on the city that initially got me here. No matter who was around, I was determined to conquer this new challenge, this unknown entity called "The City." Equipped with faith and a fierce competitive nature, I immersed myself in my graduate program, eager to dive into my studies and learn more about social work in an urban context. I was intrigued with the unique ethnicities around me, curious about how I would translate my previous small town professional experiences into this concrete environment. I hadn't yet decided if I'd stay in the city after I completed my degree. I missed the open sky and green hills of upstate New York as well as my Christian friends there. And while I enjoyed the cultures and activities of the city, it didn't rejuvenate me quite like nature had in the past.

The call from the streets, however, was becoming harder for me to ignore. I was assigned an internship with a not-for-profit social service agency in the South Bronx, the poorest congressional district in the country. As a student intern case manager in one of the agency's prevention programs, I learned strategies and methods to prevent homelessness, drug abuse, domestic violence, and to help keep families together.

Three mornings a week for a year, I left my fifth-floor walk-up apartment in Manhattan and rode the subway as it brought me into the Latino world of the South Bronx. Spanish music blared at me as I walked down the street, past the bodegos and Latina vendors selling their mangos, limes, and avocados. Everywhere I looked, I saw a sea of brown-skinned faces: mothers holding their babies, vendors selling Spanish Bibles and T-shirts, grandparents walking with toddlers.

Thirty percent of this neighborhood was also African American, and most mornings I smiled as I strolled down East 149th street with all its rich diversity, watching children play, women shop, and men gathered around one another laughing or talking or whistling. Sometimes they even teased me—in Spanish—as I walked by, thinking my dark brown hair made me Latina. I would wave back and hurry into the office, still completely aware of my pale Waspy skin.

I spent that year in counseling sessions, such as one with a young Latino man who was trying to stay off crack cocaine, or in group therapy sessions with men and women in the out-patient drug treatment program. I worked with an elderly alcoholic and a single mom with three children whose estranged husband was beating her. Many of our clients were unemployed or undereducated. Some were on welfare, living in subsidized housing, and paying for groceries with food stamps. I began to understand how to work the system for the clients and how to advocate for them, teaching them how to advocate for themselves as well, especially at some of the government social services offices.

Going to appointments to get your welfare check or reapply for Medicaid so your child can get medicine when she's sick can be dehumanizing, time-consuming, and painful because of all the bureaucracy. But when clients know someone cares about them, that someone is *for* them, that gives them hope enough to endure the daunting world of social services.

And hope enough to try to kick drug habits, find recovery, or escape the trap of the only security they have ever known: having a boyfriend. I understood. From personal experience.

Fears about relationships and anxiety about rent or safety for their children can immobilize urban neighbors. One of the biggest struggles in urban poverty, I quickly discovered, was that many people believe everyone is out to get them. Life becomes a survival game. So if I was going to help my clients, I had to learn how to win their trust. Some are more willing to accept help; others have a strong sense of pride and are resistant to help. And, of course, there are some—though not as many as the media would sometimes like you to believe—who are convinced they deserve this because of what society has done to them, because of how badly they've been treated.

Injustice is never neat and tidy.

My graduate studies were equipping me to respond to such urban issues, but my faith in Christ was pushing me to listen. I wondered how the two could come together.

While in school, I had started attending Redeemer Presbyterian Church. A friend had invited me to this reformed evangelical church comprised mostly of young urban professionals and graduate students, like me. I was struck that the preaching was unlike any I had heard in the suburban white churches I attended in Syracuse or in the urban churches of my youth. The pastors at Redeemer dug deep into the Bible each Sunday, exploring layer after layer of meaning and truth, and whetting my appetite for more. Their sermons were intellectual yet practical, challenging yet inspirational. The Scriptures were coming alive again for me.

The more I got involved in church life, the more I noticed that the theology and lifestyles of the church staff modeled something else: a balance of faith and works I hadn't seen much with white evangelicals. In the campus ministry and the suburban churches I attended, I heard many people talking about Christ and faith; growing up in a liberal Methodist church, I watched their works. At Redeemer—like the women's center in Syracuse—I saw both.

Maybe I'd consider staying in the city after all.

Part of this "word *and* deed" approach to Christianity was a unique mercy ministry Redeemer had begun in 1990. "Hope for New York" recruited people from the church to be involved in helping programs throughout the city. I watched as the director, Yvonne Dodd, coordinated volunteers or resources with after-school programs, homeless shelters, or immigrants' centers, and I was impressed. Here I was, going to social work school, learning how to help people, but realizing all the examples in my graduate courses or training came from nonreligious efforts. The history of social work, I knew, had strong Christian influences, from the faith-based settlement houses in the late 1800s to the scores of other Christian efforts (hospitals, hospices, employment training) in caring for the hurting or suffering "untouchables" the rest of society generally ignored. Very few, if any, contemporary models of social work included this historical Christian component, and I wondered just how effective we could be without it.

Now I watched Yvonne and others at this church *doing* the same type of social work I was studying. But theirs was *Christian* social work. Now I saw Christians who cared about the community, who were as concerned about saving souls as they were the quality of a person's life. They met the physical needs of others while pointing them to the Great Physician, Jesus Christ—much like Adelle and Ji had pointed me in the right direction. I hadn't realized how disillusioned I had become from not seeing the merging of spiritual and physical ministry until I saw it lived out through these urban Christians.

Didn't God care as much about our empty stomachs as he did our empty hearts? Hadn't Jesus fed the masses with fish and bread as well as offered living water to the spiritually thirsty? When I watched the struggles and efforts of those involved with

"Hope for New York," I knew that I had not been taught the whole gospel at the campus ministry or in my early church experiences. There was a reality to these people's lives; they were living out a holistic gospel, not just offering pat religious answers.

One Sunday morning during a worship service at Redeemer, I listened to my pastor's sermon on the role of the church in the city. He referred to the Scripture that talks about the city of God in heaven, emphasizing God's vision and concern for those who've made the city their home. Much like Andy's argument, it convinced me that the Almighty had, in fact, led me to the city and that I needed to stay here. Where else would I go? I realized then that if I were to be an effective social worker, I had to be around the needs of those in the city.

With that decision came another more surprising realization: my wounded heart was finding comfort in, of all places, New York City!

But first I had to have exploratory surgery.

Mine occurred in the last place you'd expect: Coney Island in Brooklyn. During my second year of graduate school, I was assigned another internship at a prevention program in the forgotten cotton candy community known as Coney Island. I was working two days a week at the same not-for-profit agency in the South Bronx while I took the long train ride to Coney Island the other days. Thirty-four concrete public housing buildings outlined the littered beaches and glass-strewn sidewalks I walked each day to the family center.

My supervisor there had a tender toughness that made anyone in her presence—clients and interns alike—feel both instantly accepted and deeply challenged. She'd stand just inches from you, penetrate you with her gaze, pat your back, and then tell you to get your act together. She was passionate about providing the best possible care for her clients, no matter what sacrifice or pain that might require.

I respected this woman. I had to.

Mary Alice, an Irish-American ex-nun homosexual social worker, would call me into her office for regular supervisor/intern meetings. In social work, supervision is designed to help you confront your own blind spots and biases that might affect your work with clients. Mary Alice was a professional at confrontation. She gripped her coffee mug like a handgun as she fired questions my way: Did I have *any* sense of my own ethnicity or heritage? Was I aware that my white perspective was affecting the way I interacted with our black and Hispanic clients? Could I see that I was bringing into the job the biases of my cultural value system, whether I wanted to admit it or not?

"Andrea, don't you know you're a WASP?" she smiled and probed, firm and gentle as she sipped her coffee.

I squirmed in my chair, trying hard to dodge her bullets. And I defended myself, muttering something of how I didn't know a thing about my heritage—it had never mattered much before. "I'm just a mutt," I responded. "I'm just . . . Andrea."

Mirrors are sometimes too honest in pointing out your blemishes and scars.

I didn't want to admit it then, but what she said was ringing true. Throughout the year, traveling between Coney Island, the Bronx, and Manhattan, I had a lot of time to think about those supervisor meetings and Mary Alice's challenges. I watched with new intrigue the many faces and cultures that sat across from me on the subways. I didn't like the fact that I knew so little about myself, about my own culture. And I certainly didn't like how it shaped my perspective of other people. It hurt me to think of all the times I had treated someone based on his cultural identity—or mine.

It was an ugly sore that needed a gentle but powerful balm. I had to attend to this issue of race and white privilege. Yet I felt I lacked a true answer to the seemingly constant struggle I witnessed in the city. I realize now that I was seeing integration and sensitivity as only parts of the solution. The more I explored, the more I began to see that true reconciliation can only begin with

and be sustained by God, the Ultimate Reconciler, bringing healing and wholeness to his people.

Anything less produces desperate fragmentation.

One morning during my second year of graduate school, I
was taking my usual route to the office in the South Bronx. As I
exited the subway just after rush hour, I turned down a small,
dimly lit hallway to the staircase that led outside to the street. My
mind was racing ahead to the day's meetings, Mary Alice's comments, and research projects I had to do. A few people walked
past me, but I wasn't paying much attention.

I did not really see the tall African-American man hiding
around the corner, his baggy jeans hanging off his hips, his big
Tommy Hilfiger T-shirt hiding his thin frame.

But he saw *me*. When he did, he lunged for my neck. I froze.
He grabbed the gold cross necklace I was wearing, one my mom
had given me, the only piece of jewelry I ever wore. He yanked
it from my neck, turned the opposite direction, and darted out of
the subway stairs so quickly I wasn't sure what to do. I couldn't
move; my legs were bricks.

I had been mugged. At 9:30 in the morning. In the South
Bronx. Where I was trying to help people.

It happened so fast. Once I finally snapped out of it, I wanted
to run after him. Then fear gripped me—what if he had a gun?
What would I do if I caught up with him? Fear subsided into
anger that this guy had targeted *me,* a nice responsible Christian
social worker. A Wasp, true enough, but a sympathetic one.
Terror seized me again and reminded me that I had just been vio-
lated. Shock sent the message to my legs that I better get out of
there, and I ran down East 149th toward my office. Once inside,
my face turned sheet white as one of my colleagues handed me
a glass of water and told me to sit down. When I did, all I could
do was cry. And cry.

Sometimes I hated the city. But so did my clients.

I have to admit, I always felt like I was a visitor in the South
Bronx, that it wasn't my neighborhood, though I respected it. Most

of the time. Maybe I was "proving" to people that I could handle working in what some felt was the poorest, most dangerous neighborhood in the city. Most of the other times I worked there, I felt safe. That morning mugging was the only time I was harassed in any way. Usually I felt welcomed. Sometimes, though, in an odd sort of way, I felt like I fit in more there than I did at Redeemer.

That, too, began to stir in me a sense of racial justice. Like Mary Alice said, working in such a diverse community, where I was a minority, made me aware that I had to confront this race issue once and for all. I'd brushed over it growing up, and with my college friends, and I blew it off at the rescue mission as something my clients had to deal with. Not me.

I was white. Privileged. Some unearned, others earned. I was profoundly realizing that I benefited from being white in a world run mostly by white people, and I did not have to confront racial issues unless they confronted me. Now they did, every time I walked down the street in the South Bronx.

When I graduated with a master's degree—and a healthy exposure to urban need—in 1994, I was ready to merge my faith perspective with my vocation in a Christian environment. Through the church, I had been leading workshops on how to empathize with someone's pain and better help someone in need. So when Redeemer's counseling center was expanding, I was hired as a consultant, expected to build up my case load. I had learned a lot about listening to and caring for others through my academic experiences, my personal struggles, and working at the women's center in Syracuse. I led workshops; I counseled couples and individuals who struggled with purpose and meaning and life skills in a city that often isn't very patient or tender toward the hurting. It was for me a year to learn some of what it meant to live out the gospel in a Christian organization, to learn how to love better.

I had the option of taking a break from urban poverty and racism. Some people didn't.

One spring day, I came home from work and noticed my roommate had received a letter from a Redeemer staff member named Elvon Reed introducing a new ministry she was starting. The letter announced that Redeemer was going to begin looking at the issue of racial reconciliation. Immediately, I thought how brave this woman was, being a black woman on the staff of a predominately white and Asian congregation raising this problem in the church. But with all I had experienced, I was beginning to understand that this was not a minor issue, but a major one that concerned all Christians. As the only black person on a church staff of around twenty, this woman was challenging her fellow Christians to confront it *with* her. If you were interested, the letter said, you were invited to a special meeting introducing the idea.

Interested? I was excited that a white evangelical church was finally going to deal with this issue. And maybe this would help me make sense of all the different cultural experiences I'd had, of Mary Alice's challenges, and of the questions I had had for so long about divisions in the church. Maybe this would help calm the confusion in my heart.

But I couldn't wait for the meeting. I called Elvon the next day and asked if we could have lunch. I had to talk with her about this ministry. Now. She agreed.

We met at a little French cafe close to the church office. I was early. When she arrived, I talked and talked about sometimes feeling guilty for being white, about not knowing my heritage, and about not having any idea how to merge my faith with this issue. Elvon smiled and nodded and waited.

Then I listened. She told me she was convinced God wanted her to act on this ministry. For years she had lived on the border of black and white America, watching both sides struggle for reconciliation; now she knew that only the gospel of Jesus Christ could tear down the walls and build up the church. I was immediately taken by her confidence, maybe even a bit intimidated. She was so composed, so mature.

I didn't know anything. But I did know my time as a white person had come. I had to act. I could no longer think about racism and feel guilty about it. I had to be a part of the solution. I just knew I needed to be a part of this ministry. I told Elvon to count on me to be at this meeting.

The room was full of white and brown faces. I sat anxious and impressed that I saw Latinos, Asians, white, and black folk around me. Elvon introduced her vision and shared the story of how she got to New York City from Arkansas. Then she showed a video, and one of the pastors ended the meeting by talking about unity. I was riveted. Ephesians 2:14–15 came to my mind, and a light bulb really did go on inside me: "For he [Christ] himself is our peace, who has made the two one and has destroyed the barrier, the dividing wall of hostility, . . . His purpose was to create in himself one new man out of the two, thus making peace."

I don't know if people left that meeting ready to initiate cross-cultural friendships and confront racial issues, but I did. I left impressed with Elvon and encouraged that there was pastoral support. The racial reconciliation ministry at Redeemer Presbyterian Church was officially launched.

In July 1994, seven of us—Asian, Latino, white, and black— joined the planning committee for this new ministry called "Do Justice, Love Mercy," based on the verse in Micah 6:8: "He has showed you, O man, what is good. And what does the LORD require of you? To act justly and to love mercy and to walk humbly with your God."

The first thing we did was start what we called Crossing Barriers Sessions. We recruited groups of nine diverse Christians to meet on three nights over a period of a couple weeks. At each meeting, we'd look at the biblical basis of unity, examine case studies, and get into small groups to listen to one another's personal stories of discrimination. Elvon and I worked on the content together and led these. We shared a common vision, and a friendship was growing from that.

Elvon also asked me if I would meet with her weekly for prayer. I was honored. She needed support as the only black person at the church office. I needed prayer as I adjusted to my role as a counselor and as I realized—largely because of Elvon's encouragement—I needed to be back in the South Bronx. We prayed for each other, for the possibility of a church plant in either the South Bronx or Harlem, and for the hearts of our church friends to be changed.

When I met Elvon, it was as if she personalized all the emotions and questions I had been confronting for the past ten years. Her vision and support helped me to change and grow.

Our friendship deepened as we continued to partner in speaking engagements or as we led Crossing Barriers groups. I watched and encouraged her as she and Butch dated and got engaged. I went to their wedding reception. I was there when she miscarried with their first child and ecstatic when she announced they were expecting again. These experiences took us beyond the mission of racial reconciliation and into the world called friendship.

By the spring of 1996, Elvon got tired. She had been the lone advocate at Redeemer for "Do Justice, Love Mercy," and she felt her time on staff was coming to a close. She believed a white person would be better in the leadership position, that maybe the church leaders would listen more to a white Christian than to the only black on staff who was often trying to promote racial reconciliation. Elvon resigned and asked me to consider being the leader.

I hardly felt qualified. Elvon was *my* leader, and I wasn't in any position to take over. I said no. I was not ready.

For the next four months, no one led the "Do Justice, Love Mercy" ministry. And I saw again that racial justice in predominately white churches can be easily forgotten.

Then I read a book called *More Than Equals,* by Spencer Perkins and Chris Rice, the contemporary story of two men, one white, one black, their friendship and ministry together. Each time I turned a page, I was convicted of the need to be in this battle, to be pursuing unity in the body of Christ. I could not sit on the sidelines anymore, terrified of jumping into this issue, this ministry. It was one thing to be on a committee and dabble in a few cross-cultural sessions here and there; it was another to be the keeper of a vision of an issue that inherently required confrontation and agitation. I was never very good at conflict, and leading this ministry was sure to mean I would have to confront my pastors and our congregation.

I called the committee back together to reexamine what we should be about. I wanted to see Redeemer's reputation for being an upper-east-side yuppie church changed into a church with a heart for all people regardless of class, culture, or race. I could not sit by and watch the superiority and exclusivity of what is often perpetuated in the white evangelical community. Elvon had instilled in us a vision for a more reconciled church, and I realized I could not let that vision—God's vision—die. I agreed to be the point person with what we would now call the Racial Unity Ministry (R.U.M.). Our goals were to foster positive cross-cultural relationships within our church and to help raise awareness of the many issues surrounding race relationships in this country. I drafted a letter to our pastors stating our mission.

The pastors understood the seriousness of the ministry and included R.U.M. in their strategic planning, encouraging us also to start a home fellowship group as one practical way to fulfill our goal of building relationships. We did.

But before we even started the home group, Elvon and Butch moved to Pasadena, California, to be a part of a Christian community development effort started by John Perkins. I'd miss my friend and leader, but I was honored again that she asked me to be her long-distance accountability friend, to talk on the phone every other week about our Christian walks, our relationships, and our jobs.

Still, Elvon was gone. I had to admit, I did not want to do this racial unity thing alone. I felt ignorant. I needed partners.

I remembered a local meeting for the Christian Community Development Association I attended the fall of 1995 at a church in Queens. I had been interested in what CCDA was doing locally after having attended its national conference in Baltimore in 1994 with friends from "Hope for New York." At CCDA, I met more evangelical Christians concerned about justice who were also meeting practical needs for people in their urban communities. I saw black and white Christians working together. My mom and I had argued for years about how to witness to the unbelieving world: she felt the best method was just to live it out—no words necessary. She liked to tell me, "You don't preach the gospel, Andrea, you just live it, being about peace and justice, changing structural powers rather than being so concerned about changing individuals."

I felt our lives and our words as Christians should have equal effect. I felt God's Holy Spirit had to change an individual's heart if structures were ever going to change. But I wasn't always sure how to bring the two together. At CCDA, I saw them merging as I heard speakers working for inward heart changes as well as social structural changes.

I went to the local chapter of CCDA hoping to hear the same calls for change. What happened instead was that I met another African-American woman who was working at her church in ways Elvon and I had at ours. Pamela and I quickly discovered we had many common interests: reconciliation, relocation, and economic development (and, of course, men). Here was another confident black lady who had a heart for the whole gospel. I was impressed with her commitment to mentoring younger women as it was being redefined for me at the time and encouraged by her positive perspective.

Pam and I talked on the phone and sometimes late into the evening. She knew Elvon, who had helped her lead Crossing Barriers Sessions at Pam's predominantly white church. Sometimes the three of us met to plan CBS curriculum; sometimes we gave formal presentations together in other places in the city. At one point, when we were both considering relocating, we even talked about living together.

One Friday night in February before Elvon moved, the three of us and another white friend of Elvon's named Suzanne had been invited to speak on racial reconciliation at a doctor's home in Brooklyn. For the past several years, our hostess organized unique talks in her home each Black History Month; this night we were the lineup. Elvon had also invited a new neighbor of hers—a white woman named Jo—to join us, and so this interracial group of women invaded the subway system and headed southeast of Manhattan.

We arrived at this historic Brooklyn brownstone home to a crowd of about fifty. After the four of us presented our stories and a discussion began, I noticed Elvon's neighbor began to cry. Something in the discussion had touched this white woman, and tears were rolling down her cheeks. Though she was a silent observer during the discussion, her tenderness for people of color somehow made her cry. I noticed how she had tapped into identifying with an isolated people, whereas I had been primarily intellectual regarding the issue, concerned mostly with my public speaking. I wasn't entirely sure what happened for her; I just knew this woman was sensitive to the same race issues I had been confronting.

Three months later on Easter Sunday, I met Jo again. We had both been invited to a potluck dinner at a mutual friend's apartment, but we never really talked until just before I was leaving. Jo asked if we could have lunch sometime, to talk about some of the things she'd heard me share in Brooklyn. I gave her my phone number and encouraged her to call.

I knew how helpful lunch talks could be.

We met a few blocks from my office in the South Bronx over Spanish rice and plantains. She asked me where my concern for racial justice had come from, how I had gotten involved in this ministry with Elvon and Pam. I told her about my dad's commitment to cultural diversity and my mom's sense of justice, about my own experiences in college and my career that led me to this place. She nodded and listened and smiled. Suddenly, there was another white girl in my life who was convinced that this race issue was imperative to the church.

Around the time Elvon and Butch were moving that summer, I was leading a work team from church for a week-long Habitat for Humanity project in one of Baltimore's inner-city neighborhoods known as Sandtown. Jo decided to come to support me in my leadership role. We were to be hosted by a Korean Presbyterian church outside of Baltimore's city limits, put up in families' homes each night while we worked on construction during the days.

The first night, the four women on our team were taken to stay with a wealthy Korean family. As soon as we arrived in this huge three-level suburban home, they took one look at us and knew they had a problem. The problem wasn't that they didn't have enough room in their house for us; the problem was that they had agreed only to host Asian volunteers.

They had no idea we would be white! We could stay the night, they told us, but the next day we'd have to find other accommodations. I couldn't believe my ears. Suddenly I was being discriminated against because of what I looked like, because of where I came from. By Christians!

Then it hit me: *this was only one small instance of experiencing what many people of color encounter every day.*

The four of us talked about it, decided to learn from the experience, and reminded one another why we had come: to help build homes and to foster reconciliation. We assured our hosts that we did not want to offend them; we would find another place, and we were grateful for the hospitality—even if it was only for one night. The next evening, after a hard day building, we crammed into a small bedroom in the church's parsonage to stay for the remainder of the week.

At the end of each work day, Jo and I would walk through Sandtown, and Jo would just stop and talk to people sitting on their stoops as if they were her friends. She wasn't afraid of being in this low-income neighborhood. It was inviting and fun for her.

I watched as she joked with the neighbors and tickled the children. One day we even found a swing set, watched two little girls climb onto our laps, and swung for a full hour, laughing and giggling with them.

There was a lack of fear in how Jo related to people of color. She seemed free and comfortable being herself. And that modeled to me how I needed to be. She had respect for the folk she talked with, and that taught me to do the same.

When we returned to New York City, I shared with Jo the desire to relocate into a diverse, low-income neighborhood. She expressed a desire to do the same. We started looking for an apartment in either the South Bronx or Harlem, hoping to build community and learn to be good neighbors. Then Pam introduced us to a friend of hers who owned a brownstone in central Harlem, nine blocks north of Central Park, and a few months later, we were able to move in.

Living in Harlem made me even more aware of my whiteness and privilege as a WASP, that I could choose to live here like I could choose to live in Queens or the upper west side of Manhattan. Though I can never walk down the street here without being a minority, I know I can feel comfortable in almost any other part of the city. The feeling of being a minority, small and uncomfortable as it may be, has helped me understand a little more of what my sisters and brothers of color experience regularly in "mainstream" white America.

Others have helped me understand as well. My friend Melinda only lives a few miles away in another part of Harlem. She is another gifted African-American woman, who works as an attorney and a college instructor, making a difference in both. Melinda's love for Christ and for life has had a great impact on me. Because she lives close by, our friendship has grown—sometimes we'll meet for breakfast around the corner at a little Muslim cafe, or I'll go over to her apartment to watch videos, or she'll come by our house for barbecues or Easter dinner. She's shown me another perspective of how to bridge the cultural gap just by being my friend.

Neighbors on our block, friends from my church's Racial Unity Ministry, and children who come by our house to play and who are so full of smiles they can't contain themselves, all have helped me see that diversity is part of God's creative design, that the gospel brings us together; it never pushes apart.

The gospel is the only hope for this race issue. Even with parents who tried harder than most to instill in us a sense of justice and equality, I still got lulled into the mind-set of white privilege in America. All I cared about in my teen years was getting a boyfriend, wrapped up in my own psychological abandonment as a result of losing my dad. Though I was raised around many cultures, I never had a sense of history, a sense of racism or injustice, or even my own cultural identity. Yes, I grew up with black and Native American kids, but that in and of itself did not teach me racial reconciliation. Nor did it give me a sense of history. I just played with the other children in my neighborhood—who happened to be African or Native American. It was normal to me.

Now, of course, as an adult I'm grateful for the choices my dad and mom made in exposing me to people from a variety of cultures. Despite the struggles I endured with my father, I now recognize the legacy of justice and understanding he left for me. I saw it even more clearly when I recently received a letter from my mom:

> *Dear Kids,*
>
> *I am remembering that tomorrow would be your dad's sixty-third birthday. I am starting to think about what your father's work was, what his life was about. I have started to write in my journal that I think his work was to learn who he was, to be in touch with his own reality. I wrote that he accepted me as his wife and companion for sixteen years. He shared his ministry with me in the community in Baltimore and we shared our lives with you. We shared in our time in Japan as partners. He chose with me to give birth to three of you and to adopt you, Emily, making a home for you four as*

my helpmate and companion. He loved music and plants. He enjoyed nature and being in it. He cared for people in many walks of life, worked hard and had a wonderful ability to keep financial affairs. He did not judge others. He tried to be loving and fair. Much of his life he struggled with his homosexual tendencies, and he must have suffered a lot over the pain he caused me in our marriage dissolution. He just had to be truthful. He surely was aware of the pain he caused you in no longer being a parent at home. I cannot imagine what he was feeling.

I remember him this birthday as one I loved. He accepted me as his lover, wife and friend and taught me so much about life. I feel deep gratitude because he forced me to move on in my life to do things I did not know I could do. I remember him as your father. He loved all of you very much. He was as awed by your arrival into the world as I was. No parent does it perfectly; we just try our best. And I hope you will always treasure the memory of your father, forgiving him for his mistakes and loving him for what he tried to be. And then living your own lives as fully and honestly and truthfully as possible.

With my love, Mom

I can't help but believe that my dad would approve of the journey that has led me to try to live "fully, honestly, and truthfully," especially in regard to racial justice. Only as I began to look into the mirror did I understand exactly how significant that journey was. And it wasn't until Elvon entered my life that it all came together—the years of having people different from me in our home, of being in Japan and the city, and in social work—that I began to get a sense of justice, of passion, of connectedness, which included culture/ethnicity and went beyond.

From her and from others, I began to see that this is what I needed to be about. My friendship with Elvon brought together the visceral and the experiential, the sense that something I always knew was right needed to be lived out consciously and intentionally. Hearing Elvon's story, and Pam's, and Jo's, and Melinda's, and my neighbors', made me realize that growing up with a variety of ethnic kids was an incredible exception to the norm.

Regardless, there are still intense injustices that keep us apart. It took the personal story of a friend to help bring the reality of this societal tragedy home. And then to help me embrace it so I could become part of the solution.

And it has changed me. Enriching me, healing many of my wounds, giving me a community that is both a balm for the past and nourishment for the future. Life is so much slower and lighter now. I still have much to learn, so many areas to grow in. But I have more of a sense of wholeness now than ever before, of affinity, of realizing the privilege that I am part of a larger human community with all its pain, suffering, joys, and hopes. That's the gospel truth.

I'll never trade it for anything.

A Dialogue *Epilogue* for the Future

It is a beautiful Saturday and the four of us gather at our friend Meredith's home outside of the city to eat and talk about

Photo by Christopher Gilbert

how this book has affected us. Our friend Melinda, who has been cheering us on during the writing process, has graciously agreed to moderate the discussion so we don't go off on too many tangents (as we like to do). We enjoy a wonderful lunch, courtesy of Meredith, that would have made Martha Stewart proud. Now we must talk about race. (We'd rather be in hammocks outside taking a siesta, but duty calls.)

The six of us sit around Meredith's blue living room looking a little nervous and tired. Four of us have various forms of race-fatigue. Elvon is seven months pregnant and must sit propped up. Andrea is fighting a cold. And Jo and Pam are weary from writing. We pray. Meredith has agreed to be the videographer and chronicle our talk on tape. We worry about her fingers cramping during the two-hour session. We confirm that the camcorder is actually recording, and we're off.

Melinda: What have each of you discovered about yourself during the process of putting your experiences on paper?

Andrea: I wanted to remember more of the details of my childhood but couldn't. My memory isn't so good!

Elvon: Me too. The first and second chapters were hard in a lot of ways because they made me recall stuff I hadn't thought about in years. A lot of it wasn't particularly "fun." It was hard to talk about it, frustrating at times to have to remember the emotions I experienced back then. It got a little easier as we went farther along in the book. It was easier to remember five or ten years ago, as opposed to ten or twenty years ago.

Jo: As I was writing my story, I kept wondering, *Who's going to care?* I thought my early life was uneventful, so part of me still struggles with people who might read this and call it some kind of psychobabble.

Melinda: Did you identify how the issue of race became an issue of the heart for each of you?

Jo: I don't know how you felt, Pam, but after reading your first chapter, I felt we had a lot more in common as kids than I initially thought. I remember you said to me, "I just can't buy the fact that you're a white suburban woman growing up with all these things that we look at as great, and yet you were lonely." But when I read about you growing up in a white Irish neighborhood in Queens, it seems you may have felt the same way. There was a sense of understanding our feelings of displacement, or feeling like an oddball. What do you think?

Pam: I *was* the oddball. Everybody else was in some kind of club, which I visited and was allowed to be a guest at, but was not in. Writing this book at this time was a unique experience for me because I spend a lot of time in the same neighborhood where all this took place. I would walk by the same places every day, and then write about them. I even walk by some of the same people who twenty-five years ago were not so kind as they are now. It made me angry as I recalled the things that happened to me. I felt at times like I should do a TV news report: "I am standing here at the corner where I was beat up by Eugene Jackson. . . ." When I was experiencing these things as a child, I didn't really understand what was wrong. I'm glad I was sort of protected from the full understanding of racism, but I would have benefited from some type of explanation for the craziness that was occurring. Now there are unanswered questions. For instance, when I was getting beat up, why didn't anyone stop it? It was a very narrow residential street. Didn't anyone care? Yet, it all seemed like such a sane existence, compared to what I think of when I imagine Elvon's coming up in the South in the late sixties and seventies. I perceive that as a really hard time.

Elvon: Many northern blacks have that perception. And in some ways it's true. I think segregation is just so ingrained in the South that it seems normal. There's no alternative there. In the North you have a lot of white people who are sons and daughters of abolitionists. Yet Malcolm X was a child of the North.

Melinda: Have you come to understand each other better through the process of uncovering your lives, your souls?

Jo: I was especially moved in your story, Elvon, when you go to the church with the white pastor of this predominantly white church, and you are "freaking out." Yet the white pastor is so gracious and welcoming. I started crying at that because it could have been so much worse. I was just so thankful that happened. [To Andrea] I've really grown in my appreciation of how God has worked in your life. There were times when I was so moved that I had to stop and take a break.

Pam: Andrea, hearing your story again gave me a much better understanding of why you are involved in racial reconciliation and community development issues. I was impressed with your parents. I have never known older white adults who were so passionate about justice. It was in the hearts of your parents to swim upstream and to make conscious decisions over and over again. It was not superficial. There were Africans and Scandinavians living in your home day after day. You lived in a community that was multiracial. It wasn't like that typical throwback, "But, I have lots of black friends." I really liked the authenticity of it, and I really see that in you.

Elvon: If it had been false in your parents' lives, it wouldn't be so real in you. I think you would have rebelled. Even when your father left your family, he joined that group, black and white men together. He left the church, but that race consciousness stayed with him. And, Jo, I always wondered how this blond chick ended up in the inner city of several cities! I imagined you sitting in your fifth-grade classroom learning about slavery for the first time. And Pam, I always wondered what it was like for blacks who have come from the West Indies and assimilated into this culture.

Andrea: I guess I learned new things about all three of you. It feels really vulnerable to be exposing all of our lives. I loved your first chapter, Pam. Reading about those incidences with Eugene and Patrick, I started crying. Then, when you shared the fantasy of how you would have liked those situations to have turned out, I flashed back to my own experiences as a kid that were just like the fantasy. The sense of your feeling so different from the people around you and wanting to fit in really struck me. That was really a thread, especially as you traveled to Grenada, wanting to fit in there, then realizing you're American, and you didn't fit in either place.

Jo: That's true because as white women we can just go back to what's comfortable if we don't "fit in" in a certain place. We have that option. I'm not so sure our black sisters do.

Melinda: Since we are products of our parents and much of the book is about where you all came from, what kind of mind-set do you want your children to have regarding race?

Elvon: I think one of the great atrocities African Americans put on themselves and their children is, "I don't care how many ethnicities are in you, you're black. That's it. That's all you can be." I'm part Cherokee. And one of the things we're going to emphasize to our children is, "Yes, you are black. And you should be proud of that. But you are also Native American, Irish American, and German." When someone asks my son, "Want to go visit Ireland?" I want him to grab it. It's part of his heritage. There's nothing wrong with being black, but you don't have to push aside the other parts of you. It's all good.

Pam: It may be that the black parents who are saying, "You are black and that's it" are really feeling, *We don't even want to know about the other part 'cause it ain't no pretty story*. I don't think interracial couples would feel that way about it since they chose each other and are therefore more inclined to embrace each others' backgrounds. I really would like my children to have more of a sense of their identity both in Christ and as Africans than I had. Then you can add in everything else about the way my parents raised me. I write in my first chapter about the little black girls who came to visit me, how they seemed so "together" in a way I was not. I didn't want them to play with the other (white) girls because I thought they might be too together, too comfortable with themselves.

Elvon: Their parents passed their identity on to them.

Pam: I know that I will not raise my children in all-white neighborhoods. I will take steps to have them exposed culturally, to travel. I thank God my parents took me to Grenada, to England, and to other places. I will definitely do that with my children. But, what I still value is the fact that my parents' attitude was that "Everyone's OK." This is what led me, allowed me, to have white friends. I would not ever want my children to be so wrapped up in their identity as African Americans that they are separated from whites and consider that a whole separate world. That's just foolish.

Andrea: If I do get married, I think I would want to raise my children in Harlem because it's been so good for me. I realize as

I look back on my life that I am really appreciative and thankful that my parents didn't just go the status quo of a typical white family. I would want to do the same for my kids. I don't want them to have a sterile, homogenous experience. I will not raise them in an all-white neighborhood. I would want them to live in an urban setting like I do now. The probability of them being in contact with other people is greater if they are in a city, any city. Reading books, telling them stories, making sure that I have adult friends who are different from them ethnically are important. God created humanity with incredible differences and that is a wonderful thing. I want my children to need and enjoy these differences, and not fear them. I want them to see culture as a great thing and to travel and explore.

Jo: In our case (as white women), it could be real easy to live in all-white areas and just stay there. I'm humbled when I think of the children in our neighborhood in Harlem. God has always used these children in different neighborhoods to teach me and cause me to grow. I always feel like relocation has made a difference; I never would have gotten to meet these kids otherwise. I'd really want kids to have a deep sense of justice. I don't know how you'd foster that, except by continual reminders that we live in a fallen world. And to explain to them that some people, because of sin, oppress others, and that we must make daily choices to challenge that. It's about relationships and seeing differences as a blessing rather than an obstacle. The idea that everyone is a potential friend, feels very Christlike to me.

Andrea: Kids watch adults. If we're modeling respect and dignity, care and hope to the people around us, hopefully, they're going to get that.

Melinda: In your friendships, do you always see race now? Does it ever get to the point where it's not, "she's my white friend, she's my black friend," but just "she's my friend"?

Elvon: Pam's my black friend!

Pam: You're my black friend too!

Andrea: I think the reality of our history, and the reality of where race relations still are in this country, makes race something that's just there. But I don't see it as a barrier or an obstacle. I see it as a richness. I'm honored that Elvon and I are friends. I cherish the fact that we have developed a relationship over time. I see her as Elvon. I don't first see her as black.

Melinda: Although you're not color blind. . . .

Andrea: No, I'm not. I know she's very much black. Honestly, I never really had a close black friend until Elvon. I've had friends, but not the kind where we talk about deep heart stuff and struggles.

Elvon: I have had close white friends before. For Andrea and me, our friendship started out in the context of race because of the ministry. I wasn't even looking at her saying, "Gee, I really want to get to know her." And because there wasn't that pressure, the friendship just evolved. As I got to know her, she became one of my dearest friends, just because of who she is and because of the knowledge that she possesses. She's just really good in areas where I lack greatly. Soon after I was married, I miscarried; I wanted to talk to Andrea about it. At first she wasn't available, and I was devastated. But she called me the next morning and suggested an even earlier date to talk. That was a major threshold to cross, and it pushed us out of the context of race into real friendship.

Andrea: I know that I have an even more heightened sensitivity now about things I say. Sometimes I say something and think, *Oh, I wonder how that came across. Did I offend someone?* Then I look at your face [to Elvon] and can sense that you are not offended.

Elvon: I work hard not to be so easily offended. I know you and know that you would not purposely offend me.

Melinda: Is there anything you could say to someone who seeks a friendship with someone of another race, to help them, or is it just haphazard?

Jo: I remember when Melinda and I first met. One day you finally looked right at me and said, "Jo, you don't always have to talk about race, you know." That was important to me because I want to understand it and because I want to be a bridge. I also know that it's only one part of a friendship, yet it's something you can't ignore. If you grew up in England, that's going to give you a different perspective. Our heritage is one aspect of who we are, and I think it's missing in a lot of friendships. A lot of white women I know won't make an effort to get to know African American women because they're too intimidated. They see black women as very strong and very together. So they usually resort to hanging out with people who are more like them. They see the differences more than the commonalities.

Pam: When we were first batting the idea of this book around several years ago, it was going to focus on the context of corporate America, where there are a lot of white women and black women working together. There's a constant interaction in the workplace, even when they are support staff and executives interacting. That seems like an easy way to bridge the gap, but maybe not. Anything that seems too formulated to me, I question.

Melinda: Not many people are in the situation where there is genuine multiracial, peer interaction. Because of the two different Americas, doesn't there have to be some level of intentionality, of crossing over a barrier? Otherwise, we all would stay comfortable in our own separate contexts, no?

Pam: And we do that so very well. We will eat your foods, you will eat our foods. We will go to your dance or concert, you will go to ours. In my old church we constantly had those artsy events, and they were deemed such great successes because everybody came and would eat the food and clap to African songs. But further contact, beyond that, was limited. It's scary that we thought we had accomplished something, that we had done our racial reconciliation thing of the month and now we were finished until next time. Intentional cultural-exchange events are only the beginning. I asked white women in the church to tell me what their obstacles were to going further in a black-white friendship. I heard things like, "Life is already so stressful and so involved, with children and so on, that there's no time." It was perceived as being work. This *perception* stopped them. I also heard, "If I were only to cut out a little window of time to reach out then I won't be authentic because I don't have 'room in my life.' So, is it still worth it?" I think that's a bad attitude. What if Jesus treated us like that? Scheduling us into his Daytimer only when he could fit us in.

Jo: I think it is important to distinguish that it's not a cause, it's not an agenda. Jesus wasn't about a cause or an agenda. He was about relationships, very authentic ones. That should be our driving force. It has to be. There are horror stories of what happens when it's not.

Pam: And it concerns me greatly that those inauthentic experiences are representative of the Church. We'll do Christmas presents for families of prisoners, for example, who are mostly minority families, and feel great about that. But "events" like that are not being seen by enough people as a way to build ongoing relationships. In too many efforts, the goal is a one-time "handout" and good-bye.

Andrea: The flip side of that would be the Racial Unity Ministry (R.U.M.) we do at our church. We realized that we needed to be about building relationships among ourselves and to model that to the larger church so that when we did go to a cultural event, it would come out of friendship and relationship. But there is still some merit in doing events to educate.

Jo: This is typical of white culture. We feel we don't have to know about other cultures since this is a white dominated country.

Elvon: That's true now, but I think we are learning that America is browning. You don't want to use fear as an incentive, but you do want to say, "If you stay in this narrow world, you are going to be left behind." This is good because Jesus set a precedent and said we should do it. It's like, "Why praise God?" You praise God because it furthers your relationship with him. Why do you form friendships with people who are different from you? You do it because it helps you. It helps you become a better person, become more like Christ.

Jo: There's a fear that I see. Working in the predominately white Christian publishing world, there is a sense that God has brought the world here to the U.S. and in particular cities. So what happens? They (white evangelicals) move further and further away. There's something inherently fearful about differences, which represents a pretty shallow perception of God. Thank goodness the world is not becoming more homogenous.

Pam: Yet it disturbs me when I see young, black teenagers who are totally disjointed from white society. Some of them have no relationships with whites and no people to bridge that relationship. I don't know that I will live to see the day when the power structure shifts significantly from white to black. When it does, whites have to wake up or be left behind. Whites have access to so many things and so many resources. It's a testament to African Americans that we can actually get anywhere in the little frame we've had to cut out for ourselves. I've told the story a zillion times of Andrea paying for my young friend Joy (who is black) to go on a trip to Denver. So many little things like that have helped her, came out of being able to go on the trip. She had never been on a plane before. I don't know that she knew any other African Americans at that time who could have said to her, "Here, let's go." I'm not seeing blacks and whites building bridges in that peer setting, hook-me-up kind of way. For example, just by my association with Jo, I'm writing for a Christian magazine. Of course, I had to have the credentials, but they talked to me based on Jo's recommendation. That's power. So, I think there's a practical aspect as well as the emotional.

Melinda: Are folks aware of these issues when it comes to black-white relationships?

Jo: No, we don't recognize that we need each other. We're too intimidated by difference. We don't realize we're incomplete without one another. Jesus said, "They will know that you are my disciples if you love one another." We're his disciples in this world. The reconciliation piece is that we need each other.

Pam: We're becoming aware of the buzz-term, racial reconciliation, yes. But we're not on to the outworking of that which is achieving economic equality. Wasn't it Booker T. Washington who asked, "Can there be social justice without economic parity?" I think that the Church has just gotten on board on the touchy-feely racial reconciliation part, but hasn't touched economic issues. That's another story. Maybe that's why I'm so moved by something like what happened with Joy and Andrea. The idea of redistribution should follow true reconciliation. Joy was really touched that such a wonderful thing could occur. That experience with Andrea helped her in many ways. Two years ago I took her to France and Germany with me, along with two white friends. They both also chipped in to pay for some of her lodging and expenses. Now, at her job, where she meets people from all over the world, she can recognize German and even say "thank you" and "good day" in that language. These German customers couldn't imagine a young black woman was speaking German to them. That excites me.

Jo: When those kinds of relationships happen, it helps break the stereotypes. Every stereotype Germans might have about young black women is shot when they have experiences like that.

Pam: Exactly. My parents came here to make something more of themselves. But I have a lot of friends who wanted to be journalists. And their parents were afraid for them to take such a "risky" path. Planning for and living out your dreams—I don't know if enough of us think it's possible. A white woman's grandfather will bail her out if her attempt at achieving her dream fails, but what about us? Most of our grandfathers didn't have the opportunity to build wealth like that.

Melinda: How does having friends of other races change you?

Elvon: Here's the best way I can explain it. I grew up thirty miles away from Memphis, Tennessee, a relatively large city. It's a great place, across the Mississippi. I had sisters who lived there and, eventually, I got used to the city. After awhile it became routine. And then I went to New York. It was new and exciting, and there was so much more to learn. It was a brand new experience. Because it was different from Memphis, it changed me as a person. What you learn changes you; knowledge changes you. So, having black friends is like going to Memphis. But being in New York City is great too. I get to experience more and become a more interesting person. It may not necessarily be sweeter, but it makes your life better.

Melinda: How do you communicate the need for black-white relationships to the "unconverted"?

Andrea: I'm really trying to get hold of that question. I know internally that I am richer because of my friends who are different from myself ethnically, but how would I convince someone else of that? The elements of friendship are there regardless of color. I think the best way to communicate it is to model it. The fact that Elvon and I walk down the street together communicates something to those white folk. It flies in the face of history. Just seeing the two of us together as friends, it's like there's justice being done right there. Healing is taking place.

Jo: I remember hearing the choir from Voice of Calvary in Jackson, Mississippi, singing several years ago at a CCDA conference. A choir of about fifty people—thirty blacks and twenty whites. Seeing those Christians singing together—from Mississippi of all places—knowing the history and seeing those huge smiles as they sang, it was such a great picture to me. It's an example of the joy that comes when you intentionally confront the horrors and ugliness of our country. Besides, people don't usually buy just one type of flower or one color flower for their gardens. They buy a whole bunch of different colored flowers because that is what's going to look the best and the prettiest. To have that kind of variety is going to make the best garden around. It's the most aesthetically pleasing, the most reflective of a creative God. And if we don't have that in our lives, it's just so much duller.

Elvon: [To Jo] As you were saying that, I pictured the lovely gardens that I've seen. All those brilliant colors. That's real beauty, in all the different seasons.

Melinda: [To Pam] You talk about the rewards of black-white relationships, yet you find yourself more in a place of sameness now at a black church.

Pam: I'm still in process. I didn't see myself in the other church. I often had a once-removed experience of everything. Church shouldn't be that way. I needed balance. I didn't have that strong identity growing up, and I'm missing that. I'm having to get that in my adult life. In the white church, I recognized that I didn't have this and wouldn't get it there. I assumed that I would because of the "one in Christ" idea. It was quite a shock to hear, "no, sorry" and not have my culture affirmed. Now, I have no lack of cultural identity. It's beautiful. I'm overwhelmed with the privilege of being at my new church CLC (Christian Life Centre), sitting under this awesome teaching, taking in the whole brown environment. I'm serving in a ministry I love with other African Americans, using my gifts and talents for his glory to uplift my people, and all people. For once, we're not an afterthought; it means everything to me. I still have many close, white friends. What attracted me also was my pastor's commitment to racial reconciliation issues as evidenced in his involvement with Promise Keepers on a national level and other organizations on a local level. Our church has a heart for community development and empowerment in the inner city, something I longed to see launched in the white church. So I said, "Here's a black church where the pastor is on board with issues I believe in."

Jo: [To Pam] How has being there helped you discover your cultural identity? And why is that so important to you? I know a lot of white folk who are not in touch with their cultural identity. Most will talk about their identity in Christ, not their ethnicity.

Pam: If anything, it's given me a new depth in my relationship with the Lord. I see that God loves to be praised with

Ugandan dancers, bongos, maracas, and rap songs. Diversity is a sweet smelling savor to him. Getting this every week, not just as a "special guest" thing during Black History Month, has opened up another area of worship for me. Worship was one of the big issues at my old church. There were no people to play in that style so we didn't do it. My view of God has definitely broadened as a result. Evangelist and teacher Tom Skinner brought up the question that if we say we are one in Christ, "How come you don't want to live with me? How come you don't want to be involved in my dilemma?" That's the difference.

Melinda: What would be some final words of encouragement for those seeking to be more racially reconciled?

Andrea: If we're Christians, it's imperative that we be cross-cultural. Christ was the most cross-cultural ever. He came down from heaven, divine, totally separate from humans, and became one of us. That, to me, is what drives me. It's inherent to the gospel. I need to be about being cross-cultural. That would be my charge to all Christians. It's not optional.

Elvon: Relationships are hard, period. But if you are a Christian and you find that this is really on your heart, don't give up after the first time if there's a failure or just because it's difficult. There is hurt and there is pain, but there is also great reward and great joy. In the end, it's really worth it. God blesses you, so don't give up.

Pam: I am reminded of the whole story of Ruth and Naomi, and learning that Ruth was a darker-skinned Moabite. Understanding their story in that context makes it so powerful. Given the choice to go back to her land or to stay with Naomi, Ruth said, "No do not tell me to leave you. Wherever you go I will go, and your people will be my people." We should grapple with that. In John 15 Jesus says, "I no longer call you servants . . . [but I call] you friends." That's powerful (and controversial, I know) in light of our history in America. It is saying that all God has shown to me I have shared with you. I'm holding nothing back. I don't want to have something to lord over you. I want us to be on equal footing. I think that's a word for white folks. We have the blueprint for economic empowerment and redistribution right there. For me, that means doing and not talking.

Jo: Right! We need to stop talking and start listening. We need to really listen to one another's stories. We can make an impact if we start listening. If this issue is ever going to get anywhere in this country, it's not going to be because we're pointing fingers, but because we're owning up to and working on our own stuff. Not asking, "Who's got more racism?" but confessing our own sin and asking God to change us. It starts with us right where we are. When you think about this issue, it can be overwhelming, but just starting with simple truths and honesty about ourselves makes it easier. In doing that, there's a little more hope. There's more room for the Holy Spirit to work because we're dying to ourselves and becoming more available to him. It starts in our own hearts.

Pam: And the truth is that we make ourselves available for the things that are most important to us.

Jo: Yes, look at your social schedule and it will show you where your priorities are every time. If this is something you feel strongly about, it will show in your life.

23 Ways to Improve Crossracial Relationships

1. Read ethnic literature. Remember that literature and art are the heart of a culture. (Check out the suggested reading list on the following pages.)
2. Go to dinner at a cross-cultural restaurant (soul food, German, Thai, Morroccan, etc.). Don't be afraid to ask questions.
3. Watch movies with cross-cultural themes and talk with other friends afterward about them.
4. Support small business owners who are from other cultures than you.
5. Visit different churches, consistently if possible. (If you know someone who attends a black-white church, ask her if you can visit as her guest.)
6. Volunteer at an urban ministry (and show up!). Or coach a suburban little league team.
7. Ask someone in your office who is racially different than you to join you for dinner or lunch.
8. March on Martin Luther King Jr. Day.
9. Be a Big Brother or Sister to an urban child and be a friend to his or her family.
10. Go on short-term mission trips to a developing country, the rural South, or an urban area. (Habitat for Humanity is a great option for this.)
11. Serve at a local urban mission for the homeless.
12. Host a multicultural potluck dinner and invite guests to bring ethnic dishes. Then discuss some of the cultures represented, listening to various music styles, etc.
13. Attend plays (or other theater experiences) with cross-cultural themes and discuss them.

14. Start a book club on books that deal with racial issues.
15. Post a message on the Internet inviting cross-cultural E-mail pen pals.
16. Attend readings at your local bookstores or libraries that reflect culturally diverse material or authors.
17. Encourage your church to join other ethnically diverse congregations for Saturday luncheons at one another's churches. (This is a great way to meet other people in your community, see their sanctuaries, and break bread together.)
18. Plan your vacation so that your family visits some cross-cultural sites, (i.e., the Civil Rights Museum in Memphis, Mesa Verde in Colorado, spots on the Underground Railroad, etc.). Research them together before leaving home.
19. Join a community organization that is likely to draw a diversity of people—Red Cross, recreation centers, reading groups, tourist areas—and build friendships with some of your coworkers there.
20. Buy season tickets to specific concert series (Latin jazz, gospel, blues) and take friends with you.
21. Subscribe to ethnically diverse magazines. (This helps sustain what are usually small business ventures while introducing you to a variety of cultures.) When you're finished reading them, you can donate your old copies to school libraries or shelters.
22. Drop by the student center at a local college for a listing of events. Universities and colleges always host cross-cultural lectures, productions, readings, concerts, and festivals.
23. Invite a small group of diverse friends to meet together for several weeknights in a row to talk about race relations. (Crossing Barrier Sessions such as these are excellent ways to produce honest dialogue and supportive friendships.)

Suggested Reading

The following books have been influential to each of us and we recommend them to you.

General Literature

Angelou, Maya. *I Know Why the Caged Bird Sings*. United Kingdom: Stanley Thomas Publishers, Ltd., 1988.

Bakke, Ray. *The Urban Christian*. Madison, Wis.: Two Thousand One Hundred Productions, 1987.

Campbell, Bebe Moore. *Brothers and Sisters*. Ann Arbor, Mich.: Waldenbooks Company, Inc., 1995.

Chideya, Farai. *Don't Believe the Hype: Fighting Cultural Misinformation about African Americans*. New York: NAL Dutton, 1995.

Dawson, John. *Healing America's Wounds*. Ventura, Calif.: Gospel Light Publications, 1997.

Evans, Tony. *Let's Get to Know Each Other: What White Christians Should Know about Black Christians*. Nashville, Tenn.: Thomas Nelson Inc., 1995.

Gordon, Wayne. *Real Hope in Chicago*. Zondervan, 1995.

Hansberry, Lorraine. *Raisin in the Sun*. New York: Random House Inc., 1995.

hooks, bell. *Killing Rage: Ending Racism*. New York: Henry Holt & Company, 1995.

Hurston, Zora Neale. *Their Eyes Were Watching God*. Reading, Mass.: Addison-Wesley Educational Publishers, Inc., 1995.

Kehrein, Glen, and Raleigh Washington. *Breaking Down Walls*. Chicago: Moody Press, 1997.

King, Martin Luther, Jr. *A Testament of Hope: The Essential Writings of MLK Jr.* San Francisco: Harper-San Francisco, 1990.

Suggested Reading / 245

Lupton, Robert. *Theirs Is the Kingdom: Celebrating the Gospel in Urban America.* San Francisco: Harper-San Francisco, 1989.

McBride, James. *The Color of Water.* Old Tappan, N. J.: Macmillan Library Reference, 1996.

Ortiz, Manuel. *One New People.* Downers Grove, Ill.: InterVarsity Press, 1996.

Perkins, John, and Thomas Tarrants. *He's My Brother.* Ada, Mich.: Chosen Books, 1994.

Perkins, John, and Jo Kadlecek. *Resurrecting Hope: Powerful Stories of God Reaching the City.* Ventura, Calif.: Gospel Light Publications, 1995.

Perkins, Spencer, and Chris Rice. *More Than Equals.* Downers Grove, Ill.: InterVarsity Press, 1993.

Raybon, Patricia. *My First White Friend.* New York: Viking Penguin, 1997.

Salley, Columbus, and Ronald Behm. *What Color Is Your God? Black Consciousness and the Christian Faith.* Secaucus, N. J.: Carol Publishing Group, 1988.

Shuler, Clarence. *Winning the Race to Unity: Is Racial Reconciliation Really Working?* Chicago: Moody Press, 1998.

Wallis, Jim. *The Call to Conversion.* San Francisco: Harper-San Francisco, 1982.

Wangerin, Walter. *Ragman and Other Cries of Faith.* San Francisco: Harper-San Francisco, 1994.

West, Cornel. *Race Matters.* Vintage (Random House), 1994.

Wright, Richard. *Native Son.* Cutchogue, N. Y.: Buccaneer Books, Inc., 1997.

History

Feelings, Tom. *The Middle Passage: White Ships, Black Cargo.* New York: Dial Books for Young Readers, 1995.

Gates, Henry Louis, and Nellie Y. McKay, eds. *The Norton Anthology of African American Literature.* New York: W.W. Norton & Co., Inc., 1996.

Lester, Julius. *To Be a Slave*. New York: Dial Books for Young Readers, 1968.

Loewen, James W. *Lies My Teacher Told Me: Everything Your American History Textbook Got Wrong*. New York: New Press, 1995.

McKissack, Patricia and Frederick. *Sojourner Truth: Ain't I a Woman?* New York: Scholastic, Inc., 1994.

For Parents and Children

Adoff, Arnold. *Black Is Brown Is Tan*. New York: HarperCollins Children's Books, 1973.

Brooks, Bruce. *What Hearts*. New York: HarperCollins Children's Books, 1992.

Carroll, Rebecca. *Sugar in the Raw*. New York: Value Publishing, Inc., 1997.

Greenfield, Eloise. *Night on Neighborhood Street*. New York: Puffin Books, 1991.

Hoobler, Dorothy and Thomas. *The African American Family Album*. New York: Oxford University Press, Inc., 1998.

Hopson, Derek and Darlene. *Different and Wonderful: Raising Black Children in a Race-Conscious Society*. New York: Simon & Schuster Trade, 1992.

Sebestyen, Ouida. *Words by Heart*. New York: Little, Brown & Company, 1979.

Toussaint, Pamela A. *Great Books for African-American Children*. Plume, 1999.

————. *Mama's Little Baby*. New York: Penguin, 1997.

Magazines

Essence
Gospel Today
"America's Original Sin: A Study Guide on White Racism," *Sojourners* (Box 29272, Washington, D.C. 20017).